THE HEART OF CONFLICT

A Spirituality of Transformation

DR. ELINOR D. U. POWELL

THE HEART OF CONFLICT

A Spirituality of Transformation

Northstone

Editor: Michael Schwartzentruber
Cover and interior design: Margaret Kyle
Proofreading: Dianne Greenslade
Cover artwork: created using artwork in the public domain

Unless otherwise noted, all quotations from the Bible are from the New International Version, copyright © 1973, 1978, 1984 by International Bible Society. Used by permission of Zondervan Publishing House. All rights reserved.

Northstone Publishing acknowledges the financial support of the Government of Canada through the Book Publishing Industry Development Program for its publishing activities.

Northstone Publishing is an imprint of Wood Lake Books Inc., an employee-owned company, and is committed to caring for the environment and all creation. Northstone recycles and reuses and encourages readers to do the same. Resources are printed on recycled paper and more environmentally friendly groundwood papers (newsprint), whenever possible. The trees used are replaced through donations to the Scoutrees For Canada Program. A portion of all profit is donated to charitable organizations.

National Library of Canada Cataloguing in Publication Data
Powell, Elinor D. U.
The heart of conflict: a spirituality of transformation/Elinor D.U. Powell.
Includes bibliographical references and index.
ISBN 1-896836-57-7
1. Conflict management. 2. Interpersonal relations. 3. Spiritual life. I. Title.
HM1126.P68 2003   303.6'9   C2003-911012-5

Copyright © 2003 Elinor D. U. Powell
All rights reserved. No part of this publication may be reproduced –
except in the case of brief quotations embodied in critical articles and reviews –
stored in an electronic retrieval system, or transmitted in any form or by any means, electronic, mechanical, photocopying, recording, or otherwise, without prior written consent of the publisher or copyright holder.

Published by Northstone Publishing,
an imprint of Wood Lake Books Publishing Inc.
Kelowna, British Columbia, Canada

Printing 10 9 8 7 6 5 4 3 2 1

Printed in Canada at
Transcontinental

CONTENTS

PREFACE 7
INTRODUCTION: THE PLACE OF SPIRITUALITY IN CONFLICT 10

PART ONE
WORLDVIEW AND PERCEPTIONS OF CONFLICT

I – Defining Our Terms **18**
II – Modernism & The Self-Fulfilling Prophecy **27**
III – Postmodernism **37**
IV – Religion **49**
V – Culture **67**

PART TWO
THE HUMAN SPIRIT MANIFESTED

VI – Honor, Grace, & Face **80**
VII – Human Emotions & Needs **95**
VIII – Coercive Power **109**
IX – Integrative & Spiritual Powers **125**
X – The Development of Faith & the Experience of Spirit **133**

PART THREE
APPROACHES TO CONFLICT

XI – Conflict Management through Systems of Law **150**
XII – Managing Conflict by Negotiation & Mediation **161**
XIII – Identity-Based Conflict Management **171**
XIV – The Mediator in Action **187**

PART FOUR
HEALING IN THE AFTERMATH
XV – Forgiveness & Apology **200**
XVI – Healing & Reconciliation **211**
XVII – Conclusions **225**

APPENDIX: MEDITATION ON A QUARREL 227
ENDNOTES 231
INDEX 241

PREFACE

"You must see the tremendous potential for healing in conflict resolution work," someone said to me a while back. Yes, indeed. As a mediator and trainer, I have discovered a renewed sense of fulfillment in bringing people together, hearing their stories, and seeing their spirits kindled as they begin to understand each other.

A mother and her teenage son were on a collision course. Because of some property damage her son had caused, the mother, at her wits' end, saw no options other than to abandon her son to the streets, or to turn him over to the police and the juvenile courts. The son was on the verge of walking out, for he could not handle his mother's rages. A three-hour mediation opened the way for a spontaneous handshake and the possibility of their starting again.

"I thought I had lost my son," the mother remarked afterwards.

This comment reminded me of another, earlier time in my medical practice, when I was engaged in an around-the-clock, successful struggle to save a young girl in a diabetic coma. There, too, a parent had said, "I thought I had lost my daughter."

My Personal Path

My journey started in Ireland, at a time when, following Independence, the new state was seeking to establish its own identity. As a member of the Protestant minority, I was aware of the separation that existed between the Protestant and Roman Catholic communities, both in the educational system and in our social interactions, or lack of them. I was equally aware, as I became older, of the tolerance shown by my father's professional legal colleagues for his belonging to what amounted to a different culture. Members of our "enclave" continued to enjoy, in large measure, their previously privileged position, despite the changing political reality. It was also a time of economic constraint. Many young educated people had to emigrate, in order to realize their ambitions, or even just to survive.

Having qualified in medicine, I eventually joined the diaspora of the 90 percent of medical graduates who had emigrated. After a three-year fellowship associated with Harvard Medical School, I settled in Victoria, British Columbia. The discipline of internal medicine, which I joined, is based very much on the scientific, objective worldview, and requires much academic knowledge and rational sequences of thought when it comes to making decisions for the benefit of patients. My experience as hospital Chief of Medical Staff gave me experience in wider issues affecting medical practice.

It was shortly after I joined the peace movement and the International Physicians for the Prevention of Nuclear War (winners of the 1985 Nobel Peace Prize) in the early 1980s, that I started to search for alternative ways to manage disagreements and conflicts, both at the international and personal levels. I wanted to know how more people-oriented approaches might apply in the real world. Could they be realistic, or were they merely idealistic? What was realism, and what was idealism? Might we perhaps have got the terms mixed up?

I gained a certificate in dispute resolution at the Justice Institute of British Columbia. Later, I served on the board of the now defunct Canadian International Institute for Peace and Security.

In pursuing the quest for nonviolent alternatives to warfare, my travels have taken me to the United States, India, South Africa, China, and Europe, including Russia.

In Canada, locally, I have been giving courses in conflict resolution from a Christian perspective at the Anglican Church of St. John the Divine, in Victoria, British Columbia. Here, participants and I have been seeking an answer to the question of what a spiritual, holistic, and realistic approach to conflict might mean. The Dispute Resolution Centre, a downtown community organization, and its training arm, the Institute of Conflict Analysis and Management, at which I teach as a faculty member, are on a similar quest.

In 1999, my association with the Centre for Studies in Religion and Society, as Community Sabbaticant, gave me the opportunity to research philosophical and theological reflections on human interaction and ultimate meaning, and how those bear on the reality of conflict and its management. At the end of the term I gave a lecture on what I had discovered. This book is an expansion of the themes presented in that lecture.

Writing this book has been a personal journey of discovery and reflection, a rediscovery of a language few of us are comfortable using. That language dares to speak of hope. Hope is both an experience of well-being in the present, as well as an anticipation of a future filled with purpose and meaning. This book affirms the basic presence of spirituality in human beings, while celebrating its complexity and its meaningfulness. It identifies this quality in the work of many writers in the field of conflict management, whether they dare to speak its name or ignore it. The book portrays a dialectic; it is part report, part reflection, and altogether a spiral that is intended to bring its author and its readers closer to an awareness of the Divine Intention. It is a message particularly relevant at the present time.

In writing this book, I have drawn from the writings of many seekers of the spiritual way and from conversations with valued colleagues. I would like, in particular, to acknowledge Richard McGuigan, John McLaren, Michael Hadley, Marcia Williams, and Mary-Wynne Ashford. To all, a hearty thanks for your inspiration and guidance along my path.

INTRODUCTION

THE PLACE OF SPIRITUALITY IN CONFLICT

Unless we change our way of thinking, we drift toward unparalleled disaster.
Albert Einstein

I have set before you life and death, blessings and curses. Now choose life.
Deuteronomy 30:19

We are spiritual beings. Our spirituality is an inborn part of our nature, the essence of who we are as aware, sentient, and intuitive human beings. An appreciation of the spiritual in our lives enables us to probe to the deepest layer of our being, for ourselves, for our relationships with each other, and for the world beyond. It is the thesis of this book that the spirit is most surely put to the test and thus most clearly manifested when we are faced with challenge and conflict.

Some people deny the existence of anything called spirit or spirituality. Others search for the essence of spirit in the empty spaces of beautiful scenery. If spirituality is associated with conflict at all, it is traditionally restricted to the "feel-good" time of forgiveness and reconciliation. This book suggests instead, that not only does our spirituality exist, but it is to be found right from the beginning of a conflict, in the midst of the turmoil. It is especially to be discovered at the moment when we confront difficult issues and our wounded relationships. This notion of a spiritual essence to conflict may appear to be radical, and I would agree. It is radical because it is rooted in the experience of reality and it is radical because it opens up avenues of approach that lie before our eyes but that have mostly been overlooked.

The denial of spirit and its replacement by a sardonic vision of the world as machine, controllable by human beings, has turned out to be a belief system of hopelessness, despair, and apathy. Our methods of control by coercive power or legal sanction have fallen short of their promise of justice, peace, or security.

The current upsurge of interest in things spiritual and a rediscovery of the value of our spiritual essence suggest that we may now be entering a period which could be the birthing ground of hope and engagement. Like most human birthings, it combines elements of both pain and celebration: pain, because a realization of the spirit takes us into and through our deepest concerns; and celebration, because by recognizing the spirit we can get in touch with what it truly means to be human.

This book takes a fresh look at our conflicts, their meaning, and how we deal with them. It sets forth an interpretation that is my own, but that incorporates many of the findings of other researchers and practitioners. It re-examines those premises and ideas that have steered and defined private and public relationships between human beings.

Einstein, in his famous conversation with Sigmund Freud, did not tell the half of it when he said that "unless we change our way of thinking, we drift toward unparalleled disaster." Ways of thinking are not the only things that have to change, if we are to avoid disaster. We need to change our attitudes toward each other and to the globe which sustains us. We need to review our beliefs about human nature and how our potential for collaboration may be fostered more effectively. Beliefs and attitudes change slowly, even when based on convictions that have been shown to be false. The belief that the threat of overwhelming coercive power is an effective means of social and political control is demonstrably untenable. Yet deadly conflicts continue to break out in dozens of places around the globe, despite the presence of control systems so powerful that they could annihilate all life on earth several times over. Moreover, we pursue a belief in unlimited economic development, while exploiting global resources beyond the earth's productive and restorative capacity. A profound shift is necessary in unsustainable belief in limitless expansion, and in our approaches to managing global and local strife.

A reappraisal of human interconnections and stewardship of global resources is urgently needed. Such a review will widen our mental horizons to encompass our understanding of the nature of reality, our nature as human beings, our relationships with each other and with the world from which we derive sustenance. The splitting of the atom has changed our relationship with the world and with each other in profound ways. It is a metaphor that shapes our culture, a metaphor for ultimate alienation, for death. But equally, we could claim it as a metaphor for rebirth, if it leads to an appreciation and awareness of the predicament of our own time in history.

Put out a wetted finger to test the winds of world affairs just now. Can't you just feel the undercurrents that were already seething under the surface of our apparently tranquil Western life? Since the events of September 11, 2001, these undercurrents have burst upon our conscious minds, but they were already being expressed prior to that date in the concerns of many. The magnitude of the reaction to the focused and criminal attack on the World Trade Center – a metaphor of Western commercial enterprise – indicates our general sense of insecurity and vulnerability. While wars had raged in dozens of countries worldwide, we had felt immune, separated by distance. Our response to the attack speaks to a dissonance within contemporary thought and action. Are we blighted to retaliate to defend material wealth, while sidestepping our responsibilities to the common good and to the Spirit that is the supreme creator, judge, and guide for all human endeavors?

A maelstrom of ideas and energy challenges us to make sense of current issues. In our more pessimistic moments, these forces often appear to be beyond our control. Over the past century, some philosophers have declared our world to be meaningless, and therefore beyond either care or hope.

Many others, however, refuse to be overwhelmed by such nihilism. Nor are they dismayed by the scale of the current crisis in our global ethic. They are prepared to expose the false certainties that impel our journey into a downward spiral, and are equally prepared to construct together a more hopeful and stable future, one imbued with life-giving spirit. In such company we take the challenge of stepping into the vortex, into the chaos of this "postmodern" historical period, in the sure hope of finding there a new perspective, a new sense of the possibilities that wait to be rediscovered. In the eye of the storm, we may yet rediscover a purpose for each one of us, and for humanity, on this finite, beautiful globe we call home.

All around us there is evidence that we are embarked on a course of renewal. We are both reappraising the value of beliefs previously taken as revealed truth, and discarding as old-fashioned many others. This work is being done by institutes of learning, by workers in the field, by grassroots organizations, and by thoughtful individuals acting independently. Foremost in these discourses is the phenomenal rise in the interest in things spiritual, appearing simultaneously in many spheres. These include the revitalization of a wide variety of quite distinct spiritual traditions, from ancient sources from China, India, Africa, and the shamanistic traditions of aboriginal cultures in the Americas. New forms of spirituality are being discovered in eco-feminism, in liberation theology, and in the ecumenical movement.[1]

There is also a search in progress for ways of dealing with conflict that will restore, heal, and reconnect individuals, groups, and nations. This book is an effort to combine these streams, to discover and describe the spirit within the pursuit of more effective conflict management.

The turmoil and dismay of the present can provide the energy for transformation, but it is not an easy road. Ambiguity and uncertainty await us as we seek small islands of hope. It is unrealistic to try to abolish conflict, for it is an inevitable part of everyday life and an indicator that change is necessary. Conflict will always be present in our lives and in our social and political arrangements, for no human system is perfect. Besides, circumstances and contexts change. Conflict is a signal of problems afoot, a challenge that tells us that evaluation, reflection, and action are needed, either in small scale or large. Such challenges put into focus the basis of our beliefs, values, understanding of reality, and our spiritual identity.

When the causes of conflict lie unaddressed, or are addressed in totalitarian ways, when conflict escalates until it becomes intractable and overwhelming, it drives human beings to despair and brings about numbness, indifference, alienation, and even self-destruction in suicide. These phenomena are evidence of the death of the soul, the human being's central core of meaning.

Alternatively, they may indicate the determination of some to refuse to accept the soul's destruction, which they see as the ultimate injustice imposed by their oppressors.

If, however, these challenges are effectively addressed, they can become turning points, birthing grounds for transformation, for new ways to meet human need. They can provide opportunity to bring the possibility of healing, justice, and truth to a world sorely in need of these qualities. The pain, the energy, the movement, and the capacity for creativity are all evidence of the transforming potential of the spirit in conflict.

A word about metaphors, especially figurative ones, for I plan to use them freely. Metaphors are essential components of language; they are the way we exchange the meanings by which we strive to make sense of the world. Metaphors enable us to share experiences with others on a subjective level, in vivid images. We have, for example, such striking images as the transformation of swords into ploughshares, or the symbol of our legal institutions: justice as a beautiful blindfolded woman, holding up the scales of impartiality. We talk figuratively about the heart as the center of our motives and desires. We describe our spirit as a breath: the flow of life-giving oxygen inward and of spent oxygen outward, back to the plants for renewal. Yet the metaphor holds even more. It conjures up a sense of transcendent mystery which transforms as it passes.

Metaphors invite active participation. Each contains a concealed invitation to the listener to make sense out of the implied meaning. Even the most mundane and rational description of our observations relies on metaphors of space and time.

Figurative metaphors allow us to express the numinous images of the transcendent beyond the power of more pedestrian language. Even before the appropriate graphic verbal image comes to mind, the search itself is creative. I have often found during workshops that the collective silence which accompanies the pursuit for an apt analogy is itself ripe with creativity. When combined with the mutual exchange of each person's ideas, the experience brings a resonance to the moment.

In the field of conflict management, we may ask, is a negotiator like a gladiator or a bulldog, a diplomatic agent or a partner with a mutual problem to solve? Is a mediator like a conductor of music, or a director of an impromptu play; is he or she a catalyst, or a servant leader, or something else altogether? Are the parties involved pawns or dictators or engaged shareholders in a common enterprise? The experience of the role gives rise to the reflection and the image. The choice will reflect our tacit beliefs about the role and how it is to be personified.

More than 3000 years ago, the prophet Moses exhorted his people, saying "I set before you life and death, blessings and curses. Therefore choose life." Which choice, toward life or toward death, shall we make at this time? Having chosen the option of life, can we gather the momentum to live out that choice together as a global community?

Language Clarification

The words used to express ideas in the area we are speaking about often mean different things to different people. Conversely, one writer will describe concepts using one phrase or word, while another chooses a different word or phrase to express something that seems very similar. Some words have fallen out of favor with readers because of negative associations. For me, the word "soul" describes a useful essence of the human makeup. But it has come to have evangelical overtones, and this I want to avoid. So I use the words "human spirit" with greater ease. Psychologists tend to avoid the word "spirit," preferring the concept of Freud's "ego." (Not all would agree that they describe similar entities.) But the Sufi theologian Helminski uses the term "ego" differently, as a sort of moral weather vane, either "false" or "true." I will avoid the use of the word "ego" altogether.

Sociologists such as Paul Sites and mediators such as Jay Rothman apply "identity" to something close to the essence of one's being. As these pages will show, identity and human spirit are indeed closely allied, and a worthy focus of our attention. I will use lower-case "spirit" for the human essence, and capital S "Spirit" for the indefinable Designer of the Universe. In their context, I trust these meanings will be easy to follow.

English, unfortunately, does not have a collective word for the singular personal pronoun. I wish to use inclusive language, so I have used "he" and "she," as well as "him" and "her" throughout. When not making a direct quote, I have changed masculine pronouns as used by earlier writers, when it appears that they meant to include both genders.

This book is an attempt to get at the heart of our concerns: to seek the purpose and meaning that lie behind the ultimate aspirations of human endeavor. Any such attempt in 256 pages will merely scratch the surface. My hope is that these comments will lead to further discussion, criticism, development, and application.

PART ONE

WORLDVIEW & PERCEPTIONS OF CONFLICT

I

DEFINING OUR TERMS

CONFLICT

Say not the struggle naught availeth,
The labour and the wounds are vain,
The enemy faints not nor faileth,
And as things have been things remain.
Arthur H. Clough

Suppose that a business deal between me and my partner has gone sour. The fight might be over some minor asset owed by someone else: say, $500 for a house repair job. I discover that my partner, whom I had previously deemed a trusted friend, has talked without my permission to the debtor. Furthermore, I believe that my partner has told the debtor that I am willing to settle for half what I was demanding. I feel betrayed. The conflict is no longer over the debt, but about our fractured relationship. Soon neither of us is willing to talk to the other.

Later, I learn that the actual reason my partner met with the client was to broker peace. His action was not a betrayal, but a gesture of goodwill. And so we reconcile, recognizing that the personal relationship between us far transcends the monetary value of any transaction.

Psychologists define conflict as "a state of tension arising between two or more individuals or groups because they perceive differences and because they desire outcomes that appear, or are, mutually incompatible."

While every word of that definition is true as far as it goes, it hardly describes the intensity of the storms, the traumas even, that we experience in the real world, where people break up, feel betrayed, and sometimes turn to wreak vengeance. Nor does it describe the experience of having gone through the heart of the fire to find reconciliation, forgiveness, and healing. The psychologists' definition simply doesn't convey the meaning, the passion — and the consequences — of the strife in our lives. It points to the desire we may have for a specific, preferred outcome, but it ignores our innermost, deeply felt needs as human beings. As a result, its usefulness as a description is limited to the sorts of altercations that deal only with material goods on a transactional basis. These disagreements should be distinguished from more meaningful conflicts, where the problem lies more deeply. Here, the parties come to feel that their identity as real people may be at stake because some basic human need has been denied.

John Burton is a pioneer in the field of dealing with difficult and protracted quarrels. In a book co-authored with Frank Dukes, *Conflict: Practices in Management, Settlement, and Resolution*, he applies the term "dispute" to situations where the psychologists' definition fits and people's material interests are negotiable. He reserves the term "conflict" for issues that relate to ontological human needs that cannot be compromised.[1]

Burton's distinction is an important one, because it separates disagreements over allocation of material resources, which may be met in a variety of ways, from those engagements of deeper meaning, which involve more non-negotiable needs and values. It is in this latter realm that the human spirit is most engaged, but we should not totally disregard disputes over tangible assets, because they are often symptomatic of something deeper, where the spirit is aroused.

As the story above illustrates, when it comes to conflict, the concern being disputed may be real or imagined. Imagined betrayals often hurt as much as real ones, and may be all the more difficult to mend, because mutual trust is shaken and communication has broken down – the pain is too great to be articulated.

Conflicts may arise from very human characteristics: concerns about honor, respect, dignity – the very sense of identity of the people involved; their particular history, culture, and how they see their circumstances. The more escalated the conflict, the more salient the human factors.[2] Conflict can bring into conscious awareness and focus the core values and sense of identity of the individual or group involved, in ways that would not have been apparent in more tranquil times. Oftentimes, the conflict turns out to be about issues that have sacred meaning to the parties.

But it's not just *what* we fight about that's important. Equally important are the *methods* we use to deal with conflict. Our choices will depend on our beliefs about human nature and how we influence others. Do we put a priority on coercion, force, or deception to deal with differences, because we believe that everyone is out to thwart us? Do we rely on the influence of some apparently objective system or code of law to provide stability and to determine who is right and who is wrong? Or do we seek, as the first priority, to enhance dialogue and understanding, to take responsibility for identifying and meeting our own and the other's needs, in the belief that people respond better to affirmation than to threat? Are we prepared to meet the other and enter into dialogue?

I believe it is this latter option that provides the greatest potential for benefit in the midst of life's storms. Such a dialogue may be an experience of discovery and risk, of encountering the full complexity and richness of the human condition. It may indeed be transformative – and spiritual.

While conflict is usually thought to have a beginning, a middle, and an end, it may be more useful to think of it as a phenomenon that waxes and wanes over time. Perhaps an issue may not have been adequately addressed in the first go-round, so it needs to be re-examined. New facets of the case may come to the surface; other variables suddenly appear and need clarification. With the passage of time, new events arise, new actors appear on stage. The process becomes circular, perhaps spiraling toward escalation or reconciliation, waxing and waning. The Buddhist idea of a continuing engagement with conflict and its causes as a property of life may be closer to experience, closer to reality, than the belief that conflict is the abnormal state and peace and stability the normal state of affairs.

REALITY

A wise man built his house upon a rock. The rain came down, the streams rose and the wind blew and beat against that house; yet it did not fall, because it had its foundation on the rock.
Matthew 7:24–25

How we perceive reality, then, has a lot to do with how we experience and enter into conflict.

Since earliest history, human beings have attempted to define reality in ways that give coherence and stability to life. In his book *The Eye of Spirit: An Integral Vision for a World Gone Slightly Mad*, Ken Wilber, a contemporary writer and philosopher, summarizes key ideas held in common by philosophers and mystics through the ages and across cultures.[3]

In his summary, Wilber represents these ideas in an ascending order of "levels" or domains in a schema called "The Great Chain (or Nest) of Being." I prefer to call it our Great Foundation of Being, choosing this modification because a foundation is something to which we can attach social systems, including worldview, religion, and culture.

In Wilber's schema, reality is portrayed as a flat construct of concentric circles, each larger circle embracing and including the one before and adding its own special dimension. Concentric circles make a readily visual and natural metaphor, representing at once the eddies of a whirlpool leading us down to the center, or conversely, ripples radiating out when a stone is thrown into a quiet pool.

Because Wilber's schema provides a basis for the development of the themes in this book, let's review each of his levels in detail.

Solid Earth – Matter

In the central spot, Wilber places the material substance of our earth, planets, and stars. This is the field of the physicists: matter, the physical world. No one doubts it exists, especially when you stub your toe on a rock! Matter is the substance of which our bodies and our living places are constructed. When examined at the level of atoms, however, matter is found to contain its own paradox. Apparent solidity turns out to be largely empty space. Einstein found that energy and mass are exchangeable for each other. Light is at once both particle and wave. Werner Heisenberg asserts that nothing is certain, for the act of observing a phenomenon appears to change it.[4]

What an analogy for human understanding and intervention in conflict! When all seems solid and unchanging, it may still be possible to bring about transformation by changing our perception of the facts as presented.

For example, a conflict may arise over tangible assets, such as land use. The discussion may be going nowhere, because it centers on competing rights. A redirection of the argument to include shared obligations and a responsibility to care for the land may set the stage for resolution. Fair outcomes may be discovered when both rights and responsibilities are acknowledged and combined. Issues entail both privilege and responsibility.

Life

Encompassing matter and adding a further dimension is life, with its ability to reproduce and diversify. Life on earth emerges, in ways yet mysterious, from the primordial building blocks of natural but lifeless elements. The sun's energy is taken into the earth's own substance, the plants, to form new, self-perpetuating entities. The material of the earth is incorporated into complex organisms that provide the resources on which our life depends. The life domain is the sphere of increase, of sustenance, and of metamorphosis; of renewal, growth, and decay.

The domain of living things is also the territory of limits, set by the finite potential of the earth to reproduce its bounty in fixed timelines, and its vulnerability to exploitation, pollution, and desecration.

Mind

At the next level, mind includes the rational, the emotional, and the intuitive. It combines ideas, observable fact, and experience into concepts of knowledge, wisdom, and motivation. These we share through language, both verbal and nonverbal, oral and written. At this level, we can reconstruct reality through our own reflection, understanding, and mutual communication.

This aspect of our capabilities is especially important in the area of conflict, because our self-reflective beliefs about human nature and motivation determine our actions. These in turn have an uncanny way of being fulfilled, both in the consequences of our acts, and in how we subsequently justify our behavior. In other words, our free-will choices create, to a very large degree, our future.

For instance, suppose your new neighbor comes over ranting and raving about the way your car is parked in his or her spot. It is very likely that you will respond in the same way, with equal anger. If, on the other hand, he or she comes over to make your acquaintance first, and only *then* mentions the matter of the car, you will be likely to move it at once with a quick apology. In each situation you have, apparently, a free-will choice about how to respond, but you automatically take your cue from the other's approach.

Soul

Encompassing these three domains is the soul. The soul is that life principle that lies at our core. It is not so much something we *have*, as what and who we *are*. Here we discover our truest humanity. The soul is where we experience fully that we are valuable in our own personhood.

When we engage the soul, we discover a power and appreciation beyond the intellect or senses, a power and appreciation of being, knowing, sensing, and loving, that extends towards life in all its abundance. We connect with others through the exchange of stories and images. Through the meeting of souls, we build our relationships with others and find meaning in our collective lives. From these we develop beliefs and understandings of the world, which we combine through intention and delight, through ritual and visionary language, into philosophies and religions. We do this in an attempt to find life's ultimate purpose and to connect with the infinite beyond time and space.

Spirit

The Spirit is the most comprehensive entity of all, for it includes all.

Although Wilber shows this level bounded by a final circle, its range is by definition limitless, eternal. The Spirit is the Source, the region of all our points of reference, the Ultimate. As the sun gives energy for life, the ultimate Spirit gives energy to the soul. It is the source of grace, the unknowable, and miracle. It is the domain above all mystery, movement, and transformation.

This all-embracing final construct includes elements of the material, of life, and of the world of conscious human thought, along with the intangible domains of the soul and the sacred. The Spirit is both immanent and transcendent; it dwells *within* us and the created order, and *beyond* us and everything that is.

Wilber's schema is, of course, a simplification, a skeleton on which to hang the basic categories we use to describe a myriad of experiences. These are dry bones, indeed, and we must flesh them out into three dimensions by identifying, in their particularity, the human beings that possess these bodies, minds, and souls, and the ways in which each person is connected to every other person and to all of life. The fact that our relationships extend over time adds a fourth dimension to the ebb and flow of life's currents.

A certain humility is in order here, as well. We venture at our peril if we declare that we can ever fathom the ultimate truth. We must continually subject our ideas and concepts to reflection and reconstruction, to fit new understandings of the universe as they emerge.

Even so, the quality and intensity of our experiencing will be heightened far beyond our imagining by an appreciation of the Ultimate Spirit, the ineffable mystery at the heart of the universe.

SPIRITUALITY

…something vital and non-negotiable lying at the heart of our lives.
Ronald Rolheiser

Spirituality is a practice of living.
Daniel Scott

Spirituality, as I portray it in this book, represents our attempts to grow in sensitivity to self, to others, to nonhuman creation, and to the Creator who is both within and beyond this totality.[5] It indicates the human search for direction and meaning. Spirituality is that fundamental property of our nature that affirms life and promotes it against the mechanisms of death. It inspires, animates, and pervades our thoughts, feelings, and actions. It is the principle of conscious life. Central to our nature, spirit resides in that hidden treasure of our nature, the soul. It is a heightened awareness of mystery and of affirmation. Out of this central, sacred place come messages vital to life.[6]

Spirituality can be seen when individuals or groups experience and come to terms with hardship or oppression, and from that event realize a new sense of who they are – their abilities, resilience, and identity; their ability to forgive and to create a fresh beginning. Spirituality may be expressed through a disciplined and thoughtful practice of living attentively and thoughtfully in the present moment.[7] The spiritual person is deeply connected to others and all beings. Such a person can indeed be focused and well-anchored in life's storms.

The spiritual emerges in the larger commitments people undertake for the sake of particular groups and communities. It's what inspires devotion to causes, from caring for the sick to saving the earth. Truth and beauty, freedom, justice and peace, all inspire and contribute to human spiritual commitment. Our spirituality is especially present in the intangible threads and networks that link us together. It is in the nature of our relationships with each other – relationships that include the tension of conflict and the release of reconciliation – that the experience of our spirituality is most clearly brought to our conscious minds.

Spirituality has a paradoxical quality. While denying its existence does not abolish it, acting in a way that releases this vital energy in others is the surest way to enhance it for ourselves. Crushing another's spirit reduces this quality for ourselves as well as for the person so shamed. Spirit and spirituality is about widening our horizons, not narrowing them. It is about paying attention to the smallest details, not passing them over. It is about power, morality, and responsibility, in the practical course of the everyday.

While an increasingly great number of people recognize spirituality and the domain of the soul as vital to their understanding of reality and human interaction, there have been philosophers and others, particularly in so-called "Modern" times, who have denied the reality of Spirit and the legitimacy of using it as a frame of reference. Whether we are conscious of it or not, these thinkers have had a profound influence on all areas of our lives, including many of our notions about the role of conflict. Before we go any further, then, it will be helpful to review how our world has been shaped, for good and for ill, by what has come to be known as Modernism.

II

MODERNISM & THE SELF-FULFILLING PROPHECY

*The troubles of states will not end until philosophers become kings,
or until kings and rulers really and truly become philosophers.*
Plato

*Faith in machinery is our besetting danger…
as if it had a value in and for itself.*
Matthew Arnold

For many people, the terms "modernity" and "modernism" cause confusion, because the words appear to have more than one meaning. Most people, when they hear the term "modern," think "contemporary." Yet the academics and pundits we hear interviewed on radio or television, or whose ideas we read, all tend to assume that the term "modernity" refers to a time that is now in the past.

In fact, the "modern era" that scholars and others are referring to started about 400 years ago, when a new and fresh worldview emerged from the medieval period. The "modern" world-as-machine pattern of thinking came out of a convergence of events and ideas, which, for all their conflicting variety, "presented a compelling vision of the universe and of the human being's place in it," according to Richard Tarnas, author of *The Passion of the Western Mind: Understanding the Ideas that Have Shaped Our Worldview*.[1] A mere handful of philosophers and scientists, most notably Galileo Galilei,

Johannes Kepler, Rene Descartes, Robert Boyle, and Isaac Newton, described their new understanding of reality. The universe, they said, was an impersonal phenomenon governed by regular natural laws, and could be understood in exclusively physical and mathematical terms. It was like a great and complicated machine, amenable to human understanding through empirical observation, measurement, and rational processes. These processes of this machine-world, they argued, operated independently of any guiding hand, and in that sense were random.

This approach to or understanding of reality proved most successful in the field of scientific endeavor. The period saw startling and creative invention and gave birth to a vast technology, which has brought us many benefits. It saw a tremendous growth in human potential, through the opening up of society to exchange of ideas and knowledge. It saw the rise of democracy and raised the opportunities for education.

Over time, and certainly during the last half-century, the lot of women and children has improved. Applications of technology based on the modern worldview in the field of medicine and public health have added tens of years to our lifespan and have improved our well-being throughout our lives. Through observation, testing, review, and analysis of the objects and processes of the life-stream as it passes by, we have learned a lot about our world.

Yet certain inadequacies in the principles at the heart of modernity became apparent when those principles were pushed or followed to their logical ends.

Among other things, modernism harbored an overconfidence in our human ability to master or understand nature. The idea that knowledge, in the modernist view, could be pursued independently of values, conscience, or wisdom proved to be its Achilles heel.[2]

As we now realize, the means of gaining knowledge, and the acts that follow, necessarily entail ethical judgments. Denying this is an ethical statement in itself – a statement that permits all sorts of activities, but takes no responsibility for their outcomes, including deleterious side effects on the earth and its equally vulnerable nonhuman inhabitants.

Yet this was acceptable in the modern worldview, because human beings, in thought and practice, were seen as standing apart from nature.

Indeed, they stood apart from each other. Now, of course, we are learning that we are *part* of nature.

Individualism and individual freedom grew to be the defining "virtues" of the modern age.[3] The dignity and priority of the individual was highlighted over any good that might be owed to the collective. Self-interest was stressed with little regard for others' needs or for the common good. The great advances in technology of the Industrial Age occurred simultaneously with the exploitation of human beings, both adults and children, in oppressive labor conditions. Religion, previously the determinant of public order, became a private affair, between an individual and God, divorced from public life and action.

The modern worldview, together with its sterile machine metaphor, now appear insufficient in the light of "reality" as we see it at the beginning of the 21st century. The realization that we cannot ever know everything may be the greatest achievement of the "postmodern" period, in which we now find ourselves. We are beginning to see, for example, that we need to consider different sources of knowledge than the purely empirical, or those that come to us solely by the application of reason. We now recognize as a necessary part of human consciousness knowledge derived from experience and action, knowledge that relates to the values we hold and act upon.

As yet, Western mainstream society is unwilling to acknowledge a *third* source of knowledge: that which relates to the deepest and most transcendent mysteries of the universe and our life within it, and which can be gained through contemplation.[4]

In his book *Living with Other People*, Kenneth Melchin puts the limits of our knowledge rather adroitly. There is the known, which refers to both facts and the values to which we subscribe or reject. And there is the known unknown. This refers to the range of information that is out there as part of the fund of common knowledge and the standard of behavior, but of which we do not have much expertise. And then there is the unknown unknown. This type of knowledge lies beyond our horizons of knowing and caring; we cannot even ask questions. "Our ignorance here," says Melchin, "can raise havoc in moral analysis and action, particularly if we remain unaware or refuse to acknowledge this ignorance in principle."[5]

THE EVOLUTIONARY STORY: TWO CONTRASTING INTERPRETATIONS

Can cooperation emerge among egoists without central authority?
Robert Axelrod

The traditional interpretation given to the evolutionary discoveries made by Charles Darwin provides a classic example of the limits and dangers of the modernist perspective. That interpretation has had a great influence on how we have seen the world and have formulated political policies.

During his voyage on the *Beagle* in the 1830s, Darwin found that birds isolated from each other on different islands in the South Pacific eventually developed features that were particularly suited to their varied environments. As the environment was different on each island, so the resident species became distinct on each, by adapting over generations to the different circumstances. To explain this phenomenon, and in opposition to the belief in the fixed nature of animal species suggested in the first chapter of Genesis, Darwin postulated a natural scheme of selective adaptation over many generations. Change was incremental, he said.

Darwin's discoveries and his theory of selective adaptation were then interpreted by Herbert Spencer. Specifically, Spencer believed that they confirmed a theory put forward by Thomas Hobbes (1588–1679) a couple hundred years earlier. Nature, and "man" too, suggested Hobbes, was "red in tooth and claw," to use Alfred Lord Tennyson's phrase. Only the fittest could survive.

Darwin accepted Spencer's conclusion that there must have been a competitive struggle within each species. Animals, and human beings too, were said to be in perpetual conflict with one another. The physically strong individual survived; the weaklings perished.

This theory fit in well with the themes of dominance that were popular among those who sought to make a virtue of their own desire for power. As a result, members of self-declared superior races used it to justify the harsh treatment of powerless minorities, whether they were aboriginal nations in colonial empires or minorities closer to home.

Today, a more hopeful view of human and nonhuman nature is suggested by recent reinterpretations of Darwin's observations. Now, the positive effects of collaboration have been interjected into the evolutionary story and its interpretation. Taking just one author as representative of many, Robert Axelrod, in his book *The Evolution of Cooperation*, points out that on average and contrary to the Spencerian view, cooperation wins out over competition, because animals, including human animals, learn to band in groups in which individuals have roles and tasks for which they are especially adept. They learn cooperative tactics within their own groups so that together they succeed, whereas isolated individuals might perish.[6] For human beings especially, bonding assists survival; within the time frame of childhood and adolescence, there is opportunity for education, the amassing of skills, and the appreciation of tradition. There is time to learn what it is to be a recognized and contributing member of a social group.

The evidence before our eyes suggests that a closely knit and mutually supportive family group is necessary for human development, and that we would not have reached our present level if these things had not been present. This can be seen at the birth of every human baby. There is a delicate balance between the size of a baby's head, an indicator of its relative maturity and ability to survive the postnatal period, and the survival of the mother through childbirth. The size of our brains, when mature, requires that we are born in a relatively immature state, when the head is not yet too big to pass through the maternal pelvis. The family unit and the tribal group were necessary for the raising of these relatively fragile infants. Mental sophistication, big brains, and nurturing social groups are interdependent factors in human evolution. Through a combination of mental abilities and social structures, many strengths can be built into a group, enhancing its chances of survival and enabling the members to perpetuate their genes. It may be, in other words, that the unit for survival is neither the gene nor the individual, but the group.

Species hold their relationships among each other in a network of dynamic tension, within their given environment. That environment contains both animate and inanimate pressures. All individuals within a species, and from other neighboring species, are themselves part of that environment. They exist in a vibrant, ever changing state, where succeeding generations deal with events as they encounter them. Also, the environment itself will be in a state of flux, presenting new conditions. And so strategies for survival will include both competitive and collaborative elements and the ability to adapt to change.

Competitive opportunities have the effect of honing capabilities when the relationship is one of predator and prey, or of staking out territory and new relationships during courtship. Indeed, competition is not to be dismissed: the presence of hostile outsiders or perils may enhance group cohesiveness and common cause. At other times, previously hostile groups may set aside their differences to meet a common peril or to help in harvests. Cooperation is not something our ancestors could have done without. Clearly, the interactions between people are infinitely more complex than Spencer and his followers ever postulated.

As Lynn Margulis and Dorion Sagan suggest in an article that appeared in the journal *Context*, life did not take over the globe by combat, but by networking.[7] A spirit of cooperation is abroad in a functioning human community, where all members have their roles and work together on routine and special tasks. It is abroad in the delight and sense of worth experienced by each member, as he or she participates in that community's life – a phenomenon disregarded by the earlier evolutionary theorists. Competition and collaboration are integral to the overall matrix of existence. Both, in their place, are life-enhancing and joyful!

SELF-FULFILLING PROPHECIES

The ideological world-picture in terms of which the individual experiences his or her life plays a crucial role in setting expectations and ideals of what it is possible to achieve.

Suzi Gablik

What can we learn by recognizing that there is more than one way to interpret the evidence of the past, and the present as well? How can such contradictory interpretations — nature, "red in tooth and claw" on the one hand, and surviving by cooperation on the other — gain a foothold and find evidence from later events to back them up? For at least a partial answer, we can turn to the findings of social psychologists and international negotiators.

As we saw in Chapter I, our beliefs about the nature of human beings produce behaviors in ourselves and in others that reflect those beliefs. For example, a belief in the essential flawed nature of human beings leads to judgmental attitudes, the casting of blame for perceived hostile actions, and justification for retributive penalties. At the same time, a belief in humanity's essential goodness creates the willingness and opportunity to widen one's understanding of the motivations of others. An open view of human motivation enables one to hear the full story before passing judgment. It does not excuse harmful actions, nor divergence from acceptable moral codes, but calls forth personal responsibility, accountability, and even restitution from the wrongdoer for harm done. Thus an individual at fault is given a chance to explain, and even to be accepted. This is what restorative justice is all about.

Another example of self-fulfilling beliefs can be seen where commitment to a cause creates a dynamic that paves the way to its fulfillment.

Social psychologists have studied the phenomenon of the self-fulfilling prophecy and found that there is a clear-cut relationship between a perceiver's expectation of others, their consequent behavior toward those others, and the target's behavior back toward the perceiver. In other words, the initiation of any behavior creates its own dynamic. Responses to situations become self-perpetuating. Competitors tend to elicit competitive behavior from others and create a distrustful and tough world. Avoidant people elicit avoidance and create a cold and barren world, while secure individuals experience positive interrelationships and build trust more safely and easily. Each personality finds his or her "prophecy" or belief fulfilled. To an extent greater than we usually appreciate, we create our own world through the choices we make, based on our beliefs and values, our perceptions of others' motives and capabilities.

The theory that prophecies have a way of fulfilling themselves has been confirmed in many spheres. Lee Jussim and Jacqueline Eccles, working in the area of education and writing in the *Journal of Personality and Social Psychology*, found that a teacher's belief in his or her students affected the student's success or failure.[8] In the field of politics, John Burton found that "realists" base their assumptions and consequent policies and actions on the belief that violent human behavior is biologically determined. Because of this belief, they insist that citizens and nation states other than their own must be controlled through coercion and a show of strength.

According to Burton, who has had extensive experience as an international negotiator and mediator, there is no evidence to back up this harsh and self-fulfilling theory. Political "realism" provides its own justification, failing to address the underlying causes of conflict among world nations and groups.[9] It is self-defeating – if its aim is really peace, security, and stability.

Burton has concluded, from his own experience and from political science analysis, that what has been termed "idealism" is in practice more realistic than the traditional "realist" power approach. At the international level as much as at the domestic level, peace and justice are linked to the preservation of human honor, dignity, and quality of life, rather than to control through coercive power and threat of force. There is no imperative that would dictate that the only response to competition must be competition. A cooperative or at least neutral response to initial hostility may create an immediate change in the climate between contending parties.

We have this sort of power – to change the game, to set or change the climate of our relationships with others, and the way we manage conflict. Of course, the longer a conflict goes on, the more difficult it is to change attitudes; those involved in deeply seated conflicts can resist change, at least until the cause of the problem and its history have been adequately addressed and understood. It isn't easy to be neutral or gracious in the face of attack, but it is surprising how often it works. Sometimes it may happen that the hostile person was just waiting for a chance to open up the dialogue, but was ignorant of any approach other than defense or attack.

Changing Attitudes

To be sure, the social structures derived from modernity have led piecemeal to movements that have redressed many of its worst excesses. Child labor laws and other constraints on exploitation have been introduced. Political apartheid and other forms of racial oppression and genocide are now more universally condemned than they were even 50 years ago. We are slowly coming to recognize the fragility of our ecosystem.

But these changes in attitude stem from a general sense that humankind has lost its way. We have come to recognize that modernity, despite the gains in human capacity it granted, is an inadequate guide to human interaction and global sustainability. It has gradually been undermined by its own intellectual assumptions and the consequences of applying them to technology and political structures. We are, in some sectors of society at least, beginning to recognize the debilitating sense of insignificance and personal futility, the spiritual loss of faith, and the exploitative and nonsustainable relationships that modernity has brought us.

And yet, it will not profit us to discard modernity. Rather, I think we must ask the question: can we re-evaluate it, build on its more positive aspects, and engage in the search for a more encompassing philosophy; can we encompass and develop its capabilities within a more holistic and sustainable framework? That is the question facing postmodernism.

III

POSTMODERNISM

All human understanding is interpretation, and no interpretation is final.
Richard Tarnas

It is only quite recently, in what we now call the "postmodern era," that we have recognized the extent to which our beliefs and interpretations shape our reality.

In fact, this emphasis on belief and interpretation is one of the things that makes postmodernism so difficult to define. It isn't simply *one* idea or philosophy. It's an *aggregation* of worldviews or beliefs that people have developed over time and in different places as they have come to reject the old ways of thinking about ourselves and the world.

Given the uncertainty of our times, we shouldn't be surprised that many of these ideas have been offered somewhat tentatively. Nor should we be surprised that they are quite diverse, and that some of them are complementary, while others are contradictory.

In order to give some shape to what is essentially, then, a confusion of contrasting ideas, David Griffin has simplified things by identifying two main streams within postmodernism. In his book *Sacred Interconnections*, he has labeled one of those streams "deconstructive," and the other "constructive."[1] I bless him for that simplification!

If we hope to understand the dynamics of conflict today, we need to consider each stream from a theoretical perspective and then look at examples of its influence at the international and individual levels.

DECONSTRUCTIVE POSTMODERNISM

Things fall apart; the centre cannot hold
Mere anarchy is loosed upon the world
The blood-dimmed tide is loosed, and everywhere,
The ceremony of innocence is drowned;
The best lack all conviction, while the worst
Are full of passionate intensity.
William B. Yeats

The deconstructive stream of the postmodern era came about primarily as an extension of modernist thought. During the 20th century, it was compounded by the discoveries of physicists and the splitting of the atom.

But perhaps we should trace this branch of postmodern thought to the 19th-century philosopher Friedrich Nietzsche. It was he, more than anyone else, who brought the essential thinking of the modern era to its logical conclusion. In a rationally determined world, he argued, there is no place for a God. And if God does not exist, human beings have to seek purpose in their lives in human terms alone.

Martin Heidegger, writing in the mid-20th century, went further: if there is no God, he said, then the transcendent, objective values we have accepted do not exist either. Anything and everything can be permitted. Life is essentially absurd, because there can be no ultimate meaning or purpose inherent in our existence.[2] No soul or spirit in his world!

The worldview or perspective that has led to the expression of these nihilistic and amoral pronouncements is essentially anti-world, says David Griffin.[3] It eliminates any point of reference to a sense of value, purpose, meaning, or a concern for the future. It denies the Spirit. Such a worldview tolerates as common sense and inevitable the possibility of one power group or nation annihilating another on slender justification. Nihilism's most dangerous dynamic is the monumental eclipse of hope and meaning and the incredible disregard of human life that it preaches.

Global Consequences

We live in an age of nuclear giants and ethical infants, in a world that has achieved brilliance without wisdom, power without conscience.
General Omar Bradley

It is no coincidence that the discovery of the nature of the atom and its enormous energy occurred in the same period of history as the deconstructive postmodern worldview. Inevitably, the lack of constraints on what is permissible led to the development and use of nuclear weapons during World War II.

Nuclear weapons were developed initially as a source of military might. But military strategists have long asserted that they can serve no military purpose. In 1999, General Lee Butler, Commander of Strategic Nuclear Forces during the Reagan administration, told the Canadian Network to Abolish Nuclear Weapons what it was like to bear the responsibility of this job. Butler had overall command of tens of thousands of crew members and the warhead-delivery systems they operated. He came to appreciate the enormity of the day-to-day risks involved in maintaining some 10,000 strategic weapons. (Even with 2,000 weapons, the risk is overwhelming.) While the record of incidents and accidents in the Soviet Union was chilling, that of the United States was only slightly less horrifying. For instance, a B52 bomber with four nuclear weapons on board crashed in North Carolina. On investigation, it was discovered that six of the seven safety devices had failed. There were many such incidents.

This leading militarist judged that the mutual assured destruction (M.A.D.) plan was the single most absurd and irresponsible document he had ever reviewed. "We escaped the Cold War without a nuclear holocaust," he said, "by some combination of skill, luck, and divine intervention, and I suspect the latter in greatest proportion."[4]

General Butler concludes that the presence of enough weapons to bring about "nuclear winter" many times over condemns humankind to live under a cloud of perpetual anxiety. It is not a legacy that he wants to bequeath to his children or grandchildren. It is simply a question of our political morals.

Despite their potential for annihilation, nuclear weapons are treated as metaphors for national status and security. For the past 50 years or so, we have lived with the awareness that these instruments of political control stand at hair-trigger alert. This reliance on nuclear weapons plays out in political terms the nihilism of the deconstructive postmodern philosophers. There is a sense of existential *powerlessness* and mindlessness in how nuclear nations view their influence in the world.

Whether it comes by an act of terrorists, or by national leaders dispatching a few bombers, or by some fallibility of human nature or accident, discharge of even a fraction of the available nuclear weapons would risk the extinction of all higher elements of Earth's Great Foundation of Being and leave nothing but inanimate, radioactive, barren rocks and sand.

The splitting of the atom has deep philosophical and spiritual consequences for humanity. It has changed forever the relationship between human beings and the natural, Earth-derived order that sustains us. As Robert Oppenheimer, leader of the Manhattan Project which produced the bomb, lamented, "We have sinned." Referring to the Hindu text the Bhagavad Gita, he said, "We have become Death, the shatterer of worlds." Oppenheimer realized, when it was too late, the implications of a science bereft of ethical standards. This leading scientist acknowledged the existence of a Power whose majesty he and his colleagues had usurped. In mythic terms, it might be said that we have left the Garden of Eden a second time.

Not all nuclear physicists have accepted Oppenheimer's level of moral and existential responsibility, even in hindsight. For instance, Louis de Broglie, winner of the Nobel Prize in 1929 for physics, considered that "Scientific discoveries *and their applications* of which they are capable are, in themselves, neither good nor bad; all depends on the use we make of them" (my italics).[5]

Few would argue against using our abilities and intellects to explore the unknown. But as soon as discoveries are made, we have to make a choice about how this new knowledge will be used and applied; it becomes a matter of ethics. There needs to be a closer link between the discoveries of modern science and the activities that derive from them, a link that can be extended through moral vigilance. This vigilance is best exercised in a proactive manner, rather than as a reaction to disastrous consequences after the fact.[6]

Consequences for Individuals

*I can endure my own despair,
But not another's hope.*
William Walsh

How do ordinary people experience the nihilistic ideas so current at the present time?

A negativistic way of thinking has, directly and indirectly, a profound effect on the human spirit. Many thoughtful people are aware of the debilitating alienation that disrupts and renders meaningless the cohesion and purposes of society. A sense of emptiness points in some instances to an estrangement from one's own self, or from other people, or from any sense of meaning in life. It is a denial of the human spirit and its power. This sense of debility is displayed in a variety of ways.

- Rollo May[7] sees inner emptiness as a major problem in contemporary society. Many report that they have little understanding of who they are. They even deny the validity of their own feelings. These folks see themselves only in reference to other people's approval, and become preoccupied with a need for acceptance. As a consequence, rather than be self-determining, they live as projections of other people's perspectives. Their locus of control, says Julian Rotter,[8] lies external to their own personhood. Instead of making decisions according to their personal sense of right or wrong, they look to rewards and punishments, which they receive from others. In this way they can absolve themselves from responsibility for their decisions and how they act on them.

  Other individuals struggle to overcome their emptiness through continual personal reconstruction. They grasp for material satisfaction, a source of gratification that does not sustain their innermost longings for personal integrity. Their emptiness is expressed in alienation from other people. They are afraid to make permanent commitments for fear of jeopardizing their freedom – a freedom that does not satisfy.

- Mary Clark[9] describes others who see their sole quest in life directed toward a radical individualism. They are self-centered and narcissistic, regarding their own self as a sacred object. This turning inward, away from connections with others, exacerbates the alienation.

These deconstructive, alienating, and nihilistic philosophies are being re-examined on many fronts. In the first place, they are self-contradictory. A meaningless philosophy has, by its own definition, no meaning. People are looking for a more creative philosophy of life, as the success of self-help books must surely attest. Ultimately, the deconstructive philosophy is abhorrent and unsustainable, and committed people are taking responsible steps to rectify it at the international, community, and personal levels. This commitment forms the core of the constructive stream of postmodernism.

CONSTRUCTIVE POSTMODERNISM

A return forward.
David Ray Griffin

While honoring the modernist world for its unparalleled advances, constructive postmodernism seeks to move beyond it through a creative synthesis that combines the best of modernist premises and the traditional concepts that preceded them. Constructive postmodernism involves a new unity of scientific, ethical, aesthetic, and spiritual intuitions.

New understandings of the complexity and indeterminacy of reality have come not only from theologians and philosophers, but also from those very atomic physicists who caused so much trouble in the first place. Werner Heisenberg, for example, found that observed phenomena seem to change just by the fact that they are being observed. According to Fritjof Capra, every time modern (quantum and relativity) physicists asked a question about nature, the answer contained a paradox.[10]

Fundamental uncertainties and unexpected dynamic processes discovered by the physicists cause us to revise our notions of a world of solid structure, previously thought to be static. Even our current understanding cannot be the final word about the nature of ultimate reality. Physicists, among others, now know enough to savor the fact that they are limited in what they can know, and will always be faced with such limitations. Goodbye modernity. Welcome to the era of living creatively with ontological uncertainty.

Ken Wilber is the editor of a book called *Quantum Questions: Mystical Writings of the World's Great Physicists*.[11] The physicists whose writings appear in the book, he says, came to realize that when they were exploring the physical nature of the world, they were dealing with shadows, symbols, and illusions, not Ultimate Reality. To go beyond the shadows of physics was to head toward the metaphysical and the mystical. For many of these physicists, the only way to explain the universe was to maintain that it exists in the mind of some eternal Spirit. In that sense, the universe appears to be more of a "thought" than a "machine" — a Profound Consciousness appears to lie at the heart of reality.[12]

Constructive postmodernism looks beyond surface meanings to discern the forces that shape us — our interconnections and our society. It appreciates that many influences lie beyond our limited human consciousness, within an umbrella of an ultimate transcendent reality. Constructive postmodernists persuade us to return to the Divine Essence, "because it is there."

International Political Approaches

All policy making involves choosing among alternatives.
K. J. Holsti

Vital and constructive political processes that could circumvent our dependence on the deterrent of nuclear weapons are now being pursued in the international field. These processes appear to be based on a philosophy that is at once more practical and potentially sustaining. This philosophy is well-articulated by Thomas Franck, political scientist and author.

It is not so much threat or coercive power that binds nations together, says Franck. What binds nations in treaty-keeping is a shared sense of both legitimacy and justice.[13] These qualities provide power of quite another sort than coercion or threat. They derive from a shared consciousness of people's need for order and predictability. Diplomats and negotiators such as John Burton[14] and Jay Rothman[15] would agree from their own practical experience that strategic issues and power balances are seldom the root causes of unsolvable conflicts.

Once agreements that meet basic human needs are worked out, the legitimacy of rules and treaties depends on their provenance and clarity, says Franck, so that there may be a common understanding in applying and abiding by them. Not to obey such agreed-upon rules, clearly stated, invites shame and ridicule – more significant motivators for compliance than coercion and threat. Symbolic validation, ritual, and the pedigree or historical origins of rules and treaties enhance legitimacy despite being allegorical and fragile. Their very tenuousness creates the need for collaboration. Respect and honor are created reciprocally. A modicum of security arises from accepting these principles and provides a sense of being able to predict each other's actions and responses.

Principles of fairness, credibility, and affiliation have been found to be powerful and sustaining motivators. The legitimate interests of governments for autonomy, security, the welfare of their people, and their need for status and prestige (the four main purposes of states as defined by K. J. Holsti[16]), can be granted and accepted reciprocally. We must recognize, however, that this cooperation and acknowledgement is not something that can be gained and kept. It must be continually re-created.

Nations around the globe create their own reality to the extent that they act in a trustworthy and reciprocal manner with one another. World leaders who attempt to build trust and reciprocity experience high drama through intense work and commitment. They continually re-create, perhaps without articulating it, a spiritual connection between each other, a web of interconnecting threads that creates a fabric of whole cloth from the often-tattered remnants of historical memory. There is always a danger, of course, that some untoward event will tear the fabric apart so that the whole thing will unravel before their eyes. Theirs is a life of risk, requiring commitment buoyed by a spirit and belief that the world of political actors can be held together, despite the nay-sayers and the powers of human error and happenstance that so often work against them.

Many international ventures, such as the initiatives of the United Nations, are directed by their members' combined efforts to bring cohesion and security to the world through dialogue, sustaining hope through a commitment that must surely reflect a spiritual appreciation of what can be. Nevertheless, the Councils of the United Nations, because of insufficient political will, tolerate inaction even when it has become obvious that intervention could save lives. The debacle in Rwanda is a case in point, where, although U.N. troops were already on the ground in considerable numbers, they withdrew and allowed genocide by the hundreds of thousands to occur.

The role and influence on world opinion of grassroots and non-government organizations is growing every day as their commitment and wide knowledge gain them credibility. Notable victories include the success in obtaining an opinion from the World Court, in July 1996, concerning the threat or use of nuclear weapons. (The court declared such use would be in violation of international law.) This consideration and decision was gained through an enormous co-partnership of organizations and individuals expressing their beliefs on a matter of conscience. The Landmines Treaty of 1997 was also the culmination of work done by many non-government groups and committed individuals.

Chief among continuing anxieties is the nuclear threat, already mentioned. Its resolution will deeply transform world attitudes and relationships. To the extent that this sword hanging over our heads focuses attention on global interdependencies, it generates new levels of awareness. Where this awareness takes root in institutions, those institutions may be further borne along by the dynamics of such interdependencies. What often seems a crisis of despair may be simultaneously a crisis of growth in the human community.[17]

Resiliency among Individuals

*The resilient forge their bedrock faith in a benevolent kingdom
despite childhood experiences that would predict the repetition of a dark life.
They actively recruit benevolent surrogates amongst acquaintances
and selectively internalize relationships that sustain them.
During adolescence they develop the ability to reflect,
in order to find a better path for their own life.*
Gina O'Connell Higgins

In contrast to the acceptance of victimhood described in the previous section on the deconstructive postmodernism, people with a constructive postmodern perspective display a marvelous resiliency in overcoming the effects of abuse, neglect, or oppressive domination. Not only do these people survive, they grow in maturity. Gina O'Connell Higgins, herself a survivor of childhood abuse, has written a poetic and insightful account of "resilient adults" in her book of that name.[18]

Two overarching themes emerge from Higgins' studies. The resilient had faith that they could surmount their obstacles on the way to health. And they had faith in human relationships as the source from which to base that victory. Faith, she says, is different than belief; it is a relational enterprise infused with the imagination to create a master narrative that sustains it. With the help of others, resilient people integrate positive experiences and create their own reality, within the context of their lives. This new reality does not come without a tremendous investment; it takes a great effort to work through negative experiences. But the spirit is aflame in these dynamic people. Their resilience is evidence of a force that seems to protect and foster mental health, even under the most adverse conditions. It stems in part, of course, from the support they receive from others in the community who provide them with hopeful models. This support and leadership is a shared responsibility of the emerging resilient and their associates.

The trait of resilience, of seeing hope where others see none, is also displayed by many people facing terminal illness from breast cancer, according to research carried out by Shelley Taylor and Jonathan Brown.[19] Taylor and Brown found that, when coming to terms with their situations, these apparently otherwise "normal" people interpret the world in ways that may not seem to be rational. "Unrealistically" positive views of themselves, exaggerated perceptions of personal control and optimism about their future, however short it may be, enable them to continue to care for others, to be serene and contented, and to engage in productive and creative work. They remodel their priorities and create meaning where others might see only despair. They accept reality more vividly than the rest of us and treasure the time they have left as a priceless gift. A sense of personal control, essential for self-concept and self-esteem, is regained. What to others seems a crisis of despair becomes for them an opportunity to build a life that brings meaning and integrity. Where does this quality of hope come from? It is surely not based on outcome, for they have come to terms with their impending death.

Cynthia Bourgeault talks of "mystical hope," in her book of the same name.[20] Perhaps this is what these "ordinary" warriors have experienced. Mystical hope is not tied to a good outcome, she says, but lives a life of its own, without reference to external circumstances and conditions. It has something to do with *presence*: the immediate experience of being met and held in communion by something intimately at hand. It bears fruit within us at the psychological level in the sensations of strength, joy, and satisfaction – an "unbearable lightness of being." Mysteriously, these gifts do not seem to come from some outward expectation, but seem to be produced from within. The dark night of the soul of these cancer patients has enabled them to experience the Spirit in powerful ways that give meaning to life.

Conflict and Spirit in the Postmodern Age

All things are implicated with one another, and the bond is holy.
Marcus Aurelius

"It is better to light a candle than to curse the darkness." In postmodern times, we may find ourselves dwelling in the darkness and the hopelessness of a nihilistic worldview, or within a crushing interpersonal conflict. From that dark place we may struggle to discover a new reality, something of value. We can use the candle of hope and meaning to construct a better, future worldview. We do not disregard our experiences of destruction or despair, but we work through them to find purpose and the means for transformation.

Constructive postmodern thinkers – whether they be philosophers, economists, politicians, feminists, or spiritual directors – stress not isolation or alienation, but essential connectedness. They seek not a body-mind dualism, but a holistic personhood made up of many integrated parts working in harmony. Egoistic-centered patriarchy and self-centered domination of any kind are set in perspective by inclusive feminism and consensus building; political advisers and leaders are pressed to depend for security not on militarism but on expenditures that enhance life. Constructive postmodern spirituality seeks wisdom, but a wisdom transformed. We learn that our world is one of ambiguity and intangibles, where one can search in vain for absolutes.

The awakening of physicists to the enormity of their discoveries, in particular Heisenberg's Uncertainty Principle, and to paradox, can be seen as a transforming parable; their sense that a Unity of Consciousness permeates our universe can provide a vision of a new and embracing spirituality. And that spirituality can transform the way we deal with conflict, both within ourselves and interpersonally.

An appreciation of the Spirit has been characteristic of human experience from the time we became aware of the world around us. From earliest times, human beings have channeled this awareness of the mystical into structures of belief and ritual, called religion. It is to these coherent patterns of meaning that we now turn.

IV

RELIGION

*Each religious tradition possesses such rich spiritual resources –
ideas of holiness and perfection, teachings on justice, love and compassion,
on peace and human unity, visions of true freedom and wholeness of wisdom
and experiences of contact with the eternal.*
Ursula King

"Long, long ago, beyond the misty space of twice ten thousand years," as the poet James Clarence Mangan puts it, humankind developed consciousness, and with it, an awareness of the world around it. People, in their primitive communities, sought to understand this world and how to live in right relation to it. This relationship meant more than mere survival or prosperity. Human beings sought to be at one with the created order. Their first attempts to live in tune with nature were fraught with magic and attempts to propitiate the powers that surrounded them. As their beliefs took shape, religion coordinated each group's collective consciousness of the nature of the world, through ritual and customs. It was through these rituals and customs that they passed on their sacred truths. Later, the ability to write facilitated transmission of this lore.

Throughout recorded history, guidance has come from the insights of great human spirits who transcended their times with profound messages – sages such as Lao Tzu, Confucius, Moses, the Buddha, Plato, Jesus, and Muhammad. Seeking to provide moral guidance, religions adopted some form of the "Golden Rule": *Do unto others as you would have them do unto you.* Early Christian traditions, derived as they were from the Jewish Pentateuch, expressed this imperative in two central ordinances: *Love the Lord your God and love your neighbor as yourself.*

Religion has presented a series of systems by which humankind has sought to understand and express its relationship with the sacred, with the eternal, Ultimate Reality. Many emphasize connection with a Supreme Being: the theistic religions. Others, such as Buddhism, relate primarily to right ways of living and the support of human relationships and all other forms of life. The narratives of all great religions are archetypes that connect with the deepest condition of humanity. They speak of sorrow and loss, heroism and betrayal, faith and hope. That is why they go on touching us so profoundly.[1]

Each religious tradition identifies for its adherents a specific set of beliefs and practices to bring them into the light of a common understanding. How each religion articulates both the Divine Presence or Principle and its attendant beliefs about human nature, plays a major role in how its adherents approach life and its dilemmas. Sacred scriptures have provided powerful messages that have shaped human history. But they are human structures, subject to challenge, dissolution, and reformation. We raise these ordinances to the status of "absolute truth" at our peril. Religious wars break out when a group takes upon itself the authority of Ultimate Truth, which it then denies to others. Zealots, often preaching peace, have instigated the bitterest of wars between themselves and those whom they perceive to hold rivaling beliefs. We have only to recall the Crusades of the 12th century, when not only Muslims but also many members of the Christian Greek Orthodox Church were slaughtered under the order of the Roman Pope Urban II.

When religious leaders set themselves up as the arbiters of Divine Will, as has happened in Christianity and most other religions, the result is oppression and the constraint of their own people's freedom. Imposition of such power inflicts an ultimately domesticating force, especially if it becomes identified with a political, secular regime. An example was the situation in Quebec before the quiet revolution of the early 1960s. For 200 years, the Roman Catholic Church had been the only real authority in the province.[2]

The clerics had grown accustomed to both wielding and acquiescing to political influence. The severity of the oppression and the sense of release from its bondage can be seen in the magnitude of the backlash that followed. According to Preston Jones, writing in the journal *First Things First*, Quebec is now one of the most militant anti-Catholic Western societies.

Ritual

Rituals are those repeated observances in which we engage to experience and express our common sense of the sacred. In the life of any religiously based community, rituals play a central role in enhancing collective spirituality. They shape, express, and maintain important relationships within the community. They celebrate the deep joy and honoring of life in all its sacred aspects. As they celebrate the Ultimate, they engage all our senses: the ear through music, speech, and storytelling; the eye through art and the kinetic movements of our bodies in ceremony and dance. They dramatize time, space, and movement through pilgrimage and drama. They bring people together in solidarity – sometimes in pregnant, collective silence; sometime in the breaking of bread and the sharing of a meal. Each vehicle, singly or in combination, provides a participatory metaphor that expresses the sacred and enhances interconnections between the members. Because rituals express human existential aspirations so powerfully, they enhance people's experience of life.

At the same time, rituals have practical applications. As Anthony Giddens points out in his book *The Consequences of Modernity*, without ritual and collective involvement, individuals are left without structured ways of coping with tensions and anxieties. Communal rites provide a focus for group solidarity at major transitions. The rhythms of ritual can reduce disruptive tensions arising within the group, preventing conflict. Or, alternatively, they may drum up the collective will of the group to attack a perceived enemy. To this very day, the fife and drum and the rhetoric of leaders inspire a collective awakening within our own societies.

Traditional rituals connect individual action to a moral framework and to elemental questions about human existence. The loss of ritual means the loss of such frameworks.[3] These kinds of rituals may, to a large extent, be culturally determined.

For example, many faiths and traditions have special times of instruction for teenagers, to bridge the time when childhood is passed and adult life is to begin. This period of instruction usually culminates in a rite of entrance into the community of the grownups.

In my own case, this rite occurred at the time of my confirmation. It was a rite of passage, denoting formal acceptance into the Anglican Church of Ireland. I was to undertake responsibility for the promises made on my behalf by my godparents at my infant baptism. My early teenaged years had been times of doubt about the place of religion in my life. Yet confirmation was expected of the members of our boarding school class, and we did not protest. Along with the rest of the class, I was required to learn by rote a catechism of doctrine about our particular brand of Christianity.

Duly prepared, we came at last to that special day, to the service at the local church to receive the "laying on of hands." What an appropriate expression! The prescribed readings laid special emphasis on the rite's continuity with the first apostles, 2000 years before. Thus we were encouraged to feel part of a time-honored and holy tradition. After ritualized questions and answers in front of our friends and relatives in the congregation, we received the blessing and were accepted as full members of our religion. For me, the highlight was the unexpected and inspired address by Archbishop Arthur Barton. I began to appreciate the meaning of sacred scripture, transcending formalized words. It was a transforming experience. Somehow, we came out as different people, ready to begin our adult lives expectantly. But it was not just a transformation of each of us as individuals, but as part of the wider collective of family and friends.

The use of rituals is not confined to religion. Secular institutions, such as those of the legal system, use ritual to enhance the authority of their processes. Because of their ability to heighten experience and give it meaning, rituals have a place in all human interaction, and may be especially appropriate and helpful when individuals find themselves confronting difficult problems and seeking ways to resolve them.

Religious devotees usually express and live their faith according to one of two distinct models. In the ascetic, monastic model of renunciation, the holy one withdraws from society. In the second, contrasting model, the faithful see their role as being within society, involved in everyday affairs. Sometimes monastic orders alternate retreat and contemplation with outreach into the community to instruct, guide, and help those in need. In Hinduism and Buddhism, the idea of the "world renouncer" is the stronger theme, while followers of Sikhism, Judaism, and Islam are more concerned with worldly affairs.[4] Christianity has potent streams embracing both traditions. However, it is the more practical, living-in-the-world branch of religious influence that will receive emphasis here, although the influence of contemplation and other solitary practices will not be overlooked.

My religious tradition is Christian, so I use it as my primary model. Like Islam, Judaism, and Hinduism, Christianity is a theistic religion, though it holds some basic principles in common with the non-theistic religion of Buddhism. Let's pause to identify what these principles are, for what we share in common may help us to appreciate the realities behind the Great Foundation of Being.

BUDDHISM

The thought manifests as the word;
The word manifests as the deed;
The deed develops into habit;
And habit hardens into character;
So watch the thought and its way with care;
And let it spring from love
Born out of concern for all things.
     The Buddha

Buddhists do not identify a God, but seek the principles of enlightenment.

Buddhism arose from the teachings of Gautama Siddharta (the Buddha), who lived in the fifth century BCE. Because it does not believe in any form of deity, Buddhism stands in contrast to the theistic religions of Judaism, Christianity, and Islam. Its principles focus on right actions towards other people, on a horizontal plane, in contrast to the vertical relationship between God and humanity emphasized in theistic religions.

Yet the teachings of Buddha suggest parallels with Christian notions of the Way, the Truth, and the Life. The Buddhist Eight-fold Path speaks of pursuing wisdom through right views and intentions; morality through right speech, action, and livelihood; and meditation through right effort, mindfulness, and concentration.[5] In the book *Conflict Transformation*, Johan Galtung draws comparisons between Judeo-Christianity and Buddhism. He points out that the civilization based on Buddhism and the civilization based on Christianity have strong views on harmony, with precepts such as the law of karma in the former, and the law of God in the latter. Infraction is detected by either an omniscient God, or by detraction from the general level of karma. If a sin is committed, the Christian will strive to improve his or her standing with God, whereas in Buddhism the sinner will wish to improve the karma.[6] Each of these two spiritual paths directs its followers towards an ideal, although in very different ways.

Galtung goes on to point out that, in Buddhist communities, help may also come from other members of the community in which the erring person abides – an emphasis that may be lost in modern-day Christianity. Only within that particular Buddhist community can the transgression be cancelled. Relief from error can be achieved through dialogue (identifying how the bad karma developed and how it might be improved), and by carrying out the prescribed, meritorious saving act.

Merit and demerit are not the sole responsibility of an individual, however; they are shared. Because each action may have arisen from the influence of another person, *everyone* is collectively responsible for the actions of community members. For errors not rectified in this life, the individual may be held responsible in ensuing reincarnations. Thus karma is a holistic concept transcending individual lifespans in time and place.

Buddhism is known for its nonviolence and disapproval of the destruction of life. It teaches the desirability of non-injury, of treating all creatures as gently as possible. The paramount Buddhist virtue is compassion. Because all living beings suffer from ignorance, they are entrapped in the meshes of the cycle of death and rebirth. That's just how it is. A Buddhist's focus, then, is to labor for the salvation of all, both the wise and the unenlightened. Each devotee is required to sacrifice or postpone his or her own achievement of nirvana to accomplish this outcome for others.

CHRISTIANITY

In the beginning was the Word...and the Word was God.
John 1:1

Over the past 2000 years, Christian belief systems have developed several diverging views on the nature of God, the interpretation of its sacred scriptures, and the ability of human beings to carry out Divine purposes. One tradition envisions God as a stern though potentially merciful judge and monarch. A second tradition developed out of a belief in God's bestowal of grace on select members of Christ's redeemed church. A third tradition sees God as Ultimate Love, extended to all, and Jesus as a model to guide human thought and action.

The tradition that sees God as judge tends to portray human nature as basically flawed. Here, our actions would naturally slide toward error. The second tradition discriminates between the chosen and the rejected. The chosen will be saved; the rejected will be abandoned. The third tradition places all humanity and nature within the orbit of God's unconditional love. It asserts that we have an inherent tendency toward goodness and that we have free will to make choices.

These models have had a profound influence on world history. Our beliefs about the nature of the Divine and our own human nature matter profoundly in all our attitudes and relationships.

God as Monarch and Judge

[And God said] "I am monarch of all I survey."
William Cooper

The Christian tradition that pictures God as a monarch and judge emphasizes the transcendence of God, and holds that the Divine exists at a distance, far off in Heaven. Human beings are judged to be essentially flawed; their basic disposition is to rebel against Divine will. In keeping with this model of belief, the early church assumed the role of mediator between sinful humanity and God. It then developed political clout as an institution, adopting the power dynamics of a secular state. The blending of secular and religious authority occurred soon after the Emperor Constantine granted Christianity state recognition in the fourth century CE. But the *church* granted itself powers mightier than any secular power could claim – powers based on the control of believers' minds and hearts, and on the fear of damnation.

This emphasis on the basic sinfulness of humankind focused on the need for constant self-scrutiny, confession, and penance. It imposed a shackle from which there could be only momentary relief. Thus, the idea of a loving and merciful God, believed by the earliest Christians, was displaced by that of a tyrant, who had to be propitiated to prevent "him" from casting souls into an everlasting hell. It is a theme that continued throughout the Middle Ages and is still in evidence in some contemporary churches. With its emphasis on punishment and control, this belief continues to influence how our justice system deals with crime. It also affects our relationships with groups and nations believed to be acting contrary to our secular interests.

The Christian as Self-appointed Agent of God

> *[And Man said] "I am monarch of all I survey."*
> William Cooper rephrased

Following the Reformation in the 16th century, the perceived relation of the Divine to humankind underwent some critical changes. The power of God, previously delegated to the institutional church, passed to the individual. Church prelates were no longer seen as necessary mediators between sinful humanity and God. As individual members in "Christ's body," with direct access to God's grace, church members gained a new sense of independence and self-sufficiency. Indeed, some Christians soon began to see themselves as special, as "Chosen People," as God's "elect."[7] Their attitude of self-righteousness was confirmed in their own minds by their prosperity, gained through a work ethic and the resulting acquisition of worldly commodities. Thus, they claimed a cloak of godly virtue. Those outside the mantle of the elect were believed to be cut off from the Divine Source, and were often treated as less than human.

Certain groups of Christians are not the only ones to have identified themselves as "the chosen people of God," of course. Virtue is often claimed in ethnocentric terms and inspires much of the world's deadliest conflicts.

Still, among these Christians, belief in their "chosen people" status and in their consequent moral superiority also resulted in a change of attitudes toward the less prosperous members within their own communities. According to Richard Tawney, author of *Religion and the Rise of Capitalism*, before the Reformation, the powerful had continued to provide at least *some* measure of care for all community members throughout the medieval period. But the rise of capitalism provided justification for the powerful to dominate and control others. Virtue was found not in working with other members of society for the mutual benefit of all but in working for each person's own gain and self-interest.

Insisting that personal character was paramount and the circumstances of others not worthy of consideration, the powerful concluded that those who fell by the wayside were guilty, not of misfortune that might have been mitigated or relieved, but of moral failure. Riches were no longer an object of suspicion, but a reward for working within the mandate of God. Thus, the essence of Christian virtue was almost exactly reversed, from love of neighbor to exaltation of self.[8]

The scriptural pronouncement that humanity has a God-given mandate to rule all of nature (Genesis 1:26 NIV), or to dominate it (according to the King James version), combined with a sense of moral righteousness, has encouraged many of the worst excesses of global exploitation. It has had drastic consequences for human populations and the ecology on which we all depend, especially in recent times because of the scale of our technological abilities. It has produced a philosophy of individualism whereby the individual pursues his or her own self-interest and the function of society is merely to control the worst excesses. It is a theology of alienation that has brought us to a century characterized by the most brutal war mythology of all time.

God as Love: *Agape* (αγαπη) and the Welfare of All

*The reduction of the universe to a single being,
the expansion of a single being even to God, this is love.*
Victor Hugo

Finally, we come to the tradition that emphasizes God as love and human nature as reflecting that love in its search for an authentic relationship with the Divine.

A good place to start is with the early part of the Hebrew Bible, the Jewish writings known as the Pentateuch. In his book *Spirit Matters*, Michael Lerner points to the Pentateuch wisdom tradition and says we have been born out of God's love and the love that permeates the universe.[9] We have every reason to see each other as created in the image of God (the more visionary part of Genesis 1:26) and to treat each other as such. If all people are born in the image of God, then it follows that our nature will be basically virtuous. Sin is not automatic, although we may fall into error if we act heedlessly, or through ignorance, when presented with moral dilemmas. However, the fact that we have this awareness and the ability to make choices also means that we are burdened by the need to take responsibility for our actions, in parallel with a deep desire for what is good. Here, our human task, given by the Divine creator, is to be trustworthy stewards of all creation.

In the New Testament account of the Sermon on the Mount (Matthew 5:1–16), Jesus, in pronouncing the blessings of a virtuous life, assumed that we were capable of responding graciously, even in difficult, soul-numbing circumstances. Our desire for the welfare of all, which is the concept of *agape* love (Matthew 5:43–44) must include even our enemies. This special word for caring – *agape* – also appears in Jesus' commissioning of Peter.

Jesus confronted Peter after the latter had denied knowing Jesus during the time of the trial. Jesus did not reproach him; instead he asked him if he loved him. Each time Peter asserted that he did love him, Jesus stated

"Feed my sheep." The wavering of loyalty was in the past, and having been reaffirmed, Peter could be entrusted with the care of the disciples.

The word *agape* also appears in Paul's first letter to the Corinthians. Love is patient, love is kind. It does not envy, it does not boast, it is not proud. It is not rude, it is not self-seeking, it is not easily angered, it keeps no record of wrongs. Love does not delight in evil but rejoices with the truth. It always protects, always trusts, always hopes, always perseveres (1 Corinthians 13:4–7, New Greek English Interlinear New Testament).

Jesus' gospel stresses the redemptive and soul re-creative effects of suffering, and the exercise of hope. *Agape* love has more to do with grace than with passion. It has everything to do with intentions, with the commitment to serve one another, and with a willingness to be vulnerable in the context of that service. Openness to life's predicaments, which underlies such love, is evidence of a full and unconditional commitment to the other's "completion," to the willingness to help the other to become all that he or she can be. Through that completion of others, we ourselves come to completion.

Agape love means succoring and bringing justice to those lacking the essential needs of daily life, to those without status, or who are subject to humiliation or marginalization at the hands of the more powerful. The spirituality of liberation theology strives to empower the oppressed and the poor. Gustavo Gutierrez, a strong exponent and practitioner of *agape* ministry, asserts that such poverty is a scandalous condition, inimical to human dignity and contrary to the will of God, the God who has a special concern and compassion for the poor.[10]

For people with this perspective, the Good News of the gospels cannot be good news unless it is put into practice by bringing healing, liberation, and new life into the pressing and particular circumstances of life. *Agape* love is truly relational. It is tough love, centered on the individual, on personal responsibility, on the "I" in the center of the storm. It is disciplined, caring, resilient, reflective, and aware.

Using the concept of servant leadership, Robert Greenleaf articulates this theology of care and commitment to the welfare of others.[11] This kind of paradoxical leadership acknowledges and respects the freedom of the other and seeks to enhance the other's celebration of who they are. It is characterized by listening and seeking to understand; it is not afraid to hear the message of the other, and, if necessary, to withdraw and re-orient oneself; it is not afraid of silence. It accepts others and has empathy for them. In some sense, the servant leader is a companion to those going through the stress of challenging times. He or she is tolerant of imperfections – of his or her own imperfections, as well as the imperfections of others. Through intuition and foresight, the servant leader displays wisdom – sometimes seeming to know the unknowable and foresee the unforeseeable, sometimes having a feel for emerging patterns before they are obvious.

Innumerable community-service agencies – some run by Christians, some by secular authorities – practice servant leadership by providing care, support, and leadership for the less fortunate. These efforts enable people to attain true equality as valued citizens who can help themselves and in turn help others.

Wherever it is exercised, *agape* love, embodied in servant leadership, results in an astonishing increase in zest, creativity, and productivity, while bonding people into communities of mutual caring.[12] It is indeed a flowering of the Spirit, a manifestation of God. It is also the spirit we can bring to peace-making and conflict management.

ISLAM

Allah loves those who act in justice.
The Qur'an 49:8
N. J. Dawood, *translator*

In recent months and years, the religion of Muslims has increasingly gained the attention of Westerners, though much of that attention has been negative. Still, Islam is the fastest growing religion in North America. More importantly, the great majority of Muslims in North America live peaceful, industrious lives, raising families while devoutly continuing their religious practices. They enjoy the freedom provided by our more open society, for many have come from regions where despotic rule is the norm.

It is important to note, therefore, that the concept of *jihad* is not, as modern Islamic fundamentalists would have us believe, a form of spiritual warfare against unbelievers, or a weapon of retaliatory violence used to redress grievances. This interpretation and call to arms is embraced by only a tiny minority, according to internationalist Scott Appleby.[13] Originally, the term *jihad* was used to signify the need to master oneself, including one's uncontrollable passions, lack of spiritual discipline, and tendencies toward illegitimate violence.

The Islamic holy book, the Qur'an, speaks of God (Allah) as a single entity, Compassionate and Merciful. Allah loves believers who submit and make peace in equity and justice, the Qur'an teaches. Islamic societies have effective rituals of conflict management and reconciliation, and it is through these that justice and healing may be brought about.[14] One of the principle Islamic practices is to give alms so that widows, orphans, and other people in need may be cared for. Attention is focused on one's duty to the community and its cohesion.

All these precepts point to the constructive aims of Islam. However, the priority of looking after its own members has often meant that distinctions are drawn between the insiders of a group and those outside, to whom a lesser duty is required.

It should be noted that Islamic practices, while stemming from the guidance and pre-eminence of Muhammad, vary widely between sects and nations, and many reflect local custom. The choice articulated by Moses – for life or for death – is echoed in Islam by the ongoing tension between peace and the use of the sword as a means for carrying out Allah's wishes.

But is this any different from the Christian story? In the search for peace with justice, history has shown that Christians, too, have resorted to violence in the name of righteousness to redress wrongs, and have brought about further suffering and injustices as a result.

RELIGIOUS INSTITUTIONS & THEIR RELATION TO THE STATE

The various modes of worship which prevailed in the Roman world were all considered...by the magistrate to be as equally useful.
Edward Gibbon

Religious institutions the world over have worked out a variety of relationships to the governments of the countries under which they operate. For instance, Christianity, after being accepted by Constantine, became co-opted by the state and thus took on political attitudes, strategies, and powers. Some believers, however, were *not* enticed or co-opted by such worldly promises. Secularization of Christian institutions and practices led many early hermits to seek purity by withdrawing to solitude and prayer in the desert.

Throughout history, when state and religion have joined forces, the state has donned the mantle of these religious traditions in times of war. Each country, therefore, asserts that God is on its side and that its acts have divine sanction. Thus, wars are no longer based solely on the interests of the contending sides, but have become ideological in nature.

A battleground also exists in the civil realm. This battleground lies between the established hierarchy of the church and state, and those who wish to liberate themselves by working for the poor and the dispossessed. For those who carry themes of *agape* love further than their religious and secular masters are comfortable with, the risk of personal sacrifice is very real. In such instances, martyrdom usually comes at the hands of the religious and political leaders, and is not one of the aims of the workers.

Others, however, *do* seek martyrdom as part of their aim, though agape love is only rarely part of their motivation. The difference can be seen in two examples: the martyrdom of Buddhist monks in Vietnam, and the "martyrdom" of suicide bombers in Palestine and North America. In both examples, martyrdom was sought in order to make a political point. However, the monks killed only themselves in their attempt to raise public awareness, whereas the bombers took many innocent victims with them. The former action drew attention to the sacrifice and cause, while the latter brought about an even more violent reaction.

In many states run under the auspices of a religious belief system, religion and politics are indistinguishable. In some countries, many of them Islamic, there are no separate secular governance structures. In regions where Buddhism is practiced, government leaders identify, at least in name, with Buddhism, although this teaching is modified to suit the secular power and culturally determined systems of government. For example, during the Second World War, the invasion of China by Japan was seen as a war fought in keeping with Zen Buddhist principles. A teacher, Harada, equated battlefield loyalty, marching, and shooting, with the highest wisdom of enlightenment.[15] Spain, at the time of the Inquisition, provides an equally iniquitous Christian-fostered example; people were put to the torch if they did not submit to the orthodoxy of church and state.

These co-opting practices of church and state have caused profound disillusion among many Westerners, and have led to a rejection of the whole notion of religious adherence and practice, and even to the rejection of the notion of God. In consequence, many people in the West feel estranged from any sort of organized belief system. They feel betrayed by formal religious institutions. Many other people have become cynical about the very idea of the sacred, or the soul, or the Spirit.

Summary

Yet we cannot deny the presence of the sacred. It is there, whether we accept it or not. Rather, we need to review how the idea of the sacred has been pulled from the eternal skies and manipulated for our own, often shortsighted ends. We cannot allow ourselves the luxury of cynicism or indifference to what is happening in world religions and the practices derived from them, for that would deny that there is hope to be found there. Instead, we need to once again study and interpret the essential teachings and inspiration of the great leaders who spoke, and continue to speak, words of wisdom in grace and truth.

We need our religious institutions. They provide rhythm and ritual that bring us together in common understanding, and a sense of comfort that the path is before us. But how we walk that path, whether as part of a great and common impetus of humankind toward the Ultimate Good, or as an elite claiming a monopoly on truth and goodness denied to others, determines our collective hope for the future. There is a paradox here. The intensity of our beliefs will often determine the intensity of our commitment to our faith. To the extent that that faith reflects the Way, the Truth, and the Life of humanity's best aspirations, it can inspire and draw us together in peace and justice. To the extent that it boasts of our own perfection, it may turn out to be demonic.[16]

The time was never more critical to turn, not with hostility, but with concern and respectful curiosity, to listen to each other's religious truths, to bring communities together and to share our teachings, our rituals, and our holy places in awe and reverence. It is not enough merely to tolerate each other; we must learn to appreciate each other's uniqueness. We need to recognize our differences and our diversity. We need to engage each other, to listen and to internalize each other's messages. But we cannot do this adequately unless we are grounded securely in our own faith and its principles.

An important component in the shaping of our spirituality and religious practices is the part that culture plays. Many of the traditions that have arisen in different parts of the world stem not only from the religion honored by the tribe or group, but also from the societal customs that have grown up over time. Culture provides the unique lens by which we view the world and our relationships, a major factor in creating differences and conflicts that we ignore at our peril. And so it is to culture that we turn next.

V

CULTURE

He who knows only his own culture, knows no culture.
David Augsburger

At a recent workshop I attended, an aboriginal participant was asked, first, to imagine that she was facilitating a group in peace-building, and second, to provide a metaphor or image for the sort of person she wanted to be in that process. She chose the image of a wolf. Now, people from a European background might see the wolf as a sneaky predator, one who snatches innocent children from unprotected communities. For the aboriginal participant, however, a wolf represented someone who was loyal, strong, protective, intelligent, and a steadfast warrior! As a member of the wolf clan herself, she was proud to own its honorable status.

In this chapter, I want to emphasize the importance of cultural identity, as it relates to conflict and spirituality, because the Western world is largely oblivious to the fact that its own constellation of values and perceptions is simply one pattern set among many others. And, as David Augsburger states in our opening quote, he who knows only his own culture, knows no culture.

So what do we mean by culture? Culture is the taken-for-granted way of doing things that groups of people who live and work together develop or design over time. It is a pattern for living, based on the accumulated knowledge of a people over its history. Out of our culture, we design order in our world, to give it intelligibility and to define ourselves in relation to our social group as well as to outsiders. Culture defines our worldview; it determines what we pick out as important, and what we ignore as unimportant. It defines the way things are done.[1] It provides our social reference point.

Culture, as a network of shared meaning, is elaborated in gesture and language. In fact, it is *conveyed* by language in all its forms: verbal and nonverbal, written and oral. Many different interpretations may be placed on an utterance within a culture and these differences will be even more evident when meeting people from other cultures. Culture, therefore, is vitally important as a factor in mutual understanding, especially in the context of dealing with those whose traditions are different from ours, as the opening story illustrates.

Defining Our Own Culture

In its quest for freedom, the Western world has accepted as normal and right a profound distancing between people. In the last few hundred years, we have become increasingly individualistic and have placed more and more emphasis on individual rights. We assume that each person wants to pursue achievement on their own, and on their own terms. Yet we still seek acknowledgment and recognition from others for our achievements, so perhaps our wish to stand alone does not go very deep. When we wish for personal affirmation for ourselves but are less willing to offer it to others, we are actually shouting for recognition in a land of the deaf. We decry our alienation, and, at the same time, continue practices that enhance it. Inevitably, this incongruity spells avoidable tension.

Other cultures have very different attitudes toward human relationships. They put much greater emphasis on community solidarity and networks of relationships than Western society does.

Anthropologists see the differences between our own culture and the culture of many other societies as so remarkable that they have put them into two separate categories. This categorization is based on the cohesiveness of societies, or lack of it, and the richness or paucity of the social network or "context" seen in these two contrasting types. In this schema, ours is a "low-context" or individualistic culture. Those communities that place greater emphasis on community solidarity and connections are designated "high context" or community-focused cultures. Each of these contrasting traditions has its strong points as well as its weaknesses. A greater awareness of the assumptions implied in these ways of life may enable us to better understand and live with each other across national and ethnic divides.

THE COMMUNITY-FOCUSED, HIGH-CONTEXT PATTERN

When talking about something that [he has on his mind], a high-context individual will expect his interlocutor to know what's bothering him, so that he does not have to be specific. The result is he will talk around the point, in effect, putting all the pieces in place except the crucial one.
Placing it properly – this keystone – is the role of his interlocutor.
Edward Hall

China, Japan, the countries surrounding the Mediterranean Sea, and many North and South American aboriginal or First Nations tribes have cultures that are grouped by anthropologists into the high-context pattern of relationships.

Members of community-focused, high-context societies tend to be oriented strongly toward the following.
- Family and group interdependence. Family relationships are of great importance. In contrast to the Western model of child rearing, where young babies may be left on their own to encourage "stamina," in high-context societies, according to Edward Hall, author of the book *Beyond Culture*,[2] babies are held closely, both literally and metaphorically, by their parents, and never lose that sense of attachment. This metaphorical umbilical cord provides a special connection between parents and children throughout the life of both. Bonds with parents, grandparents, and even ancestors are not to be severed, but are to be maintained and reinforced. In these cultures, the young person strives to separate not from other members, but from his or her own child-

hood, and moves into the larger world of the adult through formal community rites and rituals, such as the bar mitzvah of Jewish cultures. Thus, he or she maintains an identity within the community and retains an integral part in it. Family-like connections may also have a place in work-based relationships in these cultures.

- When a conflict or disagreement arises, people may feel threatened more by the possible loss of inclusion or approval by others than by loss of personal freedom. Any conflicts that arise are dealt with at the local, informal level. Preferred third parties brought in to act as mediators are already known and respected by both sides, and are usually chosen from within the group or community. This is particularly true in Arabic society.[3] In Canadian aboriginal or First Nations traditions prior to Western contact, each person, depending on their age, position, and reputation for wisdom, had a say in decisions that affected the group, and solutions were worked out by consensus. Hereditary succession was common among leaders, who had been reared from early childhood in anticipation of their adult role.

- Members tend to work through personal networks. In China, for instance, according to Victor Li,[4] citizens learn proper behavior through a painstaking process of socialization and education. Thus authorities aim to provide ordinary citizens with the information necessary for proper decision-making, and to delegate power to the lowest levels, within certain parameters of acceptable conduct. Everyone belongs to one or more small groups. These groups are organized by place of residence or work. Social pressure applied by the group or leader is extensive and effective. Cohesion within groups and tribes is close, in distinction to that of other tribes or nations in the vicinity who are considered outsiders. Identity is seen in relation to what a group believes itself to be, and what it believes itself not to be. It establishes its own identity as separate and preferred over those it designates as "other," or strangers.

- Members of high-context societies tend to communicate in a non-confrontational style because harmony is important within their own social group. They may use ambiguous, subtle, and indirect communication strategies. Because of their close association, they may use language that conveys meaning among themselves, but is unintelligible to an outsider. To the extent that they see themselves as "blended" with each other and even with their ancestors, the meaning and processes of dealing with conflicts may be subtle and discreet. Conflict does not have a clear beginning or an end; it is more often cyclical.[5] Because of the greater cohesion between members, and the constant interaction among generations, high-context societies may place great expectations of wisdom on their leaders. Traditions are passed down from one generation to another in oft-told tales of great significance. Much of the knowledge of the group is tacit – so embedded that it does not seem to need utterance.

- Where there is a defined religious tradition, the respect for elders and for a spiritual basis to the members' relationship with each other and the created universe provides a holistic perspective. Spiritual beliefs are likely to determine the obligations and responsibilities of the individual to his or her community and the Creator.
- The notion of honor is strong. Loss of "face" implies embarrassment in relation to one's place in the community and is a powerful social force for cohesion and maintaining acceptable conduct.
- Communities with a strong sense of cohesion are relatively resistant to change, and where change is thrust upon them, they suffer greater trauma than would the more loosely knit individualistic society. When a revered leader comes along from within the group with new ideas, however, change may be swift and all-embracing; the community is capable of moving as a single unit. These changes may not always be for the best, as the economic leadership provided by Mao Tse-tung for mainland China demonstrated.

It is important to emphasize that there is tremendous diversity between the groups that make up communities with a high-context cultural pattern. This diversity may be especially evident in the way groups resolve conflict. There are also differences in how groups, tribes, or nations apportion rights and responsibilities, create political processes, and exercise power. Even the degree of maturity expected of those who exercise political control varies across different cultures.[6]

While community-focused cultural patterns may appear ideal when viewed from the outside, they contain their own dilemmas. In the face of pervasive pressure for loyalty and harmony, for example, problems within the group may become difficult to deal with; those with status may be relatively immune from being called to account for hurtful acts done toward members with lesser status. Ordinary members of the group may not have access to the individual freedoms and rights that low-context society members take for granted. Because of the strong web of control within hierarchical governance structures and because of group solidarity, nepotism, paybacks for favors, and outright corruption may become entrenched. Members of high-context cultures may accept these as the "way things are" and see no possibility of or benefit from changing them.

THE INDIVIDUALISTIC OR LOW-CONTEXT PATTERN

Every individual has a place to fill in the world and is important in some respect, whether he chooses to be so or not.
Nathaniel Hawthorne

In contrast to high-context cultures, people of northern European origin have created a more individualistic culture. They have taken their culture with them into the lands they colonized, many of which had been peopled by high-context, cohesive cultures.

Members of individualistic cultures tend to be oriented toward the following.
- They prefer to be autonomous and appear relatively impersonal and professional. They place less emphasis on roles and more on individual expertise and personality. Because of their desire for autonomy, they draw their support system from within themselves by being competitive, ambitious, and able to respond rapidly to changing situations

and demands. Each person strives for his or her own goals. Each is determined to achieve individual success.
- They search for "facts" and use logic and direct communication, seeking finite solutions in a time-limited way.
- They develop specialized knowledge and expertise in particular areas. Thus, difficult problems are delegated to specialists. Issues tend to be broken up into realms of expertise, with the result that the parts working separately may become less than the sum of the whole.
- They show concern for their own personal prestige. Loss of "face" is related to one's personal idea of prestige. Individualists fear making themselves appear childish or incompetent in the eyes of peers or of society in general. The place of honor in relationships appears to have less relevance than in more high-context societies. Nevertheless, it is still present between business associates and at the international level.
- Individualistic patterns of social interaction tend to sort people into those who "measure up" to perceived norms of status and behavior. They thus tend to marginalize those who do not fit because of race, occupation (or lack of one), or status.
- They rely on codes of law and their rights within those laws.

Belief in the autonomy of the individual, to the extent it does not interfere with others, is evidence of an enduring customary practice in itself. An insistence that people are honored to the degree to which they confine themselves to rational arguments, devoid of feeling or passion, creates its own confining, community pressure amongst so-called individualistic societies.

All societies will have elements of both high-context and individualistic cultural patterns. Many informal and closely knit communities are to be found in small towns, even in individualistic societies. They can also be found where constant interaction – at work, or through professional or leisure or school or parent association activities – leads to cohesive, inclusive, interfamily socialization. Quite frequently, a person may be individualistic in a work or professional setting, but enjoy rich and diverse connections with family and friends at home. Even the most individualistic societies are composed of individuals who come from specific families with their own ways of doing things, and who join associations, unions, and professions, all of which have their own unique and implicit culture.

It is in our mutual relationships with others that we find our immediate anchoring and our sense of comfort, in the society in which we live. We all face social pressures that mold us and determine our ability to "fit in."

CUSTOMARY PRACTICES

Custom is the great guide of human life.
David Hume

In any society, whether high- or low-context, social competence is displayed by conforming to the niceties of polite behavior. This behavior in turn fosters a sense of self-worth and status. These niceties, often unconsciously practiced, are culturally determined and vary widely between groups. It is only as one mingles with colleagues from other social groups, and transgresses social practices, that one learns of these differences.

Customary practices can deal with many things that cannot be legislated, including those aspects of behavior that are traditional, moral, and religious.[7] These practices rely on tacit knowledge and the consensus of the community as to how things are done. As unstated rules of behavior, they are more evident in high-context societies than in individualistic ones. Yet we all have a sense of how we should sit down at formal dinners, come and go at meetings, greet each other and say goodbye.

Rituals are the more formally identified customary practices. As we have seen, they are powerful agents for cohesion within any community, but they play significant roles for individuals as well. According to Evan Imber-Black and Janine Roberts, authors of *Rituals for Our Times*, rituals

- mark transitions for the life of the individual. They provide recognition of the end of one period of life for the individual, and extend a welcome into his or her new level of maturity;

- help to bring people through change and to overcome adversity. They also *create* change; they bring about healing and recovery from loss by acknowledging traumatic events;
- make change manageable and safe by using familiar symbols and words, the underlying meaning of which is also familiar;
- celebrate the deep joy and the honoring of life in community.[8]

Rituals will have a special emphasis in any spiritual approach to conflict management because they operate at a symbolic level. Parties involved in an intractable conflict may attribute two very different meanings to the same material objects. Their reality, framed by language, metaphor, and symbol, will have significant meaning for them, but may not be shared by the other party or group. Once these differences are recognized, they may be resolved by each party or group re-narrating their experience and perception of history. When we recognize the symbolic worlds of the contenders, through narrative and ritual, says Clifford Geertz in *The Interpretation of Cultures*, "the world as lived and the world as imagined, fused under the agency of a single set of symbolic forms, turns out to be, after all, the same world."[9]

THE CONSTRUCTION OF REALITY & THE CLASH OF CULTURES

The general mobility of people today is one of the defining features of contemporary life. In our own culture, we witness this mobility as people pursue business interests or search for economic security for themselves and their families. But we also witness mobility on a global scale in the tragic tide of displaced people, moving away from persecution, scorched homelands, and wars. Peoples from many cultures and with long, painful memories are thus brought into close proximity. Some of these close neighbors will be members of former enemy groups; many will be strangers.

To see what happens when cultures and powers clash, we need look no further than our own North American context. In both Canada and the United States, a high-context, aboriginal culture was overtaken by a dominant, individualistic (European) one. Our attitude toward this land's original inhabitants has been extraordinarily dissonant and contradictory. On the one hand, a special Act gave them separate status, but kept them dependent under a confused governance structure. At the same time, it preached assimilation, while segregating First Nations peoples from both their families of origin and mainstream society. The effect was to disrupt their worldview, to break up their whole social context and their identification with nature. Psychological and physical barriers made access to the mainstream's cultural objectives of progress and productivity extremely difficult. It is only in recent years that we are coming to terms with what has happened. Thankfully, we are beginning to recognize and appreciate the wisdom and spiritual and cultural values of our First Nations peoples. We have much to learn from them.

Of course, the collision of culture and values plays out in a variety of ways, as we are continuing to learn. For example, immigrants who come from individualistic societies (many for economic reasons) may have little trouble learning our customs and ways of doing things. They assimilate readily. Others, from high-context cultures, often come with a desire to make a new life here. They, too, learn our public customs fairly readily. However, at home and in their communities, they continue their own cultural observances. Thus they preserve their identities within the larger society. It is the already marginalized immigrant – someone who through war or other disaster has lost family and other connections; perhaps meeting racism and other barriers along the way – who finds it hardest to be restored in spirit, or to gain equal status with other citizens.

Summary

The power of cultural influences lies in the fact that they can divide us, if we allow ourselves to narrow our horizons and build barriers of prejudice and separation, or they can lead to cooperation and goodwill, if we enhance our appreciation of society's rich diversity.

It is my prayer, of course, that we will choose the latter path, and learn to discern how they may enrich our lives and our interactions, both with those who share our worldviews, beliefs, and customs, and with those who may not.

No account of the values inherent in any particular culture would be complete if it did not address two pre-eminent themes, those of honor and grace. Yet these powerful forces in our social life are seldom discussed. The next chapter will consider these all-important qualities.

PART TWO

THE HUMAN SPIRIT MANIFESTED

VI

HONOR, GRACE, & FACE

> *Little has been written about honour in the social sciences and almost nothing about grace. Yet honour has caused more deaths than the plague and grace is what we all yearn for – whether in the form of favour, luck, pardon, gratuity or salvation.*
>
> J. G. Peristiany and Julian Pitt-Rivers

Honor has caused more deaths than the plague? Grace is what we all yearn for? Scant attention has been paid to these all-important themes in human dynamics and conflict management, to say the least. Yet questions of honor and its negation address a central, key issue in that they point to one of the most profound human needs of all – that is, the need we all share for a sense of self-worth. All of us long for personal significance and affirmation, and this longing lies deeper than many of the issues acknowledged by the rational mind. Take, for example, a newspaper report by Paul Adams and Paul Koring that appeared in the May 4, 2002, edition of *The Globe and Mail*.[1]

It was after the incursions by Israeli forces into the Jenin refugee camp. Donations of tents were made to replace the homes that had been destroyed by the tanks. But a crowd of homeless Palestinians set the load of donated tents and bedding ablaze.

Why would they do such a thing? The packages bore a U.S. flag, a country they saw as a major contributor to their predicament. The town had been a refuge for Palestinians since 1948, when the state of Israel had first been formed. The refugees had been displaced from their original homes at that time and had remained in this anomalous state for more than half a century. They were without status and had few opportunities for employment and none for re-settlement. Now the camp and its hovels had been destroyed once again.

A female resident was seen to draw her finger across her throat in a slashing motion. "I'll kill myself if they give me a tent," she is reported to have said. "I'll have a house, but I will not live in a tent again."

What outrage, what indignity, what denial of justice, what violence to her identity and pride as a human being was she experiencing! And what an expression of her undying spirit was expressed in that gesture!

Both honor and grace are intimately related to the sacred, as it is identified within each individual and each society. A person's honor is sacred. For those who have feared or experienced its loss, it is something more precious than life itself.

Grace is a corollary notion to honor and refers to something extra, something that is not obligatory or predictable.[2] Grace consists of giving and receiving service for nothing. Divine grace points to something transcendent – a gift bestowed by the eternal Spirit. The bestowal of grace creates a sacred dimension in which it may be acknowledged and reciprocated.

In addressing these complex, very subjectively experienced qualities, we move into a realm of ambiguity and generosity, with a pinch of paradox thrown in for good measure.

Nowhere are the issues of honor and grace more important than in the field of conflict management: its prevention, its conduct, its transformation, and its resolution. We cannot manage conflict – from the most apparently mundane to the most intransigent – if we do not address, however tentatively, the subtleties of honor and grace.

Before discussing honor from a spiritual perspective, let's review some pertinent findings about social dynamics from the field of social psychology. These may resonate more readily with those brought up in a rationally based, humanistic society. When examined, however, even these findings display a bemusing paradoxical quality

Caryl Rusbult and Paul Van Lange[3] summarize what they call "interdependence processes." Specifically, they talk about decisions made on the basis of people's relative dependency on each another, and the extent to which people are able to control each other's behavior. Decisions made with this methodology will be based on costs and rewards. Parties, they say, may also be motivated by their sense of working toward a common – or contradictory – goal, something that needs resolution one way or the other. The working relationship in these instances is centered on the assumption that the partner will reciprocate any given favor or concession in the future. Otherwise, the one proffering the gesture is likely to feel duped. The interaction is understood by each to be a quid-pro-quo affair.

These factors provide strong motives and undoubtedly form the underlying basis of many of our interactions. But they are not enough to explain the complexities of human behavior. Interaction among individuals is not merely an economic exchange; it is also a social fact and a symbolic act. Our interactions govern much more than the exchange of useful goods and functions. One can exchange all manner of less-tangible assets – pleasure, woes, secrets, insults, vengeance, hospitality, conversation, stories, and gifts – where the economic exchange is subsidiary. Some acts are quite clearly motivated by something beyond logic. They belong more to the heart and soul than to the head. We tend to assume that the only measure of generosity is economic value. Yet the parable of the widow's mite indicates that her bounty is of more worth in moral terms than were the rich people's gifts. The latter represented only a fraction of their wealth, while the widow gave all that she had.

Consider, for instance, the matter of altruistic behavior. Here the social psychologists enter the realm of paradox. Why does one act altruistically? Cynics question whether anyone *can* have purely altruistic motives: those carried out solely for the benefit of another, often risking harm to the actor. A scoffer would dismiss all generous acts as self-enhancing. Social psychologists Dale Miller and Rebecca Ratner[4] report that this tendency to denigrate all genuinely benevolent actions is alive and well.

So what are the implications of this fact for human interaction? Inevitably, it perpetuates the myth of self-interest. According to the cynics, only a self-interested person will take action on a particular issue. But this is circular, dead-end reasoning, supporting the belief they set out to prove. Pure altruism is assumed to be non-existent, despite our experiencing it so many times in our lives.

The myth of self-interest is further strengthened by society's sanction against proclaiming one's pure motives in any beneficent act. This sanction affects the accounts that people offer to one another to explain their behavior. Often, when people engage in acts of generosity and compassion, they use language that emphasizes their own self-interest. In this instance, we're not dealing with cynicism in action, but with a wish to downplay one's positive motivations and thus avoid reproach or accusations of boasting, especially from the cynics.

The route to acceptance in our society is strewn with many contradictions and subtleties that are difficult to express, for they vanish like morning dew when exposed to analysis. It is not a simple matter to evaluate the intentions of another person.

Personally, I believe the debate about altruism arises from too narrow a view of social conduct. While community is built when people help each other and work together for the common good, it is also necessary in a community for people to remain modest when evaluating their own deeds. The level of modesty required depends on the unwritten customs of the society in question. In our individualistic society, where competition is the order of the day, altruistic behavior is frequently belittled. "Nice guys finish last," we proclaim, and "No good deed goes unpunished." Yet we continue to act in constructive ways.

Attempting to measure or weigh reciprocity and beneficent acts is really an inadequate way to understand human relationships. Rather, we must appreciate more consciously the spiritual ties of kinship and friendship, the hidden incentive, the act of forbearance, the incalculable benefits of favorable decisions, and the aim to please that cannot be evaluated[5] but on which our human affiliations depend.

HONOR

*These ties are primordial, the very tissue of social relations.
In the end they bear fruit at the macro-level of society
and distort the calculations of those who suppose they can be ignored.*
J. G. Peristiany and Julian Pitt-Rivers

Honor, the authors of our quote state, is too intimate a sentiment to submit to definition. It must be experienced. Further, one cannot regard it as a single concept. Rather, it is a conceptual field within which people find the means to express self-esteem, and to acknowledge their esteem for others. Honor pertains to that realm where accepted truths are placed beyond question by a conviction impervious to reasoning because it lies deeper than consciousness, at the heart's core. It commands an attachment that springs from the center of the self.

There are two kinds of honor: ascribed and acquired.

Ascribed honor accompanies one's birth; it is the honor one is afforded because of the society one is born into, or because of one's status, race, or gender. The privileged tend to take this kind of honor for granted, whereas the less fortunate will be *very* aware of its scarcity in their own circumstances.

Acquired honor is honor we attain as we grow up and accomplish status by our own initiative. No one is entirely self-made, however. Each of us is given more or fewer opportunities by society to develop our potential. Luck as well as commitment and talent also play a role. Having acquired a certain status, honor is legitimated and affirmed by society as it provides affirmation of that status.

Even in a low-context, individualistic society such as ours, issues of honor and shame are important, although they appear in a more subtle form than in high-context, community-focused societies. For example, in our society, when people perceive that their sense of personal worth is under threat, they may be reluctant to acknowledge that perception, because to acknowledge the threat may be to make the discomfort all the more real, at least temporarily. Again, for example, in Western societies in the public arena, women have, officially at least, equal status to men and will therefore feel loss of honor in the same ways that men do. However, our implicit social norms have not yet fully recognized this fact. As a result, women may experience humiliation if their need to save face is seen as a weakness peculiar to women. Thus, the perceived threat to their self-esteem cannot be brought into the open.

Honor is not a fixed quality across nations and societies. What is considered honorable in one community may be seen as deviant in another. It depends on the vantage point of the actors and the perceivers. In Western societies, our concentration on individuality and equality before the law obscures the fact that an inequality often exists, based on status and access to resources and social networks. Privilege gives one the power to ignore or snub others who may be without such assets, and who may be dependent on those in more favorable circumstances. The marginalized do not have the same access to honor and may come to find, because of their low status, that it is difficult to establish their worth according to the norms of middle-class society. In order to win honor, denied by legitimate society, they may set up their own structure of honor among their peers. Thus gangs and suicide bombers are created.

The drive for honor is so vital to our well-being, suggest J. Peristiany and Julian Pitt-Rivers in the book *Honor and Grace in Anthropology*,[6] that when its existence is threatened violence may break out in its defense.

Sometimes this violence is a manifestation of a search for something transcendent, says Arthur Koestler in his book *The Ghost in the Machine*.[7] It is tied up with the need for belonging, for being part of a group that characterizes the individual's identity.

The urge to be identified with a tribe, nation, church, or cause is often a stronger motive than selfishness in the resort to violent behavior, Koestler continues. He identifies integrative, self-transcending tendencies, rather than self-assertive ones, as the more potent factor contributing to violence throughout human history. In the process of transcending the self and joining with an entity of symbolic significance, the individual comes to surrender responsibility for the actions he or she performs within that entity. Rather, he or she delegates responsibility to the leaders, who come to value loyalty and unquestioning allegiance above all other virtues. As a result, individuals within the group may act with ruthless cruelty toward others outside the group, at the behest of those same leaders.

Those who are *outside* the group are not seen as individuals, but as symbolic representatives of the whole, hated "outsider" group. They can therefore be targeted for violence, whether they are personally guilty of crimes or not.

The destruction of the World Trade Center on September 11, 2001, illustrates Koestler's point with stunning impact. I am talking here of the motivation of the actual suicidal hijackers, not the motivation of their leaders. The terrorists who actually carried out the mission may well have been acting out of a transcendent idealism, difficult as this is for us to understand.

Such people can be found in the many refugee camps or other degrading ghettos where people have been denied their essential needs as human beings.

Others possess a religious zeal and take on the role of proxies who seek to protest and correct the injustices suffered by those they claim to represent. Despite being raised in more prosperous, middle-class surroundings, these people may reject the values of the open secular society, preferring instead to join a group that portrays a fundamentalist, narrow, and retributive theology, and that promises personal salvation to come.

The challenge in dealing with this latter group is to re-introduce them to the more compassionate, inclusive, and sustaining theology of their faith, be it Islam, Judaism, or Christianity. As Jim Wallis, editor of *Sojourners* magazine, has said, "We must speak of the need to drain the swamps of injustice that breed the mosquitoes of terror and find a way to make this a teachable moment rather than merely a blame game."[8]

Of course, even if we do this, we cannot say or promise that all will be well thereafter. Efforts to control terrorism by direct means both at home and abroad will still be needed. But at least a salient cause of hostility – that of unremedied injustice – will have been addressed.

HONOR & FACE

Face is a universal characteristic of being human.
Joseph P. Folger, Marshal Scott Poole, and Randal K. Stutman

The other side of honor is the notion of "face." Face and face-saving is frequently seen as particularly characteristic of Asian and Mediterranean cultures, but it is of universal importance. Many people in Western societies, including world leaders, make decisions based on a felt need to save face and protect either their own honor as individuals, or the honor of their country. However, even the parties involved may be unaware that this is a motivation for their action.

The need to maintain "face" can be so dominant in some individuals that they come to depend on it for their sense of self-worth. This dependency is unspoken, deeper than consciousness, and connects to the person's sacred core of the self. It marks the sense of identity from which the individual seeks affirmation. People may be willing to sacrifice substantial rewards if they perceive they are being threatened with humiliation, or loss of face. Likewise, conflicts may arise or be exacerbated solely because an interaction is seen to threaten face. Thus, these individuals' sense of personal worth leads to difficult conflicts, which appear to have little logic to explain their intensity.

Once face-saving is recognized as a motivator, however, a redefinition of what the particular conflict is all about can be suggested. Disputes over material resources, for example, sometimes become unmanageable because the disagreement is really over something much deeper. The apparent presenting cause of the conflict may have to be set aside until the issue concerning personal worth is dealt with. Perceived loss of face can influence people to take extreme positions and "go for broke," or to walk away from a situation. In such circumstances, effective interaction cannot usually proceed until the threatened person feels satisfied that enough has been done to acknowledge and restore the desired image.

This concern for face-saving may be less overt in our society, but to deny it exists at all is to fail to understand the full range of concerns under which the protagonists in a dispute may be laboring.

It has been said that the person who feels most secure about his or her honor is the least prone to defend it. Conversely, it may be a sign of insecurity when people absolutely insist on the honor they think society has denied them. In this postmodern age, a surprising number of people feel themselves to be victims, or are constantly seeking to justify themselves in their own eyes and in the eyes of society. At every opportunity, they strive to reconstruct their image of themselves, because they have never felt secure about who they really are. Their simplest interactions take on the characteristics of an escalated conflict, with arguments over trifles and an unwillingness to accept goodwill on the part of others. Such a case can be seen in the following example.

> The wooden fence between two neighbors rotted and needed to be replaced. As it was only going to cost $100, one neighbor, let's call him John, went ahead and did the job. He then asked the other neighbor, let's call him Fred, to contribute half. Fred refused. John insisted, and even called to Fred's house to get his money. The more John *persisted*, the more Fred *resisted*.
>
> Finally, it came to mediation. Both men signed an agreement saying they were committed to work through the problem in good faith. But as time wore on, it became obvious that we were getting nowhere, so I took each party aside to ask what was going on. It turned out that Fred felt he needed to prove he was not a weakling, a perception he feared others would have, were he to give in to the demands placed upon him. Honor was more important to him than settling the bill, which, if he had done it, would have been a small price to pay to end the hostility.

Of course, this is not a story about a small bill. It became obvious that the fence bill, which was trivial yet so firmly resisted, had a far greater symbolic meaning. However hollow his victory might seem to others,

Fred left the meeting with an enhanced sense of self-esteem, at least in regard to this incident. He had proved to himself that he was not someone who could easily be pushed around. His need for self-affirmation exceeded his need to accommodate his neighbor.

"I fight, therefore I am" seemed to express the core of Fred's worldview, as it related to his sense of identity. Perhaps his attitude arose from an overwhelming sense of impotence, dating from childhood. In any event, his belligerence destroyed what until then had been a neighborly relationship.

John's understanding, meantime, remained at the material level of the money at issue.

In the end, I was unable to help these two men, who had such different worldviews, achieve consensus. But perhaps that was something neither intended in the first place.

GRACE

"You are accepted." Period, full stop.
Marcus Borg

As I've already noted, the term grace, as generally understood, refers to something extra, something that is beyond the obligatory or predictable. If honor is something demanded, then grace is something freely offered. Divine grace points to something transcendent: a gift bestowed by the eternal Spirit. Like the Spirit itself, grace is there, whether we are prepared to accept its existence or not. Grace offered between human beings is also something more than can be quantified by yardsticks or balance sheets.

As the quotation from Marcus Borg suggests, divine grace is something we have, without asking for it. Yet even those who believe in the existence of this gift in principle are often reluctant to acknowledge it out loud. Such an acknowledgment of grace might suggest a sort of spiritual arrogance on the part of the receiver; or it might suggest that the claimer takes it for granted, rather than as a reason for humility, gratitude, and celebration.

The concept of grace as the free gift of God is central to Christianity, and can be found in other religious traditions as well. Writing from a Christian perspective, Marcus Borg stresses the easy accessibility of divine grace.[9] Grace is experienced in God's acceptance of us, apart from our work and effort. In the Hebrew scriptures, the idea of grace and compassion turns up in both psalm and story as a given quality of God. In the Qur'an of Islam, it is God the merciful who rules and judges. Faith in the existence of this grace was the only condition of admission to the Pure Realm.

This notion of grace can be contrasted to the idea of the self-fulfilling prophecy, described by the social psychologists, where every human effort has its natural consequences. Grace is something extra, unexpected, beyond cause-and-effect relationships. It is present before we act or ask. Its very existence asserts that "out there" and "in here, in my heart" dwells an entity, a gift waiting to be received.

The bestowal of grace may come when we least expect or deserve it. Just being open to the possibility of grace, regardless of our circumstances, can change the climate of an interaction; it can change our perspective of a dilemma or predicament. An openness to grace can give us a new interpretation of what is going on, and a sense of confidence, well-being, and hope.

To be sure, the notion that grace is freely available is a radical thought, which can only be proven by acting as if it is available. And that changes everything. But such is the nature of paradox: the paradox of the Spirit.

I won't presume to recount when I have been conscious of receiving divine grace. However, when, during mediation, two previously hostile combatants suddenly see the issue with new eyes, and recognize a spark of humanity in the other's motives and intentions, and when the dynamics of this transformation elude me, or when I have goofed and it turned out for the best anyway, it *does* seem like divine grace to me!

The notion that grace is given regardless of merit is very egalitarian, according to Borg.[10] The more one understands and accepts this quality of the divine, the less one will feel self-righteous and self-made. How many of our pretensions to being self-made stem from arrogance? How many of our own achievements are a result of genetic inheritance, and the family and economic circumstances into which we were born? How much of our success depends on luck, on the coming together of apparently unconnected events, on synchronicity? A myriad of events occurs in our lives over which we have little control. The more we understand grace, the more we can replace false pride or hubris — and its corollary, the judgment of others — with gratitude.

The notion of grace is more than egalitarian, however. As a concept of completeness or perfection that is only within the capacity of the Divine to bestow, human beings come to recognize a truth about the nature of reality — that there *is* a limit to our ability to deal with all the contingencies that may present themselves. As Michael Ignatiev points out in his book *The Needs of Strangers*, there is no secular equivalent to the state of grace.[11] This is a humbling realization and essential to our understanding that we are limited in our ability to manage daily affairs and conflicts. An openness to the working of the Divine Spirit is to receive the grace so abundantly available.

Grace between People

So far, I have addressed the bestowal of grace to human beings by the Divine Spirit. But where does grace come in, in our relationships with each other? Here it takes on a more earthly flavor.

There is a donor as well as receiver and both enter a graceful dance of social niceties. On one level, the notion of grace is essentially opposed to that which is rational, predictable, and calculated. Certainly it is not legally obligatory, nor does it create a right to reciprocity. Rather, it creates a quality of intangible "value added." Grace seems most evident when the gesture comes out of the blue, unexpectedly.

And yet, where a favor has been done, is not the return of grace usually anticipated? Given appropriately, the polite word or "thank you" acknowledges that the receiver of a gift is cognizant of the social niceties of the cultural group. In critical circumstances, a slight, in the form of a failure to return grace, could provoke a resentment that may far surpass any that might result from an evasion of contractual obligations. The person who fails to make the expected gesture is shamed, or declared uncouth. In other words, much more than material interests are at stake; the individual's intimate self is damaged by the failure to follow customary norms. The balance between reciprocity and gratuity or grace is indeed a tenuous one, depending as it does on culture, history, contexts, personalities, and roles.

Here we must tiptoe gently through the dialectics of meaning. Ties of kinship and friendship, the good feeling stemming from decisions made in our favor – all these things express the quality of grace within our relationships. As each small graceful gesture is offered, and perhaps exchanged, the mutual quality of life is enhanced! Graceful gestures are incalculable and primordial, the very tissue of social relationships.[12]

Sometimes the graceful gesture in its observance or neglect can mean the difference between consolidating a friendship or causing disruption, as the following case studies indicate.

Case 1: A member of an international organization was giving a speech at a dinner held for colleagues on both sides of the Cold War divide. He had just been given a very expensive silver salver by his erstwhile political opponent, in recognition of his work on détente. He embarked on his speech after only the briefest of thanks, because he wanted to tell his audience of the great work in building friendship that the organization had accomplished. His failure to deal with the need to acknowledge the gift and even to protest his unworthiness to receive it from the donor totally changed the image of the receiver in the eyes of that donor. The very goodwill that he was so ardently promoting was jeopardized. "What can you expect from those savages?" muttered one observer to another. "We've got to make allowances," said the other.

Case 2: In Ireland, it has been the custom in the country to return a small sum as "luck money" to the buyer of any goods, such as a horse or a chair, on concluding a deal. Once upon a time, two traders could not agree on the price of the goods on offer. It was beneath their dignity to accept the other's figure. An intervener suggested that the difference could be exchanged in the form of luck money. Thus the buyer could tell his friends of the great deal in the form of the lower price, and the seller, equally, could boast of the better price. And when the friends got together, they could exchange the joke about the neat way the issue had been resolved! There was a sense of playfulness and grace, to everyone's delight.

Humor may be an effective way to sidestep issues of honor, especially if the joke is offered by the person who is at risk of losing face. In another culture, the discovery of such an arrangement might not have been seen as a joke to be shared, but as a matter of losing face for both protagonists in that they could be so easily satisfied.

In conflict management, the quality of grace can be especially manifest if its existence is recognized, either tacitly or openly. Grace enables us to live both within and outside an interaction, by viewing it simultaneously both objectively and subjectively; by accepting ambiguity and uncertainty; by not insisting on control and closure, but by being tentative and experimental.

Total understanding may be an unattainable goal: such is the mystery that surrounds our being and our interactions. No one can fully understand another person, nor even him- or herself from one moment to the next! The messages being sent may not be understood so much by the words spoken, as by the unconscious reactions portrayed on the face and by the gestures of the receiver; as well as by the feeling of relational empathy that is established between parties as they come to a deeper understanding of each other.

Grace is the quality that can give life to the tension that inevitably lies between people in their encounters with others. To the extent that we seek not to set aside our perspectives and prejudices but to recognize their influence and to integrate them into the reality of the dialogue, we demonstrate the power of grace. Grace enables us to work through our own perceived reality and to hold in honor the reality of the other. It enables us to focus on co-creating with the other a *shared* reality. It involves the attainment of a higher universality that can encompass the perspectives, the frailties, and even the mistrusts and resistances, embedded within the engagement, its antecedents, and its outcomes.

Summary

Grace is that imponderable that serves to nurture human life and spiritual growth. Its mechanism is beyond the rational and is never completely understood, its origin residing partly beneath human consciousness. Grace may be brought to an encounter either fortuitously, or by an act of will by participants, or by interveners who have learned to read the messages "between the lines" and who see an opportunity for progress.

It has been my experience that, when I raise issues of honor and grace in my workshops, the participants seize it as something beyond their ordinary discourse, yet as something of the utmost importance. Together, honor and grace bring a profound sense of well-being and enhancement to any dialogue. Indeed, both are something we all yearn for, because they have been so discounted and forgotten in our individualistic and alienated society.

Grace and honor may be either affirmed or denied. Our emotions will be aroused in either case, pleasantly or otherwise. For honor and grace are both tied up on our sense of self-worth. The next chapter deals with these vital manifestations of the spirit: the emotions and our needs as human beings.

VII

HUMAN EMOTIONS & NEEDS

*Anyone can become angry – that is easy, but to be angry with
the right person, to the right degree, at the right time,
for the right purpose, and in the right way – this is not easy.*

Aristotle

When a conflict erupts, we all know what happens. No matter how much we promise ourselves that we will keep our cool and behave in a calm and rational manner (i.e., unemotionally), somewhere along the way, someone pushes our buttons and all our best intentions are forgotten in an instant. From that point on, passion is the name of the game. Later, when the fire has cooled, we are likely to belittle ourselves for our inability to stick with the plan.

Emotions get a lot of bad press, especially when it comes to conflict situations. This is because, in modernist worldview, they are seen as somehow beneath serious consideration compared to rational-based thinking and problem solving. Our rationality, we have been told, is the superior faculty, separate from desire or feeling. Thus, the rationalists have sought to belittle subjective experience – that is, experience which emerges in the lived moments of our existence.

This modernist view of rationality divorced from feeling is in keeping with the puritanical mindset that sought to deny the existence of an emotional life. Yet, in seeking to deny them, emotions sprang up with renewed vigor, often with tragic results. Violence ensued when emotion escaped its constraints and erupted with explosive force.

Rather than suppressing emotions, for we cannot, we would do well to acknowledge them and learn their message.

Our emotions, both positive and negative, signal our most profound values and relationships with the world outside; they signal our reason for existence, the essential meaning from which we can live authentically. If we are prepared to investigate what has prompted them, our emotions and the underlying needs to which they point can indicate the core values of our souls, as theologians James Whitehead and Evelyn Whitehead contend.[1] Therefore, we suppress them at our peril.

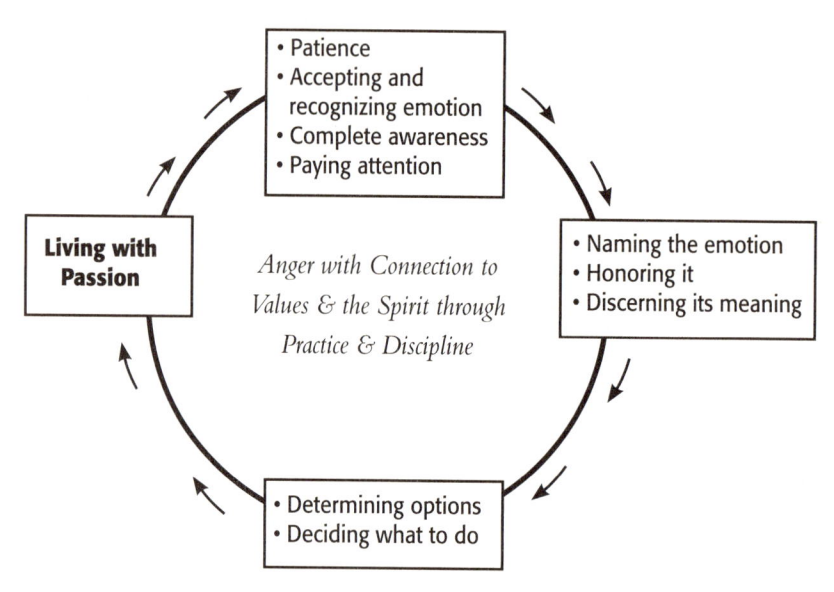

```
                  • Patience
                  • Accepting and
                    recognizing emotion
                  • Complete awareness
                  • Paying attention

  Living with      Anger with Connection to      • Naming the emotion
   Passion         Values & the Spirit through   • Honoring it
                   Practice & Discipline         • Discerning its meaning

                  • Determining options
                  • Deciding what to do
```

FIGURE 1 Connecting with and understanding one's anger

Anger

Anger plays a unique role in terms of its effects upon the spirit. Anger may provide energy for effective and necessary action, in which case it can be the impetus for creative change and an enhancement of the spirit for all the parties involved in a conflict. Something has mattered enough that anger is born!

On a physiological level, when anger triggers high levels of arousal, when hearts beat fast and faces redden, adrenaline redirects the blood circulation away from the brain and into the muscles. People do not do their best thinking in those circumstances, as most of us will have experienced! In this situation, the overloaded anger becomes a different sort of instrument. Our conscious minds allow it to overwhelm our finer intellectual processes, so that we react in ways we may later regret when conscience returns. Alternatively, we may use our anger as a cudgel to display power over another. In this case, we are not using our anger to indicate real needs at risk, but rather to inflict psychological abuse. Here anger may be used to attack or oppress, in which case the object of our wrath may suffer humiliation and a profound quenching of the spirit. We need to remember, always, that our own spiritual banks cannot be filled by robbing others of their spiritual treasures.

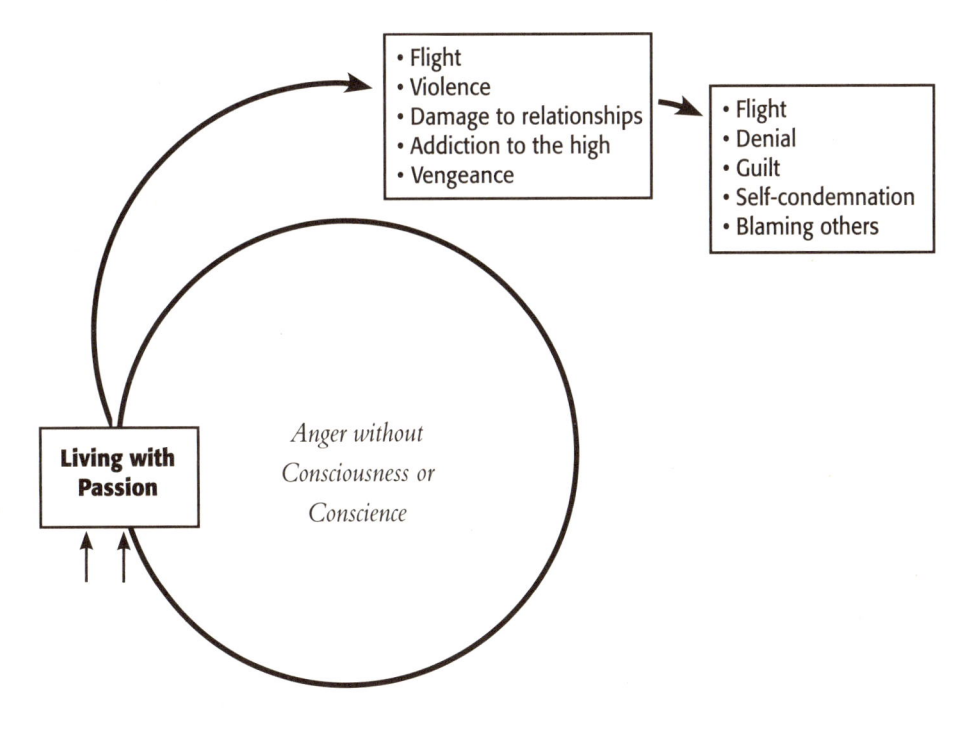

- Flight
- Violence
- Damage to relationships
- Addiction to the high
- Vengeance

- Flight
- Denial
- Guilt
- Self-condemnation
- Blaming others

Living with Passion

Anger without Consciousness or Conscience

FIGURE 2. Anger unhinged

Another reason we should be both aware and wary of anger that has grown beyond control is because of its effect on the one consumed by it. Excess anger and the coincident secretion of adrenaline contribute to such health problems as high-blood pressure and heart attacks.

Moreover, if we allow our passions to rule us, we become their victims. If they are beyond our control, then we can deny responsibility for them, as well as for the consequences of what we do under their influence.[2] In his book *Angry All the Time*, Ron Potter-Efron describes the anger high, where people become emotionally dependent on the arousal anger brings. This dependency is like an addiction. He suggests that we cannot restore relationships or build new ones until we make a commitment to foreswear the anger rush. People who use anger as a mighty sword often feel justified; the anger rush gets confused with a spiritual high. To the extent that it damages relationships and is self-perpetuating, anger will be an instrument of oppression, mistaken for spirit.[3]

On the other side of the emotional coin are those who manage, as a survival mechanism, to suppress their anger. It may be that they have experienced violent conflict in their own lives, and have learned that it would be dangerous to express their feelings. Particularly if they are women, they may have been raised to believe that the expression of anger is not acceptable, in terms of social norms of behavior. The drive to suppress anger may become so ingrained that these people go to great lengths to avoid its honest expression, with the result that they also end up denying their basic needs, even to themselves. Thus, they become locked in prisons of self-protection and victimhood. Often, they deny any chance of self-restoration, for it is only by identifying and acknowledging feelings that a person can develop an agenda for healing. They abandon hope and forgo the right to personal authenticity.

Our spirituality is a biological potential built into the human species, and our emotions are clearly linked with it. Acknowledging the spiritual dimension signaled by emotion integrates our cognitive and emotional abilities into a holistic reality of passion and authentic living in the social world. In the process, we can rediscover meaning: our essential grounding in our communities and in our sacred connections with our world and the Divine Creator Spirit.

ESCALATION OF CONFLICT

*In situations of high involvement, actors will tend to
over-perceive the level of violence in the actions of their adversaries
and overreact to the actions of the adversary.*
Ole Holsti, R.C. North, and R.A. Brody

The trading of hostile emotions, such as anger, is one of the primary reasons conflicts escalate and get out of hand. Each side contributes to the escalation of anger, feeding the storm from each other's reactions. In situations of high involvement, as the quotation suggests, perception and action from one side inspires the same motivations and behavior from the other.

A conflict rises up between people. Why? Inevitably, people perceive differences between themselves and others. But they do not always address the issue as a problem to solve or as an indication that a relationship is awry. Instead, they start to press their point of view with increasing insistence and vigor. Then the other side presents their perspective, which is not acceptable to the first side. They both get upset, and the conflict escalates. What is going on here?

Speed Leas of the Episcopal Church in the United States gives us a general description of the path of escalation, from his experience dealing with church conflicts.[4] Lest you think otherwise, let me assure you at the start that Leas' graphic description is not an exaggeration; when I have shown his scale of escalation to members of congregations in trouble, they have spontaneously placed themselves far along this perilous slope. In fact, the pattern of escalation happens universally when issues matter. If we are aware of what's going on, however, we can deal with the pattern more constructively.

According to Leas, at the lowest level of dealing with a difficulty, the parties exchange information until the problem is resolved. While they may have conflicting goals and values, each side works together and exchanges enough information so that a satisfactory outcome can occur. If tensions arise, they are short-lived. Much hard negotiation occurs at this level. People direct their energies to seeing the truth of the situation and each other's perspective, and to sorting out complexities in order to reach a resolution that will suit both parties. They remain willing and able to deal with the problem objectively. There is a to-and-fro energy and a commitment to a common goal, an engagement of the two sides in working things out. Satisfaction and perhaps an appreciation for each other's expertise and discernment can emerge from the quality of the dialogue and the mutual respect of the parties. Here there really is no conflict at all, but possibly a mutual honoring of each other's commitment and creative thinking.

If, however, the discussion breaks down because of some misunderstanding, some trigger pushed or fear provoked, Leas has seen how the human dynamic brings out less constructive behavior. Personalities become confused with issues and vice versa. Shrewdness and selective holding back of information begin as mistrust arises and grows. Each participant feels the need to defend him- or herself against the other's perceived or real attacks. It is not uncommon that one or both parties believe the other side has a hidden agenda. As the tension escalates, the conflict comes to be seen as a win-lose proposition. Now the focus is more on the person on the other side of the table, seen as enemy, and not purely on the issues. Distortion now becomes a major problem. Information sharing happens only within one's own caucus and to justify one's own perspective. Our court system requires its clients to pursue conflicts at this level!

At the next, higher level of escalation, the participants actually seek to hurt the other in some way. They have now concluded that the other is incapable of changing. Each side becomes coldly self-righteous. Each is unable to listen to information contrary to his or her own beliefs about the other. Each is deaf to hearing any good of the other. Each talks now of opposing "principles"; the issues are identified as being ideologically based.

Eventually the conflict may become intractable. By then the initial issue has become lost; it is the personalities that have become the issue. Exchanges become vindictive, with each party seeking to destroy or get rid of the other regardless of the cost. Through it all, each side sees its own actions as justified, as it responds to its own negative interpretation of the other's action. Vengeance, possibly involving violence, may be contemplated as a rough-hewn way to mete out justice.

Why would church members be so prone to this destructive pattern of mutual punishment? Why do members of religious factions fight so aggressively, when their basic messages are about peace and love?

Members of religious groups may well feel that they have a direct line to the Divine, to the source of truth, so that they are closer to the "Answers" before they and others have even asked the questions. Others, with the same sense of the Divine ear, may have quite contradictory perceptions and beliefs. They may also have higher expectations of each other regarding their peace-making abilities and their willingness to accept peaceful overtures, and suffer greatly when these abilities and overtures are misunderstood or disregarded. Mennonite Bernie Wiebe has reported that pacifist communities, including his own, are often filled with stress, confusion, and anger. He believes that the confusion and angst arise because the members are not used to putting things squarely on the table. Peace is maintained through denial.[5]

Either by being too aggressive or too passive, church members appear ill-equipped to follow their vision collaboratively.

Such intransigent levels of conflict are not restricted to church groups. Loraleigh Keashley finds similar instances of irreconcilable conflicts among the professional groups with which she has worked. "One thing I have noticed in dealing with these various professions is the intensity with which they experience their conflictual situations. What they have presented to me as the main source of difficulties could not explain the anguish and intractability of their experiences. There is a sense of something surprisingly personal, given the professional group context. Something very fundamental is being threatened."[6]

She suggests that the explanation may lie in the protagonists' competition over "turf." This in turn reflects each member's professional sense of who they are, contained in the value of what they do, and their "pecking order" in relationships with colleagues and other persons with whom they work. Despite their expertise and social standing, they feel insecure. Their commitment to their profession is their whole life, yet they are unable to confirm each other in their contribution to society's general welfare, the goal of their mutual vocation.

Members of both these groups – the church and the professionals – share the same intensity of identification with their group or calling. Yet each individual within that group has a sense of vulnerability, arising from fear of attack or criticism from colleagues or the wider society. In our individualistic culture, it may be difficult to build reliable and stable relationships because the necessary, basic trust is not assured. Such conflicts point to the deepest level of societal and cultural values, which may need to be articulated by its members, in order to meet their material, emotional, and spiritual needs and bring about a more functional relationship. Above all, "things need to be put on the table" in good faith, however painful and risky this appears to be.

It is worthwhile to compare the individual's common response to threat with that seen in international affairs, involving countries and their representatives, who obviously take the honor of their nation very seriously and personally. Terrill Northrup talks about the manner of communication in escalating conflict. She identifies four stages beyond mere problem solving.[7] Threat, the first stage, occurs when one of the parties says or does something that is perceived by the other party as invalidating their sense of identity. That person may in turn use counter-threats against the other as a form of defense.

The second stage is distortion. Northrop sees this as a psychological response to threat. The message is absorbed, but its meaning is denied or altered in order to reduce the sense of threat. The party may be trying to reconcile the message with the belief system that underlies his or her worldview and community values. The distortion is an attempt to adjust to the alien world as presented, and to protect the self at the same time.

The third stage is rigidification. The protagonists build a wall of protection, each seeking to distinguish the self from the "not-self," the other. The hostile imagination systematically destroys the humanity of the other, until the other is perceived as less than human. Parties now find their identity needs satisfied by the continuance of the conflict, which comes to define their main purpose in life.

The final stage is collusion. Yes, collusion. The opposing parties come to assist one another, not in problem solving, but in emphasizing reasons for maintaining the conflict. The original threat and conflict take on all-important, self-defining characteristics. In this situation, the conflict becomes profoundly embedded as the core meaning for life, the only reason for living. It is its own source of drama and justification. Thus there is still connection, although a pathological one. There is a state of "negative interdependence."[8]

If a peacemaker is asked to intervene at this stage, he or she may find the situation almost intractable. The mediator must take the opportunity to change the game in some way. It may be necessary for the combatants to meet on neutral terms to learn more about each other, their history and circumstances, so that they can find some common ground from which to start dialogue. By stepping outside the altercation, and by reviewing their values and goals as a linked community, they may come to see, if they are willing, that they each bear responsibility for some of the pain and destruction. This recognition may be the first step in addressing the misunderstandings, and may bring about a transformation in perceptions so that they can get down to the important issues at stake.

Emotions are, as I have tried to show, so much of the driving force of the conflict. But they exist to protect the self, the identity of the person who feels threatened. They are there to point out what matters. Resistance and emotions are potent signs of an unmet need. It is best not to deny or ignore these indicators, but to read their message and use them to discern their underlying meaning: the spiritual core of the souls embroiled in conflict.

NEEDS & THEIR SATISFACTION

Instead of being astonished at the spiritual emptiness of the times, we should be amazed that individuals manage…to find sufficient meaning and purpose.
Michael Ignatiev

Plain and simple – need is that which is necessary. Yet the discussion of needs is fraught with double meanings and contradiction, especially among many religious people. For example, a theology or an interpretation of scripture that says one must deny essential needs or be self-sacrificing in order to live authentically and morally is surely self-contradictory. Time and again, demands for self-denial have been shown to be oppressive, the source of injustice, and a betrayal of our humanity. Such theologies become, not a path to joy or fulfillment, but rather a source of resentment and despair.

That I must preface my remarks about human need by saying that satisfying them is part of life's purpose reflects the power of a soul-destroying theology that has pervaded much of religious teaching. The question of needs is seldom brought up by patriarchal church leaders, but is frequently welcomed by members of their flocks when I raise it in discussion groups!

Of course, we have to distinguish those things that are indeed truly necessary for our existence and functioning as full human beings, and those lesser matters that are more related to maintaining privilege or idiosyncrasy – wants, whims, and the like. At the same time, we do well to remember that what constitutes a whim from one person's perspective, may represent a deeply felt need from another's.

So how do we pinpoint our needs, and make decisions about their role in life's meaning? Often we can learn about the importance of a need by its absence. A hungry person needs food, a threatened one needs sanctuary, and we all need a sense of who we are and validation by our peers. As I pointed out at the beginning of the chapter, our emotions are linked very closely to our needs, and serve to amplify them so that we notice them. Our first job, then, is to listen to our emotions, feel them, and discover where they are pointing!

Case Study: What Was the Need?

In a situation I mediated some years ago, an agent had undertaken to find a piano for a young woman, at a certain price. The agent knew the price was a bit low, but he tried anyway. Research turned up nothing suitable. He went on trying. Time went by, and he did not answer the young woman's calls.

At mediation, she was very angry, as much because of the failure to communicate as because of the non-appearance of the piano. She really felt let down, because she had wanted to make this business deal herself, rather than rely on her father to do everything for her.

After giving all sorts of excuses, the real truth about the agent's motives came out. He said how he had hated letting her down so much, that he had put off telling her of his inability to get a piano in any reliable condition for the price stated.

The young woman would not be appeased. She repeated how the agent's failure to get back to her had caused all sorts of problems. She went on and on, unwilling to hear the reasons for the failure to deliver the goods.

I jumped to a conclusion: that something more important than finding the piano was at stake. I suggested that she could not move forward until we acknowledged how upset she was about the delay, the failure to communicate, and what it had meant for her own self-image as a mature, self-determining adult.

It was as if a light bulb went on. "Yes!" she said. "That is it!"

The parties went on to clarify what had happened, in a quick and reciprocating dialogue.

"You are really quite a nice man," the young woman said eventually. They shook hands and parted in good accord. She left, apparently completely satisfied, the purchase of the piano no longer an issue.

Analysis

In this encounter, it took some time to discover that the failure to fulfill the contract was not, in fact, the meaningful issue. The situation moved from a conflict based solely on material values, to one where the self-worth of the young client was at stake. Underlying the interaction was her wish to show herself as mature and capable of managing her own affairs. To this extent, the piano transaction had symbolic meaning for her. Her need to have both the agent and myself recognize her as a fully fledged adult was greater than her need for the piano itself.

In discussing the question of human needs and their relative priorities, many authors refer to Abraham Maslow, who first sought to group them in some logical sequence.

Maslow placed and grouped human needs on a hierarchical ladder of importance.[9] He suggested that those things that are necessary for bodily survival – such as food, water, and sleep – occupy the lowest rung, because they appear to be the most crucial. These physiological needs are seen in the body's efforts to maintain a constant, normal state. If these needs are relatively well-gratified, there emerges a new set of needs, related to safety. These include the need for security and stability, structure and order. Maslow placed the desire for human connectedness in the center of his model. Here we find the need for love and the giving and receiving of affection. Maslow suggested that the rapid increase in the number of training groups and intentional communities may be motivated in part by an unsatisfied hunger for contact, intimacy, and belonging. On the next level, and allied to the desire for human connectedness, is our need for self-respect, self-esteem, and the esteem of others. These are the needs for achievement, competence, confidence, and independence. They also include the desire for reputation, prestige and status, recognition, dignity and appreciation, and the desire to be useful and necessary in the world. Autonomy and "self-actualization," or the realization of the potential of each human being, comes at the top of Maslow's hierarchy. Maslow asserts that even when all other needs are satisfied, we may expect that a new discontent and restlessness will soon develop, unless the individual is doing what he or she, individually, is fitted for. This is the need for self-fulfillment.

A more flexible, holistic view is taken by Paul Sites, a philosopher who has studied human need satisfaction in connection with conflict theory. Sites says that needs range from the practicalities of food and shelter, to more abstract concepts, such as the need to reduce uncertainty and find meaning in life. Self-actualization may be one aspect of the fruition of that search for meaning.[10]

For human beings, Sites asserts, there is the need for the survival of the self. While animals adapt to their environment, human beings have the capacity to construct, control, and change their physical and social environment. The most basic human need, then, relating to the integrity of the self, is to symbolize one's life in constructs of meaning, to imagine and to build and live in a world that has internal congruency.

Sites takes issue with Maslow's construct asserting that needs cannot be prioritized into any sort of hierarchy, because all needs are interrelated. Every aspect of all of them is necessary, all at the same time. Some will be seen as instrumental, or necessary conditions for the survival of the body. Others pertain to the sense of self, and these are key to having a life of meaning, a life sustained by spirit.

Arising out of the need for personal significance and survival of the self is the desire to have a sense of identity. Threats to identity are important causes of conflict. We have seen the extreme tensions that exist in groups of many kinds – professional, religious, as well as ethnic and many more – when they perceive they have been denied their identity. We cannot overstress identity within a social group as the means for imparting sacred meaning to human lives. Maslow and many others[11] agree that social bonding and affiliation is a primary human need and that its absence or breakdown is key to many of the dysfunctional and conflict-ridden situations of modern life. A sense of personal integrity, respect, and mutual fairness are all part of the equation.

While needs, both those pertaining to the physical body and those pertaining to the self or soul, are common to all humanity, they may be identified and expressed in different ways by different personalities, in different contexts, as a result of history and culture.

Summary

Where would we be without emotions? Life would indeed be poorer. In this chapter, I have talked more about the so-called "negative" emotions than I have about the pleasurable ones, for these come quickly to the fore when we are confronted with a threat or feel let-down. While labeled negative, emotions such as anger serve essential functions, warning us that something needs attention. We may become aware of a threat to our need to live authentically only when that need is denied to us. Emotions serve as signals to the spirit, if we honor them.

But emotions can get out of hand. When enmity persists because our needs for authentic living go unaddressed, the hostility feeds on itself. Fuel is thrown on the fire by both sides. At every step of escalation, the conflict becomes more intractable, the players more obstinate. If we recognize what is happening, though, perhaps we can turn our attention away, temporarily at least, from the primary issues at stake and instead pay attention to the destructive dynamics between the parties. We can say, "Let's take a break; let's change the game; let's get back to being the kinds of people we would like to be."

Often, in conflict situations, power plays a major role. Power can be used as a force for the benefit of those it reaches, or a cudgel used to subdue the opposition. This is the topic we will address in the next chapter.

VIII

COERCIVE POWER

The measure of a man is what he does with power.
Pittacus (600 BCE)

By definition, effective power does not necessarily threaten – it is just the ability to influence others. Some sort of power is always present in human interactions. Sometimes the attempt to influence others is carried out by dominating or coercive power, where the one exerting the force seeks to get someone to do something that he or she would not otherwise do. (I do not intend to discuss the legitimate role that police and security forces play in restraining criminal acts.) But power can also be integrative, when it is used to benefit all parties.

COERCIVE POWER

I have never been able to conceive how any rational being could propose happiness to himself from the exercise of power over others.
Thomas Jefferson

Coercive power is power that is used to threaten or to impose costs or harm on another person or group, to gain compliance solely for the self-interest of the coercive one. Our newspapers are full of examples of the exercise of such power. People from every level of society are capable of using strong-arm tactics, if they feel it is necessary to their own interests to do so – and if they think they can get away with it. Dominating power helps the user to feel adequate, to feel in control, to feel as if they are worth something – at least in the short term. Thus its use often arises from a prior feeling of inadequacy.

On the national and international political scene, history tell us that a desire for domination has been the norm for nation states and other political entities, such as tribal groups. Only 150 years ago, Karl von Clausewitz declared that "War is nothing more than the continuation of politics by other means."

Indeed, wars were, not so long ago, considered chivalrous events. When these battles were local and limited in their effects, involving only immediate combatants and a lesser number of civilian victims caught up in the fighting, they could perhaps be justified, at least by the winning side, because they often achieved their objectives with minimal cost to the conquerors.

Today, however, wars threaten our entire ecosystem, create millions of refugees and untold poverty, and are often associated with "ethnic cleansing." The possible global consequences of war and the use of chemical, biological, and nuclear weapons are now so drastic that any potential short-term gain cannot be assured. The fact that wars and threats of war continue suggests that we are collectively in a state of practical, spiritual, and moral denial.

Outside of war, people who exert dominant power may be especially destructive if they operate with the sanction of the society in which they live. The story of the last century reveals that, too often, tacit approval is handed over to oppressors. We have only to remember the *Kristallnacht* in Nazi Germany, when, on the nights of November 9 and 10, 1938, Jews were freely attacked in the streets; their homes, places of work, and synagogues were destroyed; and some 30,000 were arrested and sent to concentration camps. It was, in many respects, the beginning of the Holocaust. Or we can reflect on the apartheid regime in South Africa, not so very long ago. In each case, the victims were disenfranchised. With their most basic civil rights denied, they were treated as virtual non-citizens. In Germany, the dehumanizing reached extreme proportions. In South Africa, belief in the non-worth of the Blacks led to the most appalling atrocities perpetrated against them.[1] Dominant cultural norms are powerful agencies which, in seeking to maintain one section of society's growth and welfare over others, ignore and further marginalize those who have experienced neglect, poverty, and despair.

Society-supported use of coercive, oppressive force has not vanished even from our own towns and cities. Until quite recently, for example, police did not intervene in incidents of domestic violence. Here the power of male batterers stemmed from the patriarchal ordering of society, which was taken as common sense by those in power, because it met their interests and fitted in with their worldview. Often, people of privilege are unaware of their power and how they use it to control and oppress others in ways that are coercive or humiliating. They also tend to minimize any deleterious effects their attitudes and behavior have on others.

Power magnates typically assume that those they command must be willing to obey, or that if subordinates have problems, they will dialogue politely about how a controlling edict creates problems for them, suggests Arnold Mindell, conflict mediator and author.[2] Failing a compliant response, they are at least expected to keep a respectful silence. Often the opportunity for dialogue is denied altogether; the weaker party is either disregarded or penalized for speaking out. This insensitivity to needs can be so oppressive that it may eventually be balanced by another power: that of revenge and rebellion. Until that moment, the dominant parties may not even be aware that a conflict exists; the resentment has been brewing underground, gaining energy and spirit, until it explodes in violence.

Individuals who use dominating power may see it as the only way to get things done. Sometimes they may be working from a position of assurance about their own high motives and with a clear view that they know what is best for everyone. They forget that others need an opportunity to make choices and to be confirmed, even at a modest level, that their lives have significance. The use of such power is a frequent cause of low morale and ineffective work patterns.

The following case report illustrates the subtle, dominating power that can exist in our own community organizations, even those whose aim is to foster the spiritual health and empowerment of others. To protect the identity of anyone who may see themselves or their organization here, I provide a composite picture that reflects a common pattern.

Case Study

A board member of a nonprofit organization continually criticized and blamed a secretary for stupidity and incompetence. The secretary was a single mother who could ill afford to lose her job. She found some support from other staff members who commiserated with her and joined in growling about the board member, and indeed, about the whole board for their failure to curb the actions of the "bully." A supervisor nominally in charge of staff felt powerless and caught between the power of the board and the perceived incompetence of the secretary, which reflected on her own abilities to manage. Other staff members did nothing, for they did not want to rock the boat. The board kept aloof from the problem at first, but then, when the whole function of the agency became imperiled, decided that the situation could not go on.

I was called in as mediator. After interviewing every person privately, I engaged the principal players – the board member, the supervisor, and the secretary – in a discussion.

It turned out that the secretary and the supervisor, as is often the case, had received conflicting instructions about their responsibilities and priorities. These were eventually clarified, and the secretary given the opportunity to upgrade her skills. The board recognized the soul-destroying effect of the perpetual criticism on the secretary and the effect on staff morale. Each person agreed to undertake personal responsibility for fostering a more supportive climate within the organization. Staff learned it was better to support their colleagues by providing empathy than by taking sides. The secretary proved to be resilient. Once her pain had been acknowledged and the source of it removed, she was prepared to move ahead and gain the competence required. The supervisor accepted responsibility for failing to clarify her own terms of reference. The board member also acknowledged her role in the difficulty. However, rather than change her approach and build on the rapport gained through the mediation process, she decided to resign.

Analysis

In this situation, the domineering actions of one person in authority toward another of lower rank jeopardized the whole organization, causing pain to all those who depended on the organization for its services, but especially for the individual toward whom the condemnation was directed.

A corner was turned when each member of the organization saw how he or she had contributed to the difficulty. They regained the energy and commitment to create a new reality. These changes occurred over a period of time, with many reviews to see that the new processes and relationships were working.

Perhaps, in the end, the person with the greatest need was the board member who had caused the problem. Although she was willing to recognize her error, she could not accept the possibility that there was still a place for her in the organization. She had lost face. She could not forgive or heal her own perception of herself, nor accept that this was necessary or possible. Nor could she accept the help of others in making the needed transition. Had she been able to adjust in this way, to review who she was and how she was perceived in her approach to "getting the job done," she would have been able to learn from the experience and gain a new sense of self-respect.

When the use of domineering power is recognized, bystanders often find themselves in a moral dilemma as to how to hold the operator accountable, how to sustain both the doer and the receiver as valued individuals, all the while redressing the injury.

The effectiveness of dominant or coercive power depends on the relative power of all parties involved and the social context. In the above case study, if power had been more evenly divided, the options for the staff member might have been different. The secretary might have looked for another job, had her skills and the market been more favorable. Or she might have resorted to human rights legislation.

So often we see that when the coercive nature of their actions is brought to their attention, and the balance of power is restored, dominators quickly feel diminished. They may take on the role of victim and then need a helping hand to regain self-worth and "face" on a more equitable basis, assuming they are willing to accept the new status.

The Oppressor Pays a Price

The personal cost of coercive power to the one exerting it can be massive in other ways. For example, the person may ignore everything else as they narrowly strive to achieve a goal that, in the end, may prove to be unachievable. It is a truism that no one ever believes they have enough power over others when they seek to dominate them. As Phyllis Kritek points out in her book *Negotiating at an Uneven Table*, a focus on dominant power often prevents the oppressor from considering and experiencing other dimensions of interest and importance.[3]

People who hold dominant power are often ill-informed and limited in their thinking and judging. Fighting to sustain their position and resisting any opportunity for growth and self-expansion, they become emotionally attached to their worldview. Everyone has an inner world, which is their reality, and to have it questioned is threatening. A belief in the necessity of control essentially invokes a caste system; people who have a need to dominate seem to need inferiors in order to feel adequate. Thus a resort to dominating tactics is ultimately exposed as weakness, not strength.

Coercive power is particularly counterproductive if it pushes so far that the victim comes to feel that he or she has little to lose. In this situation, fear of possible retaliation may grow for the oppressor. Those whom we control thus control us. Dominators tend to get trapped in the constraints they set up, and experience a loss of their own personal freedom. No one ultimately feels secure as a result of wielding this sort of power. Political realism, however, still preaches as "gospel" the need to control through strength and intimidation, even when these tactics are no longer effective and are revealed as self-defeating. Violent coercive power perpetuates cultural violence.[4] It is ultimately our own spirit that we quench when we resort to coercive power.

EFFECTS ON OTHERS OF COERCIVE POWER

And shame and terror over all
Deeds to be hid which were not hid.
Samuel Taylor Coleridge

It is not easy to discuss the effects of coercive and dominating power on others, because the coercive behaviors themselves are often so repugnant.

Most humiliating and soul destroying for victims is the experience of rape. The effects of rape can last a lifetime, affecting the victim's sense of safety in society and future sexual relationships with partners. In our society, the victim may undergo double jeopardy, because the judicial system requires the victim to retell the story and relive the pain again and again in front of unsympathetic officials. The interviewers may demand an assessment of the victim's credibility, rather than of his or her need, thus revictimizing the person. Sometimes the victim gets blamed for the situation by an uncaring, judgmental audience, to which the victim has gone to confide the darkest secrets of suffering and betrayal.

In our own communities, most rapes are committed, not by strangers, but by acquaintances. With growing frequency, we are also hearing reports of how they are committed by those in positions of trust. To bring this widespread atrocity to the general attention of society is, at least, the first step in controlling it and lending a voice to the victims.

In times of war, rape and sexual violence against women and children runs rampant. Sometimes it is committed intentionally and on a massive scale, as a means of spreading terror among women, and humiliation among men who are unable to protect them. In these situations, report Leslie Shanks and Michael Schull, it amounts to an act of genocide; it results in the death of a group's spirit and reason for existence, without which it cannot survive.[5]

Dr. Shanks speaks from direct experience as a member of Médecins Sans Frontières, while Dr. Schull is an epidemiologist. Both have worked in Africa, where one faction may deliberately rape and enforce pregnancy on another as a form of ethnic cleansing. Such was the case in Rwanda, where the offspring are known as *enfants mauvais souvenir*, "children of bad memories." These children are subject to abandonment and infanticide. The mothers are often stigmatized by societal and cultural norms, viewed as defiled, rejected, left destitute, and suffer post-traumatic stress disorder. Thus an act designed to bring forth new life and hope is used as an instrument of vilification, of destroying both body and soul. "Who can heal what these women have suffered?" these writers ask. Who can heal their entire communities?

The wider international community can at least listen to their voices, validate their distress, and build systems to prevent the recurrence of similar atrocities. The new initiative suggested by the International Commission on Intervention and State Sovereignty (2001) asserts that the international community has a three-fold responsibility to protect vulnerable citizens, to react by appropriate intervention, and to rebuild where necessary. They recommend to the United Nations Security Council that it should draft a set of guidelines for such interventions. It is a new approach, and not without the risk that such interventions could cause more hardships than they prevent.

The consequences of threat and victimization of whole groups has been described by Vamik Volkan and colleagues in *The Psychodynamics of International Relationships*.[6] In situations where normal group solidarity has broken down, and with it the defense that solidarity provides, individuals experience unrelieved anxiety about real threats to their existence. They find it difficult to trust anyone, even those who might help them. Their anxiety and inability to trust is communicated from one generation to the next, in a perpetual sense that justice has been denied and that there is a need for continuous vigilance in defense of self and group. Such individuals are trapped by their arrested or incomplete grief and mourning for losses, which have neither been recognized nor acknowledged by the perpetrators or their descendents, or even by the wider society. We have only to think of the continuing effects of colonization and domination on our own aboriginal peoples.

REACTIONS & INITIATIVES FOLLOWING THREAT OR COERCION

*You may never know what results come from your action.
But if you do nothing, there will be no results.*
Mahatma Gandhi

The purpose of wielding coercive power or threat is, of course, to get the target of the threat to comply. This is not always what happens, however.

Certainly the climate between the two will be influenced adversely by the hostile gesture. As we saw in the section on self-fulfilling prophecies, the approach used by one party sets the stage for how the other will respond or react. Competition sets up competition, cooperation sets up cooperation. But competition, by its nature, implies a challenge among equals. It can be fun to respond competitively, and it can hone each person's abilities. Threats or coercion are not meant to be fun. They are intended to intimidate and to disempower, to crush the spirit.

The receiver can respond in a variety of ways, however, depending on how he or she perceives the situation. The person may experience a sense of helplessness, if he or she believes that there is no possibility of controlling the situation, and that the threats and bullying are likely to continue.[7] But there are other possibilities, which Kenneth Boulding identifies in his book *Three Faces of Power*.[8]

While some people experience a dampening of the spirit, others may find that their spirits rebound with an escalated response – though not always a constructive one. Such responses include submission, defiance, counter-threat, and flight. (Boulding omits the resort to legal processes. I shall deal with this response in a chapter of its own.) Another possibility is that the person will use his or her initiative to change the game in ways that will uphold honor for all, and that are both just and peaceful. Let's look at each of these possibilities in more detail.

Submission

First, the person may submit. Indeed, where it would be dangerous not to obey, submission may be the safest and only possible response. Unfortunately, a continuing pattern of domination and submission may be set up. Responses will depend on a number of circumstances, including the age of the person being threatened or acted against. For young children in the home, parents may provide the only model of human interaction. Early experiences of dominant, bullying behavior can affect a child's emotional and spiritual development for years to come. This kind of betrayal of trust may be felt for a lifetime, affecting the person's view of the world as a safe place and all subsequent relationships. Victims may never gain a sense of who they are, but remain empty shells with no self-esteem or identity, except as despised shadows that function at the behest of others.

Domestic coercion and violence affects not only children, but the adult members of families as well. Most often, but not always, it is the women who are abused. Only recently has intervention on the part of police become accepted. In the past, women often had no recourse, for to report their situation was to risk further violence, even death.

Measures to correct these traumas on an individual and societal basis are starting to come from the wider society. The women's movement has played an instrumental role in addressing these issues over the past half-century, sometimes causing considerable consternation and reaction from those determined to preserve the status quo. Women have come together to make themselves visible politically, breaking the culture of silence and submission. Physical injury and suffering are no longer seen as cause for blame or evidence of an individual's failings, but as rooted in previously accepted social structures. Women have moved discourse from individual personal experience to the field of public political policy.[9] Community agencies with government support now provide assistance to victims, while counseling is available from professional psychologists. Yet our cultural norms still encourage – or fail to *discourage* – the portrayal of violence as entertainment in our media.

An unfortunate result of the use of coercive power is that the abuse gets transmitted to others. A victimized person may well vent his or her wrath on other, even more vulnerable people. Similarly, a young victim of brutality, having learned no other model of relating to others, may later subject his or her own family to the same domineering tactics. Thus the circle of violence and spirit-crushing is perpetuated. This is not inevitable, however. According to Gina O'Connell Higgins, at least 60 percent of children raised in abusive families realize that the model they were raised with was wrong, and use more nurturing methods with their own offspring. They have learned what *not* to be.[10] Nevertheless, the remaining 40 percent transmit an enormous legacy of pain. Many such victims turn to alcohol or commit suicide to deal with their sense of desecration and worthlessness.

Defiance

Another common response to dominating power is, of course, defiance. The spirit rebounds! Here the one receiving the threat is not subdued, but determines that the only possible reaction is to raise the ante.

If the receiver of the threat decides to be defiant, then the one using the coercive tactics has to decide if he or she will carry out the promised action. Each has to decide their options and whether they have the power or the justification to carry out the threat or the defiance.

As we saw in the section on how conflicts escalate, the choice to hit back is indeed a common response. Each may see the other's actions as more aggressive than their own and up the ante in a spiral of action and counteraction. Or, alternatively, one or the other of the parties may decide to brush the matter aside, pretending or concluding that they just don't give a damn, the issue isn't worth it.

As the history of social action tells us, defiance of coercion or injustice succeeds best if it kindles a flame and elicits support from others with similar problems. It also has a greater chance of succeeding if it is persistent and the defiant ones are prepared to live with the consequences. Such is the spirit of solidarity against injustice! It often demands sacrifice.

Retaliation

The most robust reaction to dominance and coercion is the resort to retaliation or revenge. This should not always be construed as illogical.

According to Kenneth Cloke, revenge promises a release from the rage and shame engendered by an act against the identity and worth of the person.[11] Its initial (tacit) aim may be to make the crime and pain understandable to the oppressor by letting him experience it, by repeating it in reverse. Unfortunately, the oppressor will likely misinterpret this lesson and retaliate by instigating further punitive measures.

The justification and practice of revenge has a long history. The Greek word for justice (εκδιλησις) as used in the New Testament epistles, for instance, also means vengeance. The action has an undercurrent of a search for justice.[12] As originally conceived in sacred scripture, this kind of vengeance set limits on the actions it condoned. If used as an instrument of God's justice, it had to be free from any element of self-gratification or vindictiveness. Human initiated revenge often lacks these purer aspects!

Resort to revenge *does* allow the avenger to experience an ecstasy and sensuality of violence in ways that appear justifiable, at least to him. Revenge, of course, supports a culture of violence. When the injustice is not recognized but only the vengeful act, as is often the case, then the dominant power may retaliate in turn, exacerbating the injustice and the brutality. Revenge ultimately wounds the victim along with the perpetrator, sustaining suffering by passing it on. Soon it becomes confusing as to who is victim and who is oppressor, because they are both, in sequence and all at once.

On the international scene, when an oppressed nation gains liberation all too often it turns oppressor and institutes a mode of government similar to or even more despotic in habits of management than the one overthrown. This has been the situation in several African states, following the ousting of the colonial power. Thus the cycle of violence and oppression is renewed.

Arnold Mindell brings the uncomfortable notion of vengeance as justice to the world's negotiation tables, where he seeks to understand the motives of terrorists, usually known by their own side as "freedom fighters."[13] Disempowered groups attack the mainstream society to gain equality and freedom. What appears as random and unjustified violence is actually an attempt to compensate for the hurts the disempowered have suffered. Their goal is often to waken those in power to the necessity of social change and relief from injustice. But their methods lead more often to further misunderstandings about motives and to an escalation of the conflict and violence. While wreaking vengeance gains them, in their own eyes at least, a kind of spiritual "righteousness," it can prove to be addictive and is just as much a misuse of power as the original injustices of the government in power. Nelson Mandela's *Umkhonto we Sizwe* – the Spear of the Nation – movement against apartheid, and the actions of the Irish Republican Army in Northern Ireland against Unionists and the British government, are recent instances of such action and reaction. Conflict interveners need incredible wisdom, patience, and spirit to remain calm and nonjudgmental while they search for the source of the vengeful acts, work to change perceptions about what has transpired, and encourage each side to remedy its deepest causes and listen to the other side's case. Meanwhile, security forces must contain the terrorist acts, to prevent continuing harm to innocent citizens and institutions.

Flight

Flight is always an option where safety is an issue. But it is also seen where people prefer not to engage in argument with others; instead, as avoidant people, they decide to vote with their feet.

Where alternative placement or services are available, people may no longer feel they have to put up with dictatorships. Mainline churches are going through tremendous changes right now, in some part because patriarchal leadership has become unacceptable. The dominating/obedience model is no longer seen as an option for spiritual growth. Within the family unit, too, as a consequence of a greater variety of options, spouses and offspring flee abusive relationships and take the consequences, which may not always be much better than the situation they have left.

On the international scene, the option to flee has become a global scandal. While the number of refugees fleeing across borders had fallen to about three million in the 1970s, by 1995 it had risen to an all-time high of 27 million. People displaced from their homes but still within their original country's borders add another 30 million (source: United Nations High Commission for Refugees 2001). This situation is in itself an indication of immeasurable hardship. But it also speaks to the failure of our international and national institutions to control the actions of warring factions. We have already mentioned the new initiative suggested by the International Commission on Intervention and State Sovereignty, designed to forestall or remedy these situations.

Changing the Game

The final response to the use of coercive power, which Boulding identifies, is to change the game. This initiative may be used in relatively trivial situations, or where really important issues are at stake.

In situations where the hostility is expressed more by word than by physical threat, disarming behavior can take the form of acknowledging the perspective of the other, perhaps by reframing the adversarial statement into more positive terms. This reinterprets the attacking words into a language that acknowledges both the problem and the perception of the complainer, without painting oneself into a corner. A couple of examples of this skill will clarify what I mean.

Two colleagues plan a conference together. One day one colleague is unavoidably detained, so fails to show up on time. The other colleague, feeling pressured as the day for the conference fast approaches, blasts him, saying, "You're always late! How can I bring this conference off if you don't you pull your weight?" A reframe would seek to get to the nub of the meaning of the protest. "So sharing the workload is important to you?" Or, on another occasion, someone might complain to the chairperson at the board meeting: "This bloody meeting is not just for you, you know!" If the chairperson is on her toes, she might disarm the person by saying: "It's important to you that you have a voice in decision-making?"

In actions of a more coercive nature, changing the game might mean trying to arouse the better nature of the oppressor. An example in the Christian New Testament is Jesus' injunction to "walk a second mile" (Matthew 5:41). This suggestion is often misunderstood. According to biblical scholar Walter Wink, Roman legionnaires had the authority to order anyone to carry their load for a distance of one mile. The person so ordered was usually a peasant, a "nobody," a lowly member of a conquered race. In other words, legionnaires were used to treating peasants as of no account. The remarkable thing is that, in this situation, Jesus suggests that the "nobody" should outdo the command of the oppressor, by exceeding the demand. The action, says Wink, is a ploy to show the oppressor that the victim has a sense of honor at least as strong as the powerful one; it is a demonstration of his or her equal worth.[14]

While the powerful one might have acted from a motivation to subdue, he or she is met by a response that has the potential to transform the relationship into one of relative equality. In this case, the oppressor may see a reason to re-evaluate his or her actions and back off. Of course, if you offer generosity when you believe the other is being malicious, you run the risk that they will take advantage of you.

Sometimes the act of another person may seem oppressive, but that is not his or her intention. Here the generous offer may be met by the one receiving it with a sense of relief because the grace of the offering party is appreciated, and may even be reciprocated.

An alternative response that extends the notion of changing the game even more dramatically has been practiced by members of major religions and quite a few political enterprises: that of martyrdom. Martyrs are those who, because of a principle or cause, voluntarily and nonviolently undertake suffering, even to the point of death.

Self-denying behavior by the "victim" puts the onus on the "oppressor" to recognize injustice. Such behaviors include hunger-strikes undertaken to bring attention to a cause or principle. Some risk is involved, for dominators don't usually like to change their ways. They may, for instance, be reluctant to acknowledge that the person who suggests such changes could have a legitimate point about the fair distribution of resources; or they may feel so caught up in self-justification that they cut themselves out of any future dialogue or possibility of contributing toward a constructive outcome. They may be enthralled by their worldview of privilege, and deny the spirit that might be released were they to change their attitude and examine the justice of the other's cause. This would risk unforeseeable changes in the power structure, which might threaten their own standing and influence.

Summary

This chapter has been about brutality and dominance, the circumstances that foster it, and its effects on both the perpetrator and the victim. We traveled to distance places and war zones, then came home to see that coercive power is not absent from our own communities. We found hope when we review the many different options which hardy people have used to deal with these situations. Their actions speak to the resiliency of spirit among those affected by tyrannical power.

In the next chapter we will take these ideas of resiliency one step further.

IX

INTEGRATIVE & SPIRITUAL POWERS

Let me not be misunderstood. Strength does not come from physical capacity. It comes from an indomitable will.
Mahatma Gandhi

According to Kenneth Boulding,[1] integrative power is that which enhances freedom and power for everyone involved: both the purveyor and the receiver. Unlike destructive or coercive power, which as we have seen is likely to be self-defeating, integrative power is paradoxical in that the more you use it and give it to others, the more is available. Integrative power may be based on authority, skill, knowledge, commitment to the task, a person's own sense of integrity, or the wish to restore or preserve a good relationship. It can build upon the wisdom of thoughtful people. It is, in this definition, a power that is relational.

In the field of conflict management, this sort of power will be found among mediators who help parties discern their needs from their conversations and who encourage them to pursue mutual benefits. It is seen in the application of a wisdom that seeks to reveal truth and bring about justice. More of these applications later.

What then is spiritual power? Spiritual power is not always easy to describe, but is readily recognizable in experience. Spiritual power adds a further dimension to integrative power. In some ways, it is unique to the individual, a special consciousness directed toward developing creativity, justice, and compassion, for everyone.[2] People who display spiritual power will come across as securely anchored in their faith and values. They will have integrated this faith into their daily acts. They know who they are, their imperfections and abilities alike.

People with spiritual power impart a sense of inner peace. Their power is evidence of a tremendous investment they have made in working through their own negative experiences, their shadow side. It has been said that the stronger the light an individual displays, the deeper the shadow which serves to profile that luminescence. People with spiritual power have this quality of self-knowledge. They may well have tapped into divine resources through spiritual practices, such as prayer and meditation, in order to ground themselves in an ongoing, conscious process of spiritual development and redevelopment.

This desire to engage in a process of spiritual development is a point of contrast in many of those who set out to bring peace and transformation to the world. It is a fundamental misunderstanding for peace-lovers to focus only on the light of their own motives. By focusing only on the things deemed positive and by ignoring or repressing the rest, they simply perpetuate the polarization of light and dark forces. This further distorts and empowers the very energies they try to avoid.

True healing and spiritual power come from owning, accepting, and coming to terms with all of life's energies – both the good and the bad. When embarking on a search for truth, the shadow side comes to consciousness. It is something with which the truth seeker must come to terms. In the process, the pilgrim discovers the tangled web of complex forces that might otherwise be repressed from ordinary consciousness in a desire to avoid seeing its true nature.[3] It can be a painful path.

But the dark side must be confronted and transformed in order to release the power of the spirit within. And this transformation needs to be carried out nonviolently in regards to the self, that is, without guilt or shame.

Integrative and spiritual power in leadership extends these principles to the wider world. Even just one person with such commitment, magnetism, and discipline can change the world. Mahatma Gandhi was such a one. I could have chosen others, such as Martin Luther King Jr., or Archbishop Desmond Tutu, or Nelson Mandela, or any number of other people who have followed the path, but who have not received the same publicity.

For this chapter, I have drawn on the writing of Gerald Gold[4] because he encompasses for me most clearly the essence of that Great Soul.

Why do I choose this man as an example of integrative and spiritual power? There are many reasons. Gandhi invariably insisted on nonviolent methods and further insisted that his followers do likewise. His means were compatible with his ends or purposes. He accepted responsibility for his actions and was prepared to suffer the penalty for breaking laws he felt were unjust. He had the ability to be *present* for his people in their situation. He sought the truth, listening always to the inner voice of conscience. One can marvel at the effect this dynamic person had on the world, and search for its cause.

The authentic innocence of a nonviolent person is the source of his or her power, according to Rollo May.[5] It does not involve any blocking off of awareness, nor does it involve renouncing responsibility. Its purpose and its strength lie in the fact that the person using it does not strive for personal gain, but for the good of the community. It acts as a goad to the rulers' ethics – a living rebuke to the smugness of their establishment. The rulers cannot turn away from the sufferer, nor from the dramatization of the issue provided by a nonviolent, committed person.

(Gandhi's methods stand in stark contrast to those used on September 11, 2001, when terrorists used planes packed with civilians to destroy the World Trade Center and its innocent civilian occupants. The worldwide cooperative response of people of all faiths against this act will have been contrary to what the terrorists had in mind.)

A Personification of Integrative and Spiritual Power

Gandhi developed an aptitude for self-discipline as a youth. In England, he learned the principles of fairness and justice during his training as a lawyer. He studied Hinduism and the Bible. His autobiography shows us, in self-revelatory detail, his analysis of his own motives and behavior, good and bad.

When he went to South Africa and was thrown off a train because of the color of his skin, he learned about prejudice firsthand. This incident and his interpretation of sacred texts set him on his lifelong pursuit of truth, through nonviolence and civil disobedience. He was aware that no individual can know the entire truth in any situation. Thus, every confrontation was carried out in an unceasingly open approach to those who would oppose him, seeking always to use cooperation where possible. Pursuing truth meant adhering to his understanding of the situation and vigorously attempting to persuade his opponent to the same view. At the same time, he held his own convictions in tension with an openness to be persuaded by the other. The experience taught him how to organize, how to oppose, and how to move masses of people to follow his lead.

The way to fight injustice, he decided, was to respond with truth and love, combined with a fierce unwillingness to submit to injustice or cruelty. His "weapon" was civil resistance, openly breaking the unjust law and inspiring others by the thousands to join him. "Non-cooperation with evil is as much a duty as is cooperation with good," he said.

His reputation brought him back to India, where his actions led to the defeat of the mighty British Empire 30 years later – through the power of mass action and nonviolent civil disobedience. This action was not for want of respect for lawful authority, but in obedience to a higher law, the voice of conscience.

Gandhi proved the integrity of his motives and actions by being prepared to suffer the penalty for his disobedience. This was the only safe and honorable course for a self-respecting person, he believed. When the British rulers appeared ready to redress injustices, Gandhi called off the civil disobedience actions. But more often the British reacted with physical violence and by jailing the protestors by the thousand.

Over time, the response of the British government escalated from imprisonment, to beatings, to the final massacre of hundreds of unarmed men, women, and children at Amritsar. After this episode, the British could no longer be viewed as the champions of fair dealing and the exponents of high principle, but instead were seen as upholders of Western hegemony, the notion of racial superiority, and the exploitation of colonial people. They lost their moral prestige.

At the same time, Gandhi's reputation remained unimpugned, because he lived a life of asceticism: personal poverty, celibacy, and fasting. He was loved and revered not only because of his politics, but because he carried out in practice what he preached about poverty, humility, and goodwill. His example and action aroused the people of India to a sense of their heritage and civilization. He imbued a whole nation with spirit, through the power of his personality and his sense of justice and truth.

British imperial power was now subject to the power of the Indian masses. India had become ungovernable. The British bowed out of India, the last viceroy handing over power in 1947. Gandhi had overcome injustice by an unwavering adherence to his principles. He used a transformative power that provoked conflict in the name of justice for the colonial people, including those of the lower caste within Indian culture.

Unfortunately, Gandhi's methods, which were so successful in dealing with colonial British power, were less effective in providing stability and goodwill between the two major religious groups in India: the Hindus and the Muslims. Gandhi sought to contain the violence that erupted between the two groups by dint of his own moral standing, by going on a hunger strike each time violence broke out. This was, at best, a temporary expedient, and could not succeed.

As we are all aware, an orthodox Hindu gunned him down within a year of Indian Independence. Gandhi's method of fighting injustice by organizing resistance to the colonial order could not pull his own people together into a stable unified system of government. For that, other sources of legitimate power were required, such as the ability to administer a new political entity that could build bridges between the Muslim and Hindu populations. But that is 20/20 hindsight. It did not happen.

Spiritual and Integrative Powers in the Present

Integrative power is personified by many active groups working for social justice around the world. What was previously considered private and nonpolitical is being brought to the front of the political agenda. The accepted model of social control is starting to shift from a hierarchy of dominance and submission, to one of distributed responsibility; to an implicit partnership, where the abilities of each member can be integrated into a formidable team of mutual support. Hierarchical structures are still necessary, for each person needs to know the roles of the other, both for mutual support and for predictability as to who is responsible for what. We are, however, gradually developing new models that reflect not pain, but spirit; not domination, but collaboration. These developments are still at risk of being co-opted or taken over by special interests groups who may have a different agenda: that of pressing their own interests or of maintaining the status quo.

The spiritual dimension abiding in our souls is no longer a taboo subject but is being expressed in solidarity movements for social justice. Spiritual power is embodied in creative, healing leadership, provided without judgment, but entailing risk, for it is often seen as dangerous by those who seek to maintain the status quo.

Summary

From the discussion in these last two chapters, we can see that notions of power stretch from the crudest, most destructive or manipulative, to the most creative and nurturing; from the most spirit quenching, to the most spirit enhancing!

As a result, when we discuss power, we had best define what type of power we are referring to. No matter which type is being exerted, however, and whatever the intentions of the powerful one and the one receiving it may be, the dynamic is always relational. The relationship may be one of domination and oppression, of equality and mutual empowerment, or of altruism, which seeks only to benefit the other. The outcome depends on decisions made by both parties, and on their sense of their own and the other's worth: the quality of their interconnection.

Remarkably, while dominance power produces peace, it is peace of a negative sort, because it may be obtained only by putting the lid on other people's legitimate aspirations, without their agreement. Integrative and spiritual power, by its search for peace with justice, often challenges the status quo and therefore brings on a situation of instability or conflict until that justice is obtained. Conflict, yes, but only until the injustices have been addressed and corrected. Then comes true peace.

Our spirituality is forged and shaped as we face life's challenges and discover, in the process, what is most meaningful. We gain wisdom in the process. That experience of development is featured in the next chapter.

X

THE DEVELOPMENT OF FAITH & THE EXPERIENCE OF SPIRIT

In faith we find our fiercest fidelity to an anchored and elaborate vision of a more human life.
Gina O'Connell Higgins

Whenever I raise the topic of spiritual experience with the students who attend my workshops, or suggest that an understanding of spiritual development and growth can bring a deeper sense of meaning to life and the conflicts we become involved in, it is as if a new hope has been visibly planted within them.

An appreciation of our spirituality as a primordial gift, to be honored and implemented, provides a proactive and constructive base from which we can steer our lives and choose our actions.

Of course, not everyone reaches adulthood with a developed sense of their own spirituality, or even with a general awareness of the existence and presence of Spirit. So how does this sense or awareness develop in people?

Spiritual awareness, for people who have been previously oblivious to this dimension, may come about as the fruit of a personal crisis. Or it may arise within the framework of a conflict with another person. In any event, such experiences often lead the individual to a discovery of the underlying narratives of his or her own life. In turn, these narratives may bring a new and profound meaning to the person's life, including an awareness of their spiritual essence, and a more congruent sense of what it means to be human.

To see how this transformation actually happens, or what it looks like in the lives of real people, it is helpful to refer to the work of Diarmuid O'Murchu and Matthew Fox, who describe similar pathways of transformation, though their models are slightly different at certain key junctures.

REDISCOVERING THE SPIRIT

What a caterpillar calls the end of the world, a master calls a butterfly.
Richard Bach

In his book *Reclaiming Spirituality*,[1] Diarmuid O'Murchu describes an *awakening* stage that may be triggered by any one of a range of events or experiences, but which is usually related to questions of meaning or lack of meaning. There is no conscious religious or spiritual awareness at the beginning of this stage. Life goes on in its humdrum way. But then an event occurs that causes internal confusion. Feelings of rage or anger may arise. People may even doubt their own experience. They might try to suppress their reactions, or to rationalize them, or, better yet, to ponder the possible meanings behind the event and their own reaction to it.

If the confusion persists, it may become deeply disturbing and the person may seek counsel from others. At this point, they may discover a spiritual vacuum in their current networks; they may find themselves let down, and grow to feel disillusioned and vulnerable and misunderstood by those whose counsel they sought. Alternatively, the people they turn to may judge them, or supply them with too-easy answers that provide no help or understanding. Others may gladly accept the counsel of cult or sect leaders, who seem to have clear-cut answers. Thus, they get sidetracked from their own spiritual journey.

When and if the person gets through this stage with integrity, having sought and found some insight into their previous confusion and its meaning, the individual gains a sense of progress. They may then enter a stage of maturing depth and conviction, based on personal reflections that continue to unravel the enfolding and unfolding mystery of their unique existence.

Having gained this new level of maturity, something deep within has changed profoundly and there is no going back. A transformative experience has taken root, an experience that colors their entire life-orientation and values. The experience tends to have far-reaching consequences and often inspires the seeker to universalize his or her faith experience. A fundamental "rightness" seems to permeate all of creation.

If the initial dilemma involved only the seeker, then this process may be sufficient. But if others are part of the situation, or if the person, having gained a wider perspective, becomes aware of major social injustices that he or she wishes to change, then something more may be required. We have not yet obtained nirvana, cautions O'Murchu. The shadow side of this more active stage may surface. Specifically, the individual may exhibit a naïve optimism in a tendency to deny the pain, suffering, and injustice that others may be encountering. Many who seek to bring about world peace, goodwill, and harmony, by simplistic ideas and means find themselves in just this place. Unless they internalize their commitment, disillusionment may cause them to drop out of further spiritual development.

In the final stage of the spiritual journey, assuming the person gets that far, there is a sense of coming home to oneself as a spiritual being. A prolonged struggle has grounded the individual's conviction in a concrete and practical way. This final stage possesses several dimensions, such as
- a sense of inner peace, even in troubled times;
- a tendency to adopt ethical standards in lifestyle and work;
- the development of a spiritual discipline or praxis, such as prayer, meditation, or reflective reading;
- a steady commitment to cultural or social movements that address the injustices of the world.

O'Murchu is speaking here of an emerging spirituality that can be seen in many who address our present global dilemmas in constructive and empowering ways. Parallels to this spirituality can be seen in such mystics as Meister Eckhart of the 13th century, and in St. John of the Cross, who lived 300 years later, and in the spiritualities of Matthew Fox and Thomas Merton in our own time.

All these writers speak of the journey within, undertaken with intent, through difficult times – a passage in which we may experience a dark night of the soul.

Taking Matthew Fox[2] as our next guide, we begin again, but this time at a time and place when all is going well. Fox calls it the *Via Positiva*, where peace extends all around us. Then something untoward happens, which throws the soul into turmoil. Pain is now a very real part of life; we have entered the *Via Negativa*. Here the person experiences the dark night of the soul. There is hope, however, for those who are prepared to live through this time. As St. John of the Cross makes clear, when we're in this deep place, the intellect is left clean and free to understand the truth. "The anguish and dryness of the senses illuminate and quicken the intellect. Vexation makes one understand." Letting pain be, says Fox, is an essential ingredient in learning from it. The dark night of the soul can be a bottoming-out experience of immense spiritual depth, and a source of new birth.

Out of that deep place, one may move from despair to hope, from alienation to reconnectedness. At this point, one is entering the third phase of Fox's journey: the *Via Creativa*. As the process works itself out, something new may be discovered or created from the depths. The good news of the individual's power and responsibility to heal now comes to light and is deemed acceptable. Fox warns us that our creativity is truly fearful, because its power can be used to bring about either constructive or destructive outcomes. Our sacred power is also our demonic power.

Out of this creative phase, which is often chaotic, comes the *Via Transformativa*, a time associated with justice and compassion.

The experience of moving along these paths always changes those undertaking the journey; they are different people, with new insights and a more heightened awareness built upon their previous personality.

These insights into spiritual development through hard times become particularly relevant when addressing issues of conflict. In particular, the attention to naïve optimism raised by O'Murchu is important, for in conflict situations solutions may be reached that do not stand the test of time.

The main difference between the writers' accounts appears to be the experience of the negative time. Either it is a time of doubt, suppression, or rationalization, all of which tend to avoid the pain (O'Murchu), in which case the experience has to be relived until its lessons are learned; or the experience can be entered into fully, the pain can be allowed to have its way, and the time used to learn what the experience is trying to teach (Fox).

The two processes of development that these authors identify are compared in the table on the following page.

The following case study illustrates Fox's stages, modified by O'Murchu's insights, in a family-based conflict that I mediated.

Case Report

A junior employee married her boss.

Via Positiva. The marriage settled down, with the husband making all the decisions for himself and for his young wife. As the wife matured, however, she became uncomfortable with her submissive role and started to discuss the edicts imposed by her husband. This he did not like. As a result, he became increasingly angry. The disruptive event was not long in coming.

Via Negativa. One evening he hit her, knocking her down and bruising her. She complained to the police, and, after court proceedings, he was put under a restraining order, conditional on his keeping his distance. Later, with the permission of the probation officer, and at the request of the wife, a mediation was arranged. Their aim was to come to an agreement about joining in an important family function, and perhaps, if things worked out well, getting together again on a different, more equal footing than before.

The mediation took place after separate meetings with both parties and with the most scrupulous attention to the wife's safety, both physical and emotional. Each arrived separately, and the use of

O'Murchu's Spiritual Development Schema	Fox's Spiritual Development Process
	VIA POSITIVA All is well.
AN EVENT OR CRISIS	**AN EVENT OR CRISIS**
• A trigger challenges life's meaning or lack of it. • There is no conscious awareness of the spirit. • Rage or anger may arise. People may react by doubting, suppressing, or rationalizing their experience. • Ideally, they will reflect upon it. • Progress begins. People may seek answers from others. Disillusionment may arise if none are found. • A naïve attitude that denies the injustices of the world may develop.	**VIA NEGATIVA**
	• People are cast into turmoil and experience a dark night of the soul. • The intellect becomes free by allowing the pain and by seeking to learn what the experience teaches. • The process results in new birth.
	VIA CREATIVA
	• There is movement from despair to hope, from alienation to reconnectedness. • Something new is discovered. • Good news is now accepted. • Warning! Creativity is fearful! • Creative power can become demonic power. • But if things go as they should…
TRANSFORMATION	**VIA TRANSFORMATIVA**
• There is deepening maturity and a commitment to understand the experience through reflection.	• Justice and compassion are possible. • New insights become possible. • A heightened awareness is present.
REASSESSMENT	
• A deeper commitment and resolve are possible. • A sense of coming home is achieved.	
The individual is a different, more mature person.	**The individual is a different, more mature person.**

Table 1. Comparison of two schemas illustrating how crisis aids spiritual development.

a large room enabled them to keep their distance. Ground rules for behavior were set up and mutually agreed upon. Soon the couple entered into a conversation about their respective perceptions. At one point, the husband described how he had, in his despair and rejection, experienced a deep spiritual realization of who he was and the predicament in which he found himself. He acknowledged that while his wife had previously accepted a spiritual dimension to life, he had previously scoffed at such a notion. Now he knew whereof she spoke. He had encountered his own dark night of the soul.

Checking for naïve optimism. Great gains were made at that first session. At the beginning of the next session, I cautioned them that while there was evidence of progress, they could now expect to begin to uncover the real problems – a process that might turn out to be painful.

Via Negativa revisited. The wife then started to tell about her perceptions of the previous relationship and how it did not work for her anymore. And she was quite firm in her expectations of how she would be treated in future should they reconcile. She raised the issue of the abuse, and he insisted that he was not an abusive person. "How do you describe an abusive person?" she asked. He had no answer. As his wife painted the picture as she saw it, tension grew. He had not expected such a challenge as the price of his reconnecting with her. He ended the session by stalking out, slamming the door in anger. But a week later, he returned for the third session. In the interim, he had again walked through the dark night of the soul.

Via Transformativa. Because of this period of loneliness and despair, the husband re-evaluated who he was, accepted his behavior as unacceptable, and was ready to take a fresh look at their relationship, because he cared for her so much. And, in a new way, he was proud of her stance. The wife had already passed the Rubicon of new birth, self-empowered and deeply caring of her husband, too.

Via Creativa. Now they could, carefully and with heightened sensitivity, build a more equal and respectful relationship; they could refashion their marriage. It was a beginning. Not only that, it was a beginning imbued with hope.

Analysis

In this case study, transformation preceded the creative phase, however, both were accomplished.

What happened in this mediation was most profound for all involved: for both participants and for myself as mediator. It was part mystery, part faith, part possibility.

Some of the themes that thread their way through the book were illustrated. These include the power relationships between the pair, both before and after the abuse. The threat of sanction changed the power dynamic in the wife's favor. The legal system was invoked to prevent further violence and to allow for a time-out period. The husband lost honor in his own eyes, felt deeply shamed, but out of this dark place was moved to re-appraise his priorities from a certain humbleness of spirit. He came back prepared to listen to his wife's reality. In further respectful and creative discussion, they both gained a new sense of mutual respect and the possibility of living together in a more equal, mature relationship.

There was anger too, stemming from the husband's belief that women have a particular role in marriage. Throughout the entire process, the wife gained power as she confirmed her new sense of identity as a person in her own right.

The dialogue, always intense, brought them through the anger and the depths of despair to resilience and a new awareness of their relationship and how it could be re-created. It brought their time together in mediation to a deep level of discourse and verbal intimacy.

And finally, the husband recalled the depth of his spiritual despair in his isolation, and his chagrin at his own behavior. In the lived experience of the spiritual engagement, he discovered an awesome mystery and a reality that he had previously denied and derided.

This case turned out to be resolvable because both parties wanted to restore their relationship and were prepared to accept each other's challenge to work out how this might be done, despite the pain and anger. Throughout, the emotions were contained within boundaries acceptable to both. Of course, not all attempts to reconcile marriages through mediation turn out as well as this one.

The Mystical Experience

The most profound experiences of life, such as the one the husband had in the case study above, are mystical. They cannot be lived vicariously. No one can experience another's truth at this level. The mystical experience of the spirit is beyond language, beyond anyone's control, demanding only our respect and awe. "The mystic is one who has been turned by his or her deep, unforgettable and truthful experiences. There is a trust implicit in the mystical reliance of that experience – a trust of the universe, a trust of what is and what occurs to us, and yes, a trust of oneself," asserts Matthew Fox, in his book *The Coming of the Cosmic Christ*.[3]

Fox goes on to say that mystical experiences are unitive. One does not lose oneself or dissolve differences by having them, but there comes a perception of a unity of creativity, a coming together of different experiences. It is a return to the Source, perhaps through silence and contemplation, or through engaging in the challenges of life and having the commitment to live through them and learn their message.

The battles the mystic undergoes in the discovery of that essence teach a sense of personal understanding and compassion. This understanding and compassion extends toward the "enemy," as an outcome of having confronted one's own psychic battles. Compassion is the very origin and goal as well as the process of mysticism. The mystical experience is authentic empowerment, for the self and for the other. There is a resonating truth, which includes all creation. The mystical experience cannot be "thought"; we cannot analyze it. We just experience it.

WISDOM

Awe is the beginning of wisdom.
Matthew Fox

Knowledge is expressed in declarative certitudes, whereas wisdom must compare, raise questions, and suggest restraints.
Mihaly Csikszentmihalyi and Kevin Rathunde

As people reflect on their life experiences, searching for deeper meaning, they grow in spiritual maturity and in wisdom. Wisdom is born and grows as each new experience is integrated into a person's identity. Our society has tended to emphasize the value of knowledge built upon the acquisition of factual information. This type of knowledge is indeed necessary for performing the tasks of everyday life. But it is not sufficient. Knowledge by itself can be as dangerous as ignorance. Wisdom is essential because it helps us recognize the limits of our knowledge and understand the wider implications of life's events. We need wisdom to discern and to integrate, to stretch ourselves toward deeper truths.

Wisdom integrates all the elements of mind, morality, and spirituality and takes us back into the realm of our relationship to the world and each other. But what are the characteristics of a wise person?

In Robert Sternberg's collection of essays entitled *Wisdom, Its Nature, Origins and Development*,[4] Mihaly Csikszentmihalyi and Kevin Rathunde suggest that the great width (empathy), height, intelligence, and depth (reflectivity) of the wise person allows him or her to form a more complex (i.e., more concrete *and* more abstract) perspective on a given problem. These perspectives gain for the individual the possibility of seeing the most propitious course of action from the options available to them, and even the ability to step out of the box of conventional thought. The wise person gains rich life experience through spontaneous and intuitive emotional involvement with the world, and brings clarity and form to this experience while maintaining an intellectual distance. It is a quality that is gained from experiencing and reflecting on a life lived in the fire of events both traumatic and pleasurable.[5]

As Daniel Robinson points out in the same volume, wise people may be illiterate; many accomplished or affluent people may be unwise.[6] Some of the wisest people I have met have been those attending courses on conflict management for people out of work and on welfare. They have learned their lessons in the "school of hard knocks" rather than in formal institutions of learning. One person, although turned down for a small grant for which he believed he was eligible, mentioned how he nevertheless appreciated the fair process with which his claim was heard and how he felt satisfied because of it. Others, freely and without arrogance, were prepared to acknowledge and integrate the shadow or dark side of their own personality, just as they honored their abilities and resilience to build more hopeful tomorrows.

People who are wise are very much anchored in the present. They have an ability to integrate, often unconsciously, the multiple experiences of their lives. Wisdom develops as they live through unavoidable difficulties, where the elements necessary for a solution are unknown, or not known with any degree of certainty. Wise people can integrate a formidable array of facts pertaining to a situation: facts embedded within the cultural framework of those involved. The wise combine with these abilities a freedom of thought based on a deeply reflective knowledge of themselves, a knowledge that is emancipatory, or freeing. Wise persons are adept at finding questions to ask; they don't give easy answers to their own or friends' dilemmas. They thus encourage reflection and self-knowledge in others.

In relationships, wisdom places less stress on rights or blame, and more stress on honor, accountability, and responsibility. Wisdom gives a sense of hope and discernment. Because it draws as much on intuition as logical mental processes, and is more art than science, more spirit than logic, wisdom has been discounted in the value-systems of empirically and rationally minded pundits. In the face of current world dilemmas and conflicts, a holistic, creative, and spiritually revealing wisdom is needed now more urgently than ever.

STORYTELLING

The universe is made up of stories, not atoms.
Muriel Rukeyser

Wise people often speak indirectly by using the gift of storytelling. This allows them to give their message while avoiding blame.

A story is more than a vehicle for information.[7] Something else happens in narratives. The potential energy of the story and manner of its telling are part of its working strength. The story, the narrator, and the audience are all part of an interactive network; each listener derives his or her own interpretation in light of their experience and in relation to the purpose of the narrator. Meaning is more implicit than explicit. Each listener comes to a fresh understanding with each iteration of oft-told tales. In the telling and retelling, myths and mystical truths are constructed that speak to the core values of the group or tribe.

Ancient writers and orators introduced their moral truths through the particulars of a revealing story, sometimes telling of unsavory characters meeting inevitable consequences.[8] From these specific instances, the hearer was invited to recall his or her own knowledge of the good. This approach assumed that the listeners shared a common humanity, having the same needs, emotions, and frailties. It was an indirect way to inculcate ethical norms and behaviors.

Many of these ancient tales continue to resonate today. Indeed, in countless collectivist cultures across the continents, they are still being told and retold. Particularly meaningful in Canada are the tales of our aboriginal peoples, who have passed along their truths through a uniquely oral tradition.[9]

Stories such as these are really not about the plot, but about the character of the people involved, who act out their decisions within the framework of the plot. Individual traits are seen as a product of *who* the actors are, their history, and what happens to them. All of these characteristics of story can be seen in the following two tales. They are myths with meaning.

Do you remember the story about the sheik who died and left his camels to his sons? The eldest son was to receive half the herd; the middle son, one third; and the youngest son, one ninth. At the time of the sheik's death, however, he had just 17 camels. How could they possibly divide the herd in such a way?

The three sons searched throughout the land for wise counsel, but no one could suggest a just division. Finally, they asked a poor wise woman for guidance. Out of her generous and trusting nature, she offered her own solitary camel. Now they had 18 camels, and the division could be made. The oldest son received nine; the middle son received six, and the youngest son received two. With commendable fairness, the sons were happy to give back to the wise woman the camel she had given to them, which now proved to be surplus.

This story may appear to be just a matter of imaginative arithmetic, but it illustrates something more; it illustrates the place of both imagination and generosity, and how we can step outside the box of our narrow vision of *what is*, into *what could be*.

In the second story, which comes from the Hebrew scriptures, we learn how the prophet Nathan told a story to the mighty King David, as a way of calling the king's attention to a grave injustice he had committed. Here's the story Nathan told.

There were two men in a certain city, the one rich and the other poor. The rich man had very many flocks and herds; but the poor man had nothing but one little ewe lamb, which he had bought. He brought it up, and it grew up with him and with his children; it used to eat of his meager fare, and drink from his cup, and lie in his bosom, and it was like a daughter to him. Now there came a traveler to the rich man, and he was loathe to take one of his own flock or herd to prepare for the wayfarer who had come to him, but he took the poor man's lamb, and prepared that for the guest who had come for him (2 Samuel 12:1b–4).

When David heard this story, he rightly condemned the action of the rich man. Nathan then said to David, "You are that man." For David had taken to his own bed the wife of his loyal officer who had been absent on the battlefield, and whom David had caused to be killed. The wise Nathan used a story to hold David accountable to his own set of values.

Stories take us beyond intellectual comprehension to our intuitive feelings and often inspire great transformation as a result. This mystical capacity allows us to be united with the Source of life, and to become more aware of the everyday and the unique.

True dialogue across the table, when there is a deeply meaningful exchange between the parties, often happens as a result of the stories the participants share, and how they share them. A story is told of a workshop, held for two conflicting parties. Here's what happened.

> The facilitators brought the parties together to engage in a process designed to encourage communication. But the meeting was getting nowhere. The more the facilitators introduced their process, the more it was rejected, first by one side, then the other. Each side became more and more resistant to work through the exercises, which appeared childish compared to the real-life struggles they faced every day. So the facilitators withdrew to discuss in private what they could do to get the process moving again. Lunch hour was called, which seemed doubly unfortunate because it would mean a further disruption in the planned program.
>
> But when the facilitators came into the dining room after their caucus, they were struck by the noise and the energy they encountered. The protagonists had met in the absence of the facilitators. They had yelled insults and argued and blamed each other for their battle scars. Then the tone had changed and they began to boast of exploits, each outdoing the other to the point of fantasy. So they had laughed, and started to trade real stories. In the process, they became a single band of honorable men,

proud of their warrior status, in some sense comrades, though under different uniforms. Now they were prepared to meet as colleagues, to work out the problems between them.

Facilitators can face chagrin if they try to impose processes that do not fit the life experiences of the people they're working with. We need to learn how to work with participants so that what we do is meaningful. We need to hear the unspoken stories that may emerge from the chaos that is presented.

In the story above, the members of the two groups developed their own process, chaotic though it was, as they broke bread with each other. They delved into their suffering at each other's hands and discovered their common humanity. In so doing, they created a shared story that was theirs to own.

In his book *Talking Peace: A Vision for the Next Generation*,[10] Jimmy Carter tells of a similar situation where the opposing parties were at loggerheads. The meeting took place at Camp David, and President Carter was trying to get Menachem Begin and Anwar Sadat to agree to a proposal. Nothing would move them, and Begin was showing the greater stubbornness. In a private meeting, Carter decided to change the game. He pulled out a picture of his grandchildren to show to Begin. "He became very emotional," recounts Carter. Soon, stories about grandchildren and their pride in them became the topic of the conversation. The ice was broken and Begin lost his previous recalcitrance. "He was thinking, I am sure, about his responsibility to his people and about what happens to children in war," suggested Carter in reporting the incident. As a result, the two leaders were able to get down to business and a compromise was reached. Carter had discovered a way into Begin's heart, and that had made all the difference.

Summary

What an amazing tapestry we can weave when we draw together the threads of spiritual maturity, wisdom, and storytelling! Life gains a certain majesty, however humble or eminent the person may be. We can gain confidence in making decisions about how we run our lives, where we might need assistance, especially when faced with conflict, and how we might evaluate that assistance.

Let's now consider a variety of methods used to deal with these challenges. In each case, we will assess how well they address the qualities and needs of the human spirit. We begin with perhaps the most familiar process, our legal system.

PART THREE

APPROACHES TO CONFLICT

XI

CONFLICT MANAGEMENT THROUGH SYSTEMS OF LAW

The law is reason free from passion.
Aristotle

Since earliest times, systems of law have been set up by governments for the good ordering of society. These systems provide an alternative to violence as a means of resolving disputes. They have two main functions: to bring established concepts of fairness into dispute situations in a standard fashion, and to bring stability to the community. By their presence and their use, citizens are able to go about their daily business with a degree of security and confidence.

Legal systems have been the usual way of resolving conflicts in our society, and are still held by many to be the optimal way to do this. The process is inherently adversarial, however. Every day the court system hears disputes over titles, over breaches of contracts, and innumerable situations where someone has a grievance against someone else. Legal experts act as advocates and present their client's side. This presentation is necessarily one-sided. Even if a lawyer sees merit in the other's side, he or she will not voice the matter. That is the job of the opposing counsel, and, ultimately, of the judge.

Using the courts and its systems is often quite cumbersome and costly, and seldom improves relations between opposing parties, because the courts are not geared for that purpose. Evidence is presented according to a rational procedure that uses objective standards. Non-rational, subjective, and emotional feelings count for little, at least on the surface.

The parties, having presented their case, do not have a say in the court's deliberations, which are based on an examination of the evidence presented. A judge then makes a decision *for* the parties, on the basis of established law. Clients accept the verdict in most cases and go their way, having received a decision that enables them to get on with their lives.

Given these circumstances, can the legal system deliver anything that will support a spiritual approach to conflict management? Do we even consider the legal system in this context? Is the application of the law simply an exercise in dry fact-finding, or does it subscribe to eternal values? Does it reach the soul of those whose lives have been affected by the conflict? Does a reliance on rational procedure, and the avoidance of emotional factors, limit access to the healing of the human spirit? Are the legal procedures used within the system actually devoid of emotion, anyway? Can they be devoid of emotion if they are to serve the deeply held and legitimate values of clients, which may be related to their culture, loyalties, or social obligations? Does the legal system serve ultimate justice and truth?

Practitioners of law appear divided on the matter. Some are cynical, believing they are doing a job according to the rules, and getting the best outcome for their clients under the circumstances. Others believe that there *is* something sacred in what they do. The literature on this aspect of the legal system is sparse, because prudent writers focus more on the *means* of maintaining order and allocating resources, than on the ultimate *ends* to which the law might point.

Harold Berman is one writer who suggests that there *is* a spiritual basis undergirding our legal systems. In his book *The Interaction of Law and Religion*,[1] he suggests that compliance with our legal system will stem from a belief that the law is not just a body of rules, but a "living process" of allocating rights and duties. The law helps to give society the structure or gestalt it needs to maintain inner cohesion, he says. Law has to be believed in, or it will not work. Far more important than coercion in securing obedience to rules is the belief that such qualities as trust, fairness, and credibility are to be found there. Thus, according to Berman, there can be emotional and sacred elements in people's perception of legal systems and practices, however much its processes emphasize the rational.

If a society's members come to believe that a code of law is based only on utilitarian principles, the law cannot fulfill its functions, regardless of which code is used, Berman continues. Moreover, by thinking of law solely in terms of its efficiency, we rob it of that efficiency. "By failing to give enough attention to its religious dimensions, we deprive it of its capacity to do justice and possibly even its capacity to survive."[2] It is the *spirit* of the law, rather than the *letter* of the law, that creates a cohesive society, Berman insists, and I would agree. Yet ever since Aristotle made the famous comment that opens this chapter, the emphasis has been on the rational to the exclusion of the emotional.

More fundamental, however, is the question of whether our written codes are inherently just. Another Greek of ancient times, Socrates, tells us that we need to be prepared to challenge unjust laws. If we believe too steadfastly in the sanctity of the law, we may fail to recognize when a particular law is unjust and needs to be resisted. All laws are human constructs, after all, and can be applied too rigidly. There comes a time when the law must be examined critically and be subjected to principles of ethics, especially with regard to the treatment of minorities and people without status in society.

Berman develops his theme to say that the legal system, if it is to fulfill its role of providing structures and processes for allocating rights and responsibilities, must be more than a mere instrument of secular policy, but also part of the ultimate purpose and meaning of life. That spirit is enhanced by the drama with which the law is practiced. Ritual is used in religion to convey the collective spirituality of its adherents; the same is true in regards to legal institutions. Yet here he surely goes too far. He confuses the *means* – the ritual and the codes of law – with the *ends*, or ultimate truth and justice. We cannot expect the legal system to provide a sense of integration into the "harmony of the universe," as he suggests. The harmony of the universe? If only conflicts could be managed so as to accomplish that! What one person considers musical harmony may be jarring discord to another. Berman's philosophy gives no specifics as to how these visions are actually implemented in the everyday resolution of human differences.

Kenneth Cloke,[3] a lawyer turned mediator, who, like Berman, would like to put the essential spiritual aspect of conflict management at the center of our endeavors, has similar concerns to my own.

According to Cloke, an inherent defect in all legal systems is that they end conflicts prematurely, before the lessons of the conflicts have been learned. Cloke sees that legal systems deal only with the transaction of goods and services, and do not directly address the client's deeper needs and meanings, which may have given rise to the conflict in the first place. We learn most from a conflict when we stay with it as its lessons unfold. But our tendency is to move quickly to solutions, because the tension of staying in the conflict is uncomfortable, even painful.

Many of us have come to see ourselves – and each other – as insignificant in the great scheme of things. People have learned to delegate their affairs to experts. Perhaps, then, it is only through recourse to the court system and its experts that individuals can gain the recognition they so deeply find missing in their daily lives. If this is the case, then people must be encouraged to find their own voice and gain self-determination in ways that can empower them and at the same time build community.

At this point, it may be helpful to review the basic issues of truth and justice, because there is an idealism attached to these values that feeds our hunger for the Ultimate.

TRUTH

It takes two to speak the truth, one to speak and another to hear.
Henry David Thoreau

First, let's address the issue of truth as it is pursued within a court hearing. The fact that truth is a principle dear to the legal consciousness is evident in the requirement that when witnesses take an oath that they will speak it. But how can truth as a reflection of reality be spoken in an adversarial system?

In North America, where the Common Law of England serves as the basis for channeling evidence, witnesses are constrained by the rules of evidence to answer closed questions already framed by the advocates for either side. While the "examination in chief" may be designed to allow the party to tell his or her own story, how can the truth emerge from the cross-examination, where witnesses are put on the defensive and make conciliatory statements at their peril? The inadmissibility of contextualizing testimony, including hearsay – which may have a direct bearing on motives and actions, and which is admissible under the French legal code – can make the process appear harsh and inhuman. The North American adversarial system often deprives narratives of their richness, hidden meanings, and truths, leaving only the bare bones of "admissible" evidence.

In South Africa, a more spacious interpretation of the meaning of truth was developed by the Truth and Reconciliation Commission.[4] In addition to factual or forensic evidence, such as is accepted by the North American legal system, truth also included the personal, unique, subjective experience of an individual, expressed through narrative. It attempted to find meaning for the narrator, so that he or she could make sense of the incident. Truth was seen as a social phenomenon, revealed through the sharing of stories, and through dialogue, interaction, and discussion. "I see you seeing me," is a famed African aphorism. Revealing the truth turned out to be healing and restorative, because the process allowed facts and meaning to be placed into a context of relationships.

Bennett Sims[5] offers a fuller description or typology of truth that complements Tutu's vision.

- *Empirical truth* is the first "type" that Sims identifies. Empirical science relies on sense data and numbers to describe the universe. Facts are either false or true. The modernist worldview depends on the analysis of evidence to discern whether facts are reliable from a mechanistic point of view. The legal system, in presenting evidence to back up personal reports, subscribes to this aspect of truth.
- *Relational truth* involves the testimony of human beings. This concept of truth moves human knowing to a deeper level, for it either

provides or erodes the foundation of relationships. Truth at this level will be based on trust and on interpretation of the meaning behind the words. Legal processes, while appearing to be based only on empirical evidence, are hung up on this area of truth, playing it to its absolute conclusions: if, for example, opposing council or a judge catches a witness in a lie, the whole testimony of the witness may be rejected and his or her reputation destroyed. Here, the intention of a witness may receive an unfavorable interpretation that is undeserved. Did the person *intend* to give false testimony, or was his or her recollection marred by the framing of the question, or even by the "embroidery" embedded in his or her manner of speech? The courts do not have the time or resources to resolve these matters. At some point, expediency takes over in order to get a resolution.

- *Evolutionary truth* puts the notion of fixed truths against those that change over time. Some previously accepted "truths," such as the idea that the sun orbits the earth and not the other way around, are now no longer tenable. Evolutionary truth is also seen in the context of evolving group dynamics, as members interact with each other and develop new insights and understandings over time. The essential ingredient of this sort of truth, then, is the time needed for seeds of insight to take root within the interaction and to bear fruit, which they often do with unexpected results. Our legal system develops from precedent; in this respect, it is also continually building and changing over time. Thus it is an instrument of evolutionary truth influenced by the wider society. In other words, both the legal system and society evolve together.

- *Mythical truth*, which is usually expressed in a story, is the opposite of a factual truth of history; it is an *interpretation* of history that is concerned not so much with the details, but with the *meaning* behind the account. The legal system avoids mythical truth in its processes, but every judgment that resonates with its audience will have aspects of mythical truth. This sort of truth is very evident in religious narrative. For instance, in contemporary times, a debate rages between those who assert the historical accuracy of the gospel stories of Jesus' life on earth, and those who see them as mythic tales told for their meaning and ability to make us conscious of ultimate truth.

- The term *paradoxical truth* relates to the notion that the opposite of a great truth is another great truth. Each of us is both an individual, and part of a community. Individuality and community appear to cancel each other out, because, from a logical perspective, one cannot be a single and a plural entity at the same time. But the paradoxical reality is that every person *is* both at the same time. It takes two mutually exclusive and apparently self-canceling truths to state the totality of what is true. Those societies that foster individuality in the midst of a cohesive community – and I can think of many, including my own Irish country neighborhoods – approach most closely the social aspects of this truth.

  Paradoxical truth blends contradictory human roles in a dynamic balance that creates greater meaning. Paradoxical truth lies behind those other paradoxes of human interaction: the power used to empower others, the love that builds in others the capacity to return love, the teaching of knowledge to enhance the abilities of others to grow in wisdom. This, I believe, is the truth that most clearly portrays the quest of Mahatma Gandhi.
- According to Sims, *mystical truth* is the deepest level of truth available to human experience. The opposite of a grasped truth is a truth that does the grasping, he says. The initiative in seeking and finding such a truth is generally not one's own, but comes unbidden from outside of human resolve or expectation. While mystical truth is reported to be common in human experience, it is beyond full comprehension and difficult to articulate. It is the sensation of being taken hold of in one's depth by an exalting power that lifts one's spirit above the ordinary.

Sometimes, truth comes to us freely, when someone tells us their story, for example. Other times, it is only given up as a result of probing questioning. But truth may also appear out of silence. When understanding is dawning, and people pause to ponder the meanings behind the words spoken, a pregnant silence may bring an unexpected treasure – a whole, indescribable truth may emerge that speaks without words and that brings a transformation, an appreciation of the spirit and its message, to the assembled company.

Truth is at once an expression of everyday, temporary provability, as well as a transcendent property beyond our grasp. Truth is also the process, the regulator, that can transport us on the road from the practical to the mystical. The search for the spirit of truth in the resolution of conflict continues!

JUSTICE

Justice is the first virtue of social institutions.
John Rawls

What principles guide the search for and application of justice within our codes of law? How might we define justice?

Morton Deutsch,[6] a leading proponent of constructive conflict management, divides justice into three main principles: equality, need, and equity.

Equality will be important if the issue involves memberships in a group. In a stable democratic society, each member is due certain rights. Treating people as equals before the law builds good social relations, and where fostering these relations is the goal, equality becomes the dominant principle of justice. The disproportionately large number of people from ethnic and class minorities in our penal institutions suggests that equality is not a high priority in our social and justice systems. Evidently, members of these minorities have discovered barriers to equality, barriers that are absent for others in more fortunate circumstances.

Decisions based on the principle of *need* will seek to address the unique circumstances of the parties involved. In Chapter 7, we saw that "need" is a complex concept; it can refer to the allocation of necessary material resources, to maintenance of security and the reduction of uncertainty, as well as to the preservation of the integrity of the self – an individual's or people's sense of personal identity. Our systems of justice are crude instruments for addressing any but the most material of needs, and reduce all other needs to a postulated monetary equivalent.

Decisions based on principles of *equity*, where rewards are determined according to the contribution of the parties, fosters productivity, say Tom Tyler and Maura Belliveau.[7] But equity does not just involve the distribution of material goods. People need the affirmation and recognition they receive when their contributions are rewarded appropriately. They feel satisfied when their work is favorably rewarded and is recognized by their peers. Equity provides feedback as to how one is viewed by others; it involves an implicit evaluation of an individual's worth as a person. When principles of equity are fulfilled, people gain their own sense of significance in the essential order of things, according to Robert Folger, Blair Sheppard and Robert Buttram.[8] Individuals gain recognition as contributing and receiving participants in a meaningful social network.

Justice in the World's Religions

Issues of justice have been a prominent part of world religions. We are, at the present time, being exposed to these concepts as never before, because of the increasing presence and influence of those from many faith traditions.

David Lerman,[9] speaking from the Jewish tradition, sees justice as inseparable from spirituality. Judaism speaks of the sanctity of people in a world where the Creator places upon each of us the responsibility of working toward the completion of creation; justice reigns when this path is followed.

For Muslims, according to Nawal Ammar,[10] justice is an attribute of Allah; to stand for justice is to be a witness to Allah, even when to do so is detrimental to our own interests as we conceive them. We are to act as if in the presence of Allah.

A Buddhist would not, according to David Loy,[11] ask what a *reasonable person* would do under certain circumstances; instead a Buddhist would ask what the *moral person exercising self-control* would do. Justice, he says, grows out of mercy.

Howard Zehr,[12] a leading Mennonite writer in the field of restorative justice, observes that we tend to assume that love and mercy are different from and opposite to justice. Instead, they are complementary, he says. Both strive for well-being. Biblical justice grows out of love. Its aim is to make things right between people. Zehr goes on to say that the myth that we need a social contract to protect us from one another, articulated by Hobbes 350 years ago, implies that a state's justice must grow out of fear. Surely a social contract is needed more to provide a level of mutual predictability and trust.

John Paul Lederach,[13] sociologist, mediator and peace broker, also sees justice as the pursuit of restoration, as the attempt to rectify wrongs, and create right relationships based on equity and fairness. Justice involves advocacy for those harmed, open acknowledgement of wrongs committed, and an effort to make things right. Mercy, he says, involves compassion, forgiveness, and a new start.

Summary

Systems of law are essential to the functioning of society, because they define the limits of acceptable behavior, provide a mechanism for allocation of resources, and defend people's right to live in security and freedom.

But by its very nature, the legal system is caught in a dilemma. It assumes a shared universe of meaning, but that assumption may not be borne out in practice, especially in our pluralistic society. It also pursues the lofty principles of truth and justice, but in many situations it falls short, in part because it has adopted a procedure that pits person against person, thus aggravating the alienation that already exists between conflicting parties. As well, systems of law seem insufficient to deal with the underlying, subjective, and more deeply rooted concerns of the people who present themselves to the courts.

Perhaps we should resort to our legal codes only when coercive measures are necessary and all other avenues have been explored. Perhaps we might agree to comply with the *spirit* of the legal system, but leave the letter of the law, the blindfold and the scales, tipping only to the right hand or to the left, for those cases where such polarities are sufficient.

We need to get to the human heart's core, in order to address the more complex problems of our global life together. Our task, then, is to examine alternatives to coercive power and legal systems that may have the potential to address more directly and supportively the needs of people through every domain of the Great Foundation of Being.

XII

MANAGING CONFLICT BY NEGOTIATION & MEDIATION

The truly great person dwells on what is real, and not what is on the surface.
Lao Tzu

Neither power – of the coercive sort at least – nor legal systems have been able to reduce the amount or intensity of conflict in the world. Sometimes, resorting to these options actually makes things worse, because of their intrinsically adversarial nature. Often, they fail to address the underlying needs that are the cause of the conflict in the first place: the essential needs of human beings and their collectives for identity, security, belonging, and self-worth. We sorely need a structure that can address these more fundamental aspects of life. We need a process that can permit the human essentials to shine through.

During the past 50 years or so, Western academics and practitioners have been looking for more effective ways to manage conflict. The path has not been an easy one, for we are dealing with complex creatures: human beings. Life in community demonstrates an inescapable tension between a desire for peace and stability, and the struggle for justice and the need for change. Our ongoing journey takes us into the crucible of the often-intense interactions between people as they seek to claim their place of honor as earth's citizens. These most deeply felt conflicts are best met, we are discovering, by the power of human dialogue and a commitment to search for the meaning behind the hostility.

Just human dialogue? Yes, indeed, so it behooves us to get a lot better at it! More than 20 years ago, when I first started to engage in peace studies and nuclear weapons had already been long established as the preferred defense strategy, I asked myself the question, "Is there any alternative, since these weapons cannot be used without threatening the destruction of the entire globe and all its creatures?" The answer I finally arrived at was, "The power of dialogue!"

What a contrast! The only real answer to the absolute power to destroy us all is something that appears almost puny – our human ability to communicate. It is in managing our conflicts that communication is put so sorely to the test. But it is also through our commitment to this vital task that our spirits will enable us to endure and to thrive.

What form might this dialogue take? I will confine the subject here to face-to-face encounters and leave aside such other means as letters, phone calls, and e-mails. A few definitions of the conflict management procedures of negotiation and mediation may be helpful here. These processes and the roles required for each are best seen as quite distinctive, for they view the conflict from different angles.

Negotiation and Mediation

In negotiation, the parties or their representatives take on responsibility for both the process and the outcome. Negotiators may act on their own behalf, or employ others, called proxies, who act as spokespersons or advocates. Negotiators may represent constituencies to whom they are responsible, and with whom it is essential that they communicate in order to represent them effectively.

Mediation, in contrast to negotiation, brings a third entity into the fray – an intervener. The intervener assumes responsibility for the process, but leaves the final decisions to the parties or their representatives. Mediators seek to be impartial in that they do not favor one side over the other. They do not make judgments, although they may make recommendations. Mediators engage with the parties and seek to understand their several perspectives, experiences, and needs, and to have each of the parties understand the other in relation to the issues on the table. The mediator stands apart as a "separate" facilitator of that mutual exchange, yet is part of the whole group's dynamic. The very presence and interventions of the mediator set up a different energy from that where the parties or their representatives work out their own process without such outside help.

What follows is a brief review of a number of methods of bargaining and interest-based conflict management. These processes will be reviewed in order of sophistication and the degree to which they may include recognition of a spiritual dimension.

POSITIONAL BARGAINING

Each side takes a position, argues for it, and makes concessions to reach a compromise.
Roger Fisher and William Ury

Positional bargainers make demands for solutions that will meet their own needs as they perceive them, but may fail to recognize or grant those of the other side.[1] Thus the battle becomes one of determining who will prevail. At best, some compromise may be worked out: "You demand 2,000 to settle, I offer 1,000. So let's agree on 1,500." The process will be much the same whether the issue is dollars, sheep, or living space. In the bargaining process, the real interests that may underlie the positional statements are seldom probed. The positional-bargaining process sees the pie to be divided as fixed; the debate is limited to material-based issues. It ignores the human meaning these material resources may represent, and it certainly doesn't admit an opening for the spiritual in either the process or the succeeding relationship, which may be damaged in the altercation. It remains adversarial. Tremendous opportunities for meeting as fully human beings are often lost in the process.

THE INTEREST-BASED, PROBLEM-SOLVING MODEL

The purpose of negotiating is to serve your interests.
Roger Fisher and William Ury

The cooperative, win-win problem-solving model provided a major advance over previous adversarial models, because it directed attention to underlying interests that might be the motivators in the hostility. Initially introduced by Mary Follett in 1941, it was expanded by Morton Deutsch in 1973, then popularized by the Harvard Negotiating Team in the classic book *Getting to Yes*.[2] Let's look at what the method has to offer.

Roger Fisher and William Ury, the authors who led the Harvard team, set out four main principles for the method:
- It focuses on interests rather than positions.
- It separates the people from the problems.
- It uses objective criteria.
- It invents options for mutual gain.

It will be helpful to review each of these in turn.
- *Focus on interests rather than positions.* Positions, as we saw, are those initial solutions that appeal to one side, but do not consider the perspectives of the other. Opposing positions may conceal a variety of shared and compatible interests, as well as conflicting ones, that turn out to be important causes of the conflict. These interests include the desires, hopes, and expectations – and also the risks to be avoided – of each of the contending parties. Initial demands, such as those posed in the positional bargaining method, may not be the best or the only way to meet underlying interests or to avoid risks for either side. Other, more favorable options may be possible, if the interests are identified throughout the discussion.

- *Separate the people from the problems.* This distinction is meant to enable a mediator to deal with the people involved, and their relationship, in an empathetic and direct manner. This will make the parties, they suggest, more ready to address the material issues. It also means that they will have to step back from their personal, subjective involvement, to look with more objective eyes at the issues and what they wish to achieve.
- *Use objective criteria.* These measures, based perhaps on what is accepted in other comparable situations, can provide elements of fairness on which both sides may agree. They afford a rational context for the discussion. For instance, because nurses in Calgary have a certain wage per hour, the same professionals working in Regina may make their case for parity: similar pay for comparable work.
- *Invent options for mutual gain.* Fisher and Ury emphasize that to suggest that the resource pie is fixed might well limit options. Sometimes desires might not be in opposition. In the classic story of a fight over an orange, one party turned out to require the rind, the other the juice. When this was discovered, it was no longer seen as optimal to divide the orange in half, but to squeeze out the juice for one and give the peel to the other. Each then got all of that part of the available resource upon which they had counted.

There are many excellent ideas contained in this approach, for in every conflict there will surely be both divergent and common interests between the people involved. Perhaps the parties may have misperceived their mutual problem. Discussion may lead to the discovery that the opponents have different priorities and/or value the available resources differently. A risk for one may not be a risk for another. The parties may discover that it is more helpful to understand and respect each other's perspectives than to establish whether either is right or wrong.

As I said, this interest-based model has been a major advance in Western approaches to conflict management. It has now achieved a plateau, however. Something vital is still missing. It *does* begin to address relational matters, but it makes no claim to understand the human dynamics, the experiences, the deep needs of the parties within the reality of their context, culture, and history. It does not pay adequate attention to subjective and community-oriented matters, such as loyalty to friends, or sharing responsibility for the common good. The method may draw attention away from an emerging mutuality of spirit.

For the same reason that Kenneth Cloke criticized the legal system, the "interest-based" method tries to end the conflict prematurely, all "neat and tidy," before the deeper issues have surfaced. The approach has proven inadequate to deal with anything more than the most straightforward issues of limited duration. "Separating the people from the problem," or to use a more poetic image, "the dance from the dancer," is often not possible, or even desirable, because the problem often lies within the people and their perceptions of the altercation.

Despite these shortcomings, this problem-solving approach to negotiation, and subsequently to mediation, has proven to be helpful in many ways. It introduced cooperative strategies as an alternative to the adversarial modes of the courts. It brought people together, where they could see each other's humanity and hear explanations about what went wrong. The parties might even have come to honor and respect each other and indeed regain a sense of their own authenticity, almost by happenstance.

TRANSFORMATION MODEL

*Disputes can be viewed not as problems at all,
but as opportunities for moral growth and transformation.*
Robert A. Baruch Bush and Joseph P. Folger

One further, significant step in the development of conflict management processes was the provocative approach of Robert Bush and Joseph Folger, in their book *The Promise of Mediation*.[3] Here the priority is on the people and their relationship. In contrast to the interest-based model of Fisher and Ury, the transformational model is relatively indifferent to finding a solution. That may be why it provoked such controversy!

Bush and Folger's goal is to "use the mediation process to transform the character of both the individuals and society as a whole."[4] The purpose of the mediation process is to enable the parties to undergo human moral growth. This is brought about in two specific dimensions: individuals are encouraged to empower themselves on the one hand, and to give recognition to others, including those viewed as opponents, on the other. When parties speak with passion, the mediator probes to see what has prompted the strong reaction, what the basis of the strong views might be, in order to surface opportunities for self-empowerment. In that empowerment, each is expected to accept responsibility for their role in the events leading up to the meeting and during the mediation process.

From the beginning, the mediator elicits the commitment of each party to the transformative goal. The mediator seeks opportunities for the parties to reinterpret the past in ways that avoid negative judgments of the other. Throughout, whenever the parties talk, each is presented with opportunities to see the other differently. This allows further chances for recognition. Through the process, solutions to the problems may pop up, but this is a secondary goal to the understanding that parties gain about each other and their perspectives. The transformation sought for each of the parties and their relationship is a moral re-awakening and reconnection.

The transformative method, in its focus on the people and their strengths, has much to offer. It has become controversial because it imposes an agenda that may not be the parties' own, but rather the mediator's. The mediator sees his or her primary role as bringing about moral growth in the parties. If they are not willing to take responsibility or to accept the insights that emerge from the dialogue, but instead resist the opportunity to grow morally, in the opinion of the mediator, then the mediator should be prepared to withdraw his or her services.

The method has worked well in several corporations, where all the employees were able to become part of a corporate culture by dint of the leader's expectation and extensive training. However, in the wider society, the method can prove unworkable. It may assume an impossible level of self-determination on the part of the participants, especially those with low social status. People who, because of race, gender, or education, may have learned to censor what they say about their needs in order to be accepted at all, will not be able to muster sufficient self-esteem to please the mediator. Where automatic self-censoring has become ingrained – for instance, where a woman has been raised in a traditionally patriarchal culture and never been encouraged to speak on her own behalf for her own needs – it is possible that a person will not know what he or she wants, or be able to act assertively. It may take years of emotional growth, undertaken within a supportive and safe community, before such a person is able to stand up for him- or herself. It may take a generation, not just a few hours' empowerment in a mediation among relative strangers, to gain functional self-confidence.

On the other hand, those who have no problem with their self-esteem, and who believe that their moral growth is their own business, may not appreciate the directives of the mediator in the matter.

Bush and Folger's formula is indeed people-centered. As a result, it will be part of every constructive encounter. But to focus on obligatory personal growth may turn out to make these processes, paradoxically, less accessible or helpful. To make transformation the primary aim may be to thwart its possibility. Transformation of the parties' attitudes is likely in any mediation where each gains a new understanding of the other and of themselves, but it is something to be discovered, rather than demanded. The approach may well be especially inappropriate when dealing with people across different cultures and backgrounds. For any mediator to presume that he or she knows the path of moral growth for a person confronted by conflict could be considered presumptuous and paternalistic.

Summary

These methods of managing conflict present two extremes. Both the bargaining and the interests-based models stress the allocation of material resources, and leave the human, subjective aspects on one side. The Bush and Folger transformative model emphasizes the human element and the relationships between the parties, but beats the drum to the mediator's own rhythm when it comes to defining what the encounter is all about. We can learn from these methods, even as we continue to search for the spirit in the heart of the conflict.

Recent developments in theory and practice resonate with ancient mystical teachings about the spirit's development. From these two unlikely comrades we can perhaps build a holistic, spiritually sensitive framework for addressing conflict.

XIII

IDENTITY-BASED CONFLICT MANAGEMENT

The very situations that are so impossible can also be your greatest teachers.
Arnold Mindell

The ARIA model of Jay Rothman[1] and the world-work of Arnold Mindell[2] probe closer to the heart of conflict in that they both resonate with spiritual meaning, although Rothman avoids using such language. First, to Jay Rothman.

ARIA
(Antagonism, Resonance, Invention, Action)

Identity conflict is about who we really are and what we care about most deeply.
Jay Rothman

Rothman, who has wide experience tackling conflict in refractory areas such as the Middle East, starts by stating that passion in conflict should be seen as an intensification of the everyday! Conflict, he says, strikes at our core, our identity. The groups to which we belong are vital to us because they represent our investment and our hope for a meaningful, safe, and dignified life. Conflict can bring out the worst and the best in us. Rothman sees our need for identity as being at the heart of intractable conflict, because it probes the meaning of who we really are. Conflict can lay bare our most profound feelings about what gives life meaning, and reveals our very soul. People are prepared to fight to the end to preserve their sense of life's meaning. Simply put, their survival depends on it.

Conflict is deeply subjective; at the level of intensity we're talking about, it involves an experience that may be difficult to explain or describe. Moreover, the disputants' subjective experience of themselves and of others in the conflict is shaped by their particular cultural reality and historical context. The parties may or may not be aware of how much these factors influence their perspectives, motives, and communications.

While focusing on the issues that present themselves in the altercation, Rothman is at pains to distinguish "*identity*-based" conflicts from those rooted primarily in "interests." A focus on the latter when deeper issues are at stake may move the discussion too quickly, before perceived or real injustices and suffering have been acknowledged. This is especially the case when the real issue involves a threat to one's identity.

How do we know that an identity issue is at stake?

One reason that identity conflicts are difficult to discern as such is because they are often represented as disputes over tangible resources. One clue that a deeper concern is involved may be that a party becomes more intransigent the closer agreement or settlement appears to be. Resistance, it is said, points to an unmet need.

Another problem lies in the protean nature of identity. For individualists, identity is very much based on how the person labels him- or herself within the context of the encounter – perhaps as "parent," fighting over child custody in one situation; or as "member of a profession" railing against administration or a rival colleague in another. Same person, different identities. Yet in any of these different situations, it is only when one's core is threatened at a deep level that the values a person holds to be sacred may emerge. For the member of a collectivist society, identity will be more closely connected to the family, tribe, or clan.

In the wider society, identity issues are also of signal importance. In community-based societies where people see themselves not as individuals but as part of a valued collective, when their group's survival as an entity is threatened, each individual's attention will be focused on preserving those matters that give meaning to the whole group. These include the language, memories, history, and customs that they share.

When conflicts escalate, as we saw in Chapter 7, perceived differences between those on the inside and those on the outside of each group often become stereotyped and rigid as hardships continue over time and are blamed on the other. When conflict erupts across group boundaries, biased thinking and the resulting hostile behavior escalate the tension. Each group comes to feel justified in their negative assessment of and reactionary behavior toward the other. Eventually, the altercation becomes intractable. By then, each group's identity becomes maintained by a negative, destructive interdependence upon the other.[3]

It is from his experience working at this level of hostility in the world's hot spots that Rothman has evolved his approach, which, choosing a light-hearted mnemonic, he dubs ARIA. Each letter identifies a stage in the facilitative process: Antagonism, Resonance, Invention, and Action.

Antagonism

To begin with, when contestants meet face-to-face, we can expect them to go through a phase of antagonism: blaming each other, polarizing, attributing negative motivations, and projecting or exteriorizing their own worst fears about the other.

To emphasize and lend authenticity to the intensity of feelings emerging at this stage, Rothman actually *encourages* parties to express their hostilities freely. He allows a period of venting, which may bring buried and pent-up issues to the surface. From within this period of mutual revelation will emerge, perhaps obscurely at first, the personal suffering, the bruised and battered human spirits that are fighting so hard to survive.

The mediator, if prepared to go this route, will have explained that he or she expects the outburst of finger-pointing, and will control the process so that parties are safe to say the difficult things that need to be said. Allowing people to state their positions and their differences highlights the perceptual contrasts and comparisons. At the same time, it demonstrates how their old pattern of relating has not worked, and this, at last, can be acknowledged. When the mutual recriminations have proved once again to be a painful and ineffective way of proceeding, the parties may find the motivation to change. They get to the point where they are "willing to suspend belief that no other route is possible."[4] The "A" stage (Antagonism) comes to an end naturally, and the time of "R" (Resonance) has come.

Resonance

Parties begin to tell each other their stories, to explore their own questions about their concerns, and begin to articulate the underlying needs at the bottom of the barrel. Out of this discourse they begin to establish a resonance between them. They get to articulate what is truly at stake and why it matters so much. The individual or group's most basic "I" – their identity, values, beliefs, experiences, hopes, and fears – comes to be articulated through an encounter with the "Thou" of the other, says Rothman, using the language of philosopher Martin Buber.[5] As the sides begin to exchange stories and to identify what is really important to them, they move from a blaming stance to one that brings the conflict back into their own territory. The conflict shifts from being externalized, the fault of the other, to being *internalized*, when the parties begin to realize and accept that they may share responsibility for the situation. When feelings and meanings come into the open, parties make discoveries about who they really are. Transformation can occur spontaneously, when even the bitterest of enemies discover that they share common human needs, especially those that lie closest to the heart: issues of honor, self-worth, dignity – their identity as conscious, feeling, self-aware human beings. This transformation, this ability to recognize the shared humanity of the other, is allowed to occur naturally, rather than as a result of any influence by the mediator (as Bush and Folger had proposed).

As they gain clarity and self-respect, the parties get in touch with their values, not only on their own behalf, but on behalf of the other; it is nothing less than a reciprocity of spirit. With this level of awareness, of being in the process together, new priorities may emerge, new possibilities invented.

Invention

Now that the adversaries no longer view each other as malicious or evil, but as potential partners in a project of needed change and development, the "I" stage of Invention can begin.

"My" safety is closely tied up in "your" safety, "my" honor with "your" honor (or "our" collective honor with "your" collective honor). Whereas tangible resources such as land or water may indeed be in short supply, the intangibles of honor and identity are limitless; they grow as they reciprocate with others.

Once these identity needs are acknowledged and taken care of, the material issues can more readily be addressed, starting with broad statements of objectives, moving to formulas and principles, and then to the difficult and tedious work of ironing out specific details.

Action

The final stage is again an "A": one now of *action* that addresses the actual plans to be implemented.

One of the strengths of Rothman's model is that he recognizes the pain that lies within many unresolved and difficult conflicts. He does this to honor the people who are experiencing that pain, and to highlight it as signal of the importance of the conflict. Earlier models sought to make conflict management a pain-reduction enterprise. As a result, they didn't pay attention to the pain of the experience as a key factor in escalation, or as an impetus to the discovery of new ways to proceed. Rothman's process can be a way to engage the very spirit of the contestants and to plumb their core sense of who they are as individuals and as opponents. They can recognize that they have been "partners in waiting," suggests Rothman. Once this level of understanding is reached, their interaction has become a journey towards hope.

HONORING THE SPIRIT WITHIN

*Without recognition of what has happened,
the past cannot return to its place as the past.
The ghosts will continue to stalk the battlements.*
                    Michael Ignatiev

While Rothman builds his metaphor from a secular perspective, Arnold Mindell, in his book *Sitting in the Fire*, has no problem naming intractable conflict as it really is: a crisis of the spirit. Mindell finds that he is compelled to question his own deepest beliefs and the meaning of life when working with people in conflict. Searching for answers to global problems throws us into a spiritual crisis, he asserts. He finds these crises valuable, because the very experience of feeling insecure and vulnerable opens us to the possibility of finding some part of infinite meaning, even in the most mundane of interactions.

Speaking as a facilitator, Mindell asserts that the very situations that bring us to wonder, despair, or shock, can be our greatest teachers. Yes, the very groups that are so resistant, so strident, and so rigid, turn out to be our spiritual mentors. Mindell finds that the experience tears the facilitator's assumptions asunder, as much as those of the participants. The facilitator finds him- or herself being transformed along with the parties – no longer a facilitator, but a learner, "even a devotee of what is."[6] Mindell's love and commitment to the people with whom he works and his appreciation of their potential shines through on every page of his book.

Mindell illustrates the lessons he has learned by recounting a particular workshop he facilitated in Northern Ireland. Both sides of the "troubles" had been brought together for a weekend of dialogue several years before the Good Friday Accord of 1998. Each side had discarded nonviolent action in the fight for justice or to impose security. At one point, as he was facilitating the group process, he was interrupted by an outburst of anger from one side, then the other. His style of leadership had been construed, but not intended, as claiming expertise and rank. It was this, rather than the raising of sensitive issues, that had provoked the angry attack among people already on the edge of despair. A tirade of hostile exchanges ensued.

It was a previously silent person in the audience who acted as peacemaker. She pointed out, over the din, that the screamers were trying to express their own vital truths based on personal, raw experiences. A self-styled expert from afar, she said, could have no concept of the intensity of the lived experience of those present. At this welcome intervention, Mindell explained his role and prepared to create the space for the people to reclaim their voice. Things quieted down. Then the true and heart-rending stories started to come out.

From Suffering to Retaliation: the Creation of Freedom Fighters and Terrorists

This episode demonstrates how vital it is to recognize the unseen motives behind hostile group interaction. Such actions are cries for justice, says Mindell. The two groups were up in arms – at the meeting figuratively, and in the world outside literally – because they had experienced betrayal, breach of trust, shame, and dishonor. They had chosen to fight with guns on their home turf and with angry shouts at the workshop, rather than to leave, or to give way to despair.

Mindell has seen, firsthand, circumstances where injustice perpetrated by people in power has led to acts of revenge from the dispossessed. He has some interesting things to say about the motivation of those called "freedom fighters" by one side, and "terrorists" by the other. His remarks, written before September 2001, have to be viewed from that perspective.

In view of those events, it is perhaps wise to distinguish acts taken by violent dissidents according to their motives, acts, and targets. As targets of those violent acts, we would perhaps condone none of them, but our sense of outrage is different in each case.

First are those "freedom fighters" who have tried to draw attention to their cause through nonviolent actions, but have failed. Thus they turn to destructive, violent acts. They deliberately demonstrate their frustration by destroying strategic inanimate objects, such as train lines, bridges, and military installations. They aim to cause disruption, but have no intention of hurting anyone. At this level of engagement, the receiving body politic will realize that there is a section of the population that is quite unhappy. The civilian population does not get involved, expecting the damage to be repaired and steps taken to find the guilty ones. In many cases, government representatives eventually begin discussions with the dissidents to resolve their complaints in order to restore order. Bertram Spector calls this "deciding to negotiate with villains"[7] – which usually becomes inevitable.

At the other end of the scale of terrorist activities is the event of September 11, 2001, where there appears to have been a deliberate decision to kill civilians indiscriminately, by the thousand, regardless of their country of origin or their reason for their being in the targeted buildings. At the same time, it was seen as an attack on the political and economic systems of the United States. Here the response was immediate and overwhelming, with countries all over the globe recognizing the challenge the attack posed to all established forms of government.

Many, perhaps most, terrorist activities lie somewhere between these two extremes. Perhaps people have been hurt or killed by the dissidents, and these may be security forces or uninvolved civilians. The perpetrators may not have intended to kill, or had become indifferent to the deaths of people whom they saw as allied with the oppressive state. Our reactions to these acts may vary, depending on our own perspectives and aims.

History has shown that, too often, those in power fail to address any legitimate grievances the insurgents claim to represent; instead, they continue to suppress the violence and persevere on as before, to the extent possible.

I can personally bear witness to this phenomenon. The uprising among the Catholic minority in Northern Ireland in 1969 occurred when a peaceful demonstration was forcefully suppressed by the Unionist government. This lead to killings by the thousand, perpetrated by both sides. I visited the region in the early 1990s. Echoing the words of the previous prime minister of Great Britain, Margaret Thatcher, a professional woman told me that "We have an acceptable level of violence in Northern Ireland." This Protestant lady was prepared to preserve her privileged position – which gave her the vote, access to a good job, good housing and good education – by maintaining a counteracting violence, with loss of life, under a governance structure that denied these same necessities to Catholic fellow-citizens. The violence and the continuing death toll were acceptable to her! This attitude is, of course, a recipe for disaster.

So-called "terrorist" acts, then, often represent a fight for freedom and justice against collective domination, and are used when nonviolent methods fail or are suppressed. For example, Nelson Mandela's group, "Spear of the Nation," used a policy of sabotage in South Africa, prior to his arrest and imprisonment. While for the African National Council nonviolence was an inviolate principle, Nelson Mandela came to believe the opposite: that nonviolence was a tactic that should be abandoned when it no longer worked. The state had given the Blacks no alternative to violence. It was wrong and immoral to subject his people to armed attacks by the state without offering them some kind of alternative. People on their own had taken up arms. Violence would begin whether they, Mandela's group, initiated it or not. "Would it not be better to guide the violence ourselves, according to principles where we save lives by attacking symbols of oppression, and not people?" They formed a new group who "embarked on a new and more dangerous path of organized violence, the results of which we did not know and could not know."[8]

I put the heinous acts of September 11 into a category all their own, for that action has besmirched the reputation of those who might justifiably be called freedom-fighters. I believe Mindell is talking about this latter group, the "freedom fighters," when he talks about people labeled as "terrorists." They are, he asserts, a potential presence, or spirit – his word is "ghost" – in any group, anywhere, anytime, ready to react if they are dismissed or put down. The way to deal with angry, vengeful people, he suggests, is not to wreak further violence. His proposal runs counter to our automatic responses; we should respond constructively to their ultimatum by paying attention to the message they are conveying about the need for social change.

Mindell insists that vengeance as a response to oppression is normal for insurgents. All of us get angry and most of us know what it is to seek revenge for hurts inflicted upon us, he reminds us. "Much of childhood is about learning to protect ourselves from wounds inflicted by those who use their power unconsciously," he points out.[9] Both as facilitators and as human beings, we can learn to hear the echo of our own experiences and thoughts in the screams and attacks of others.

Vengeance, Mindell asserts, is central to religious teaching and in keeping with the biblical concept of justice! He goes on to explain his statement by pointing out that we are apt to feel a divine justification for our actions when we resort to revenge, whether by physical action or by caustic undercutting remarks. This felt sense of "justice fighting injustice" transmutes chronic violence into a sort of religious struggle against "evil doers." Each side becomes a mirror of the other, which they most despise, yet each sees the motive of the other as contrary to their own.

Mindell suggests that to address the ghost of terrorism in any genuine, effective way, one must acknowledge another ghost: that of suffering. The members of his workshops – often rival gangs and other extremely hostile groups – frequently rage and yell at each other. We need to realize that in that moment, when everyone is yelling, no one is listening. It is a crisis moment for everyone involved, a time for participants and facilitators to reach for their own anchors, their own commitment to justice, to regain their center, to listen with heart and mind, and to welcome the story of suffering and pain. The task is to dialogue with apparent enemies, because they are telling something vital – to those who will listen and to themselves as well.

ARIA and Spiritual Development

What do Rothman and Mindell have in common? While Mindell describes the ontological suffering and motivations of people who choose belligerence rather than give way to despair or apathy, Rothman describes a formal, staged process for working with similarly hostile people when they decide to meet with their opponents. In combination, they describe a process with parallels to another spiritual journey. This is the journey described by the mystics across the centuries and more recently by O'Murchu and Fox, which we examined in Chapter 10. While Fox and O'Murchu were talking about an inner transformation as one matures spiritually through life, Rothman is talking about the dynamic between the protagonists in an actual conflict. Let's compare them and see the similarities. They might surprise you! (See table next page.)

Fox's Spiritual Development Process	Rothman's ARIA Process
VIA POSITIVA All is well. [apparently]	**AN EVENT OR CRISIS**
AN EVENT OR CRISIS	**ANTAGONISM**
VIA NEGATIVA • People are cast into turmoil and experience a dark night of the soul. • The intellect becomes free by allowing the pain and by seeking to learn what the experience teaches. • The process results in new birth.	• In this stage people experience pain and frustration; • blame, polarize, and attribute negative characteristics to the other; project their own unacceptable traits to the other. • They discover that these actions do not work.
VIA CREATIVA • There is movement from despair to hope, from alienation to reconnectedness. • Something new is discovered. • Good news is now accepted. • Warning! Creativity is fearful! • Creative power can become demonic power. • But if things go as they should…	**RESONANCE** • People realize that the conflict is deeply subjective. • They articulate deep needs and values, which they may discover they share to some extent. • People move from casting blame to accepting responsibility. • A whole and inclusive picture emerges. • Objectivity is sought to transform negative conflicts into creative opportunities.
VIA TRANSFORMATIVA • Justice and compassion are possible. • New insights become possible. • A heightened awareness is present.	**INVENTION** • The process of transformation can equalize power. • People recognize that they need "the other" to make the conflict constructive. • Cooperation leads to integrated solutions and points the way to…
	ACTION
The individual is a different, more mature person.	• Specific plans are laid out together. • People may discover that they have been "partners in waiting."

Table 2. Comparison of Rothman's model with Fox's Spiritual Development model.

Rothman's period of "Antagonism" the moment of challenge when the parties are brought together, corresponds to the *Via Negativa* of Matthew Fox. The parties speak to each other in hostility, of suffering at the hand of the other. We could call it the "dark night of the soul" in the conflict, alive as an active presence in the meeting. Together, the protagonists grapple with the deep questions of why the conflict is so intractable. And they stay in this dark place so long as they project blame on one another. Yet, in that very negative place, they eventually come to suspend belief that belligerence is their only recourse. As the poet Theodore Roethke says, "In a dark time the eye begins to see."[10] The space allows them to suspend their belief that no other course is possible. It replaces despair with hope and undercuts their resistance against progress. That moment is the source of new birth, new possibilities. It leads them to the next stage, the *Via Creativa* of Fox, and the Resonance of Rothman.

There is a reconnection in which they begin to articulate their deep needs and values and move from blame to responsibility. When the protagonists start to talk to one another from the perspective of their mutual humanity, there comes "Resonance," and with it hope.

Yet there is a difference between the two schemas. While Rothman stresses the positive outcomes that emerge from the original soul-searching, Fox sees the energy generated from that dark time as moving in two possible directions. Creativity and new perspectives can be used to solve the situation to the benefit of each – or it can be directed toward demonic ends and a worsening of the relationship between them. It seems as if the theologian is more realistic than the conflict mediator!

When all goes well, the third Fox stage, the *Via Transformativa*, parallels Rothman's Invention stage. Here justice and compassion have their equivalence with Rothman's equalizing power. The new insights gained through the transformative event enable each to see the other as necessary to make the conflict constructive, and to invent mutually satisfying solutions. Then action can be taken and the ARIA is complete.

Rothman emphasizes that when parties get close to an apparent settlement, new issues may arise that have to be addressed: the process turns out to be circular. While Fox talks of spiritual development as a linear event,

O'Murchu, like Rothman, speaks of setbacks due to insufficient probing or perhaps naïve optimism. In this situation, the lessons that needed to be learned at the *Via Negativa* stage have not been adequately addressed and dealt with; therefore, they must be revisited. Thus, in either case, the process turns out to be cyclical. This observation has an air of reality about it! Conflicts and challenges often wax and wane, take on new contenders and drop old ones, or take on new issues to resolve as we mature through life and especially through tough times.

Both Rothman and Mindell permit their participants in mediation or facilitation to express their strong emotions, believing that this is necessary for each to see the humanity of the other. As we saw, Rothman reassures people ahead of time that while this emotional, stressful period is to be expected, he will keep the dialogue safe. To follow through with this assurance of safety puts a formidable responsibility on mediators. In this role, they have to have the personal strength to live with their own anxieties, to set clear boundaries while remaining connected with the parties. They will endeavor to remain very present and aware of everyone's level of comfort. It is within this emotional climate that creativity, problem solving, and adaptation to future necessities are possible. Thus, to permit a measure of disequilibrium may actually help move people from a fixation on their positions, to a consideration of each other's underlying needs.

In other situations, where a mediator has decided, through previous separate meetings with the parties and careful assessment of the degree of antipathy or power imbalance, that safety cannot be assured, then processes other than face-to-face mediation will be needed. These may involve preliminary cultural awareness-raising, historical reviews, or problem-solving opportunities for each side separately, or recourse to more formal or shuttle maneuvers before the parties are brought together.

Reflection on the World Trade Center Attack

How might the ideas expressed in this chapter be used as a basis for understanding the events of September 11, 2001? Let's start with the warning in Fox's schema. The stages outlined by Fox and Rothman described in the main a path of positive re-creation out of a dark time of suffering. But the interaction may not proceed so fruitfully. Matthew Fox reminds us that our spiritual power may also be a demonic power. If a serious problem is not dealt with to the satisfaction of the parties involved, there may come about a transformation — not toward listening, but toward alienation and violence.

Extremism is found in all religions and some secular institutions (such as fascism), according to R. Scott Appleby.[11] When powerful leaders such as Osama Bin Laden come to believe, because of their own experiences at the hands of secular powers, that the world is in spiritual crisis, they may justify violence on theological or ideological grounds. Islamic extremism appears to have started in the 1920s as an initiative by freedom-fighters to gain independence from colonial powers in Egypt, and was revived more recently against the Soviet Union in Afghanistan. Currently, Bin Laden has reinvented the movement, apparently to drive the Western presence from Islamic states, and to punish the United States for what he sees as a betrayal of his former allegiance to it.

Taking upon himself the authority of an avenging messianic prophet, he has used the structures of Western society against itself. His tactics are an example of guerilla warfare on a global scale, which has caused profound anxiety about our own security, and even our own values. Is he concerned about the ills of our society, its injustices and its corruption? Is he seeking its transformation to a Islamic theocracy as an alternative to secularism? We cannot guess, but his acts have been widely condemned by both ordinary, pious Muslims worldwide, and by states where Islam is the dominant religion. Whatever Bin Laden's motives, they are clearly criminal and cannot be justified on any ethical or accepted religious grounds. Moreover, as they appear to be carried out to destroy a society, it is difficult to conceive of how they might serve to redress wrongs or bring about justice. They appear to be ends in themselves, rather than a means to better Bin Laden's own people.

What might we do about this attack? Such events do not occur in a vacuum. We have a responsibility to examine the circumstances that may have led to the actions, both of the leader and of his followers. Jim Wallis' statement, which I quoted earlier, rings true: "We must speak of the need to drain the swamps of injustice that breed the mosquitoes of terror and find a way to make this a teachable moment rather than merely a blame game."

Who are our enemies? They are not Muslims in general, who abhor the notion of the Qur'an being used as a license to kill innocent civilians. For the Qur'an states, "If anyone slew a person...it would be as if he slew a whole people. And if anyone saved a life, it would be as if he saved the life of the whole people" (Surah 5:32). This catastrophe has been the occasion for many meetings across religious divides, and has brought greater understanding of the profound truths that each tradition provides.

It may be our purpose, then, to take this crisis as an opportunity to change the game again – to rebuild structures of justice, openness, and truth; to foster equality, democracy, and human rights within and beyond our borders; to use our influence as individuals or as members of groups working for social justice, or as representatives of political organizations and governments. Our focus must be to bring about peace and security with equity to regions where we have in the past fostered, for our own commercial interests, political regimes that continue to deny these same benefits to their citizens.

The response of states targeted by the terrorists has depended largely on militarism. Should this lead to further outbreaks of retaliation by non-state actors, then we may well find that Yeats' prediction has come to pass: that "Mere anarchy is loosed upon the world."

XIV

THE MEDIATOR IN ACTION

*Surely you desire truth in the inner parts;
you teach me wisdom in the inmost place.*
Psalm 51:6

As mediators, we continually place ourselves in the center of conflict. Accepting and being aware of the reality and energy of the spirit enables us to get to the essence of things, to seek and perhaps find meaning in the conflict. To do this well, of course, we will have taken training courses and had practical experience. We will also have had many life experiences, such as parenting, and interacting with people in all sorts of situations, that will contribute to our sense of readiness for the job at hand. However, in the following section, I deliberately focus on the spiritual preparation we can do.

CENTERING

*When you meet a being who is centered you always know it.
You always feel a kind of calm emanation. It always touches you in that place
where you feel calm. But you can't hustle it.
You can't make believe you're calm when you're not. It never works.
Everybody knows. You know. It's horrible. You must center. Find that place
inside yourself... You're doing it from that place.*

Ram Dass

Our first task, before we even meet with clients, will be to ponder our own values and beliefs about ourselves and our role as a mediator. What metaphor might we choose to describe this role? Are we traffic cops, who steer or direct the flow of the conflict? Or are we judges, pronouncing who is right and who is wrong? (The latter is certainly no role for a mediator! "Knowing what's best for them" is bound to be counterproductive.) Perhaps we're catalysts who bring about change in others, without ourselves being changed?

Few metaphors adequately reflect, by themselves, the essence of the role, which involves bringing an authentic, human presence to the encounter. I believe that a mediator is at times, and all at once, a servant, a leader, a supporter, and perhaps even a guide. The mediator influences and is influenced by the people present, and is an intrinsic part of the dynamic of the mediation session.

The Mediator Taps into His or Her Spiritual Reality

A spiritual approach to mediation is one that will deal with reality at all levels. Of course, the fact that we try to bring a spiritual consciousness to conflict management does not mean that we possess a special sanctity or purity of mind that others do not have. On the contrary, to assume or to pretend that we are especially and perfectly peace-loving would be to set the scene for concession, dissatisfaction, and potential backlash. A sure way of sustaining violence in the world is to fail to admit the place of violence in our own hearts and actions, to identify ourselves only with unaffected innocence and purity.[1] In Chapter 10, as part of the discussion of adult faith development, I mentioned the need to integrate our shadow side with our highest aspirations. This is an important point to remember. The soul is an explosive and powerful force. Through the medium of its imagination, it can accomplish marvelous things — and terrible things too.

People who are connected with their spiritual nature will, above all else, know themselves — their abilities and limitations, their reactions under stress. They will be in touch with their feelings, thought processes, values and beliefs, and will seek to make their actions congruent with these.

Gifts of discernment will have been maturing in us throughout our lives, as we engage in everyday happenings, form relationships both loving and hostile, and find ourselves moving into and out of conflicts. While different people will follow different life paths, those who plan to engage the spirit in a conscious way will have engaged in some sort of spiritual or life discipline, a process that includes introspection. In introspection, we become our own nonjudgmental observer. The most "human" of human capacities, the one that sets us off from the rest of the animal kingdom, is our ability to be aware. We are aware of the world around us and seek to comprehend the links between cause and effect. We are also aware of ourselves, and aware of ourselves being aware. If we use this capacity to witness our own thoughts, values, aspirations, motives, and actions, to be a stand-apart viewer of our essential selves, we can probe to our deepest self and, when faced with a challenge, ask, "What's going on?"

Self-knowledge goes beyond competence and skill, though it may be grounded in these things. According to organizational developer Peter Senge,[2] when personal mastery becomes a discipline — an activity we integrate into our lives — it embodies two underlying movements. The first movement involves continually clarifying what is important to us, who we are in the context of the moment. Does this issue matter, and if it does matter profoundly, why? We often spend too much time coping with the immediate problems that pop up along our path, and forget to ask why we are on that particular path in the first place, suggests Senge. The second movement involves placing ourselves in a continuous and conscious learning process, to help us see current reality more clearly. In moving toward a desired destination, it is vital to know where we are now.

Being in touch with ourselves will also mean that we become more aware of the great part of our psyches, memories, and motivations that lie *beyond* awareness, in our unconscious. However much we review our values and integrate them with daily decision-making and action, there are times when we are surprised by a thought that comes unbidden and unexpected out of some unaddressed or forgotten experience of the past. These discoveries enable us to redefine our moral horizons, to translate old experiences and find new meanings from them, says ethicist and theologian Kenneth Melchin.[3] There may be a place of woundedness that needs airing, reflection, and even healing, before we move forward and offer professional help to others. We must be true to ourselves, before we try to help others understand their motives and actions.

Insights into the qualities of that inner eye that helps our discernment can be found in many religious traditions. Kabir Helminski, writing from a North American Sufi (Islamic) tradition, would, I think, see it as a manifestation of what he calls the essential self.[4] This essential self is a fundamental energy, with many positive qualities: aspiration, diligence, responsibility, self-respect, discipline, and integrity. These qualities belong to the Source, and are reflected through us. In our self-awareness, however, there is always a risk that we will develop a conceit about our new-found spiritual depth, as the Christian mystic St. John of the Cross warned. Such a conceit would, of course, negate any such claim. We need the power of an integrated personhood – as servant, not master – in order to relate to the spirit of truth that lies within each one of us. We engage the spirit when we remain open in a way that allows for humility, creativity, redemption, love of self, and mystical connection with others. Spiritual growth, then, may take the form of reflection, which involves both the head, for congruencies and meaning, and the heart, which connects emotions and meaning to the essential self. It is experienced as much by letting go of non-essentials as it is by a firm concentration on what matters.

The notion that spiritual growth is an intentional task, best undertaken before facing difficult challenges, is also a part of Buddhist teaching. Life is a chain of opportunities to improve our karma by acts of will. Guidance is provided, as we saw earlier, by following the Noble Eightfold Path.[5] Our intention is to relieve suffering by reducing our desire to hurt others. This action in turn reduces suffering for ourselves.

Jewish philosopher Martin Buber, in his book *Between Man and Man*, emphasizes that moral action and the application of wisdom involve solitude in preparation for action. It is in solitude that the deepest questions arise: "Solitude and relation are the systole and diastole of the soul… In the ice of solitude man becomes most inexorably a question to himself and, just because the question pitilessly summons and draws into play his most secret life, he becomes an experience to himself."[6] One retires to solitude in order to become free of the world "out there," and to gather up the powers of the spirit, before engaging in the challenges of the task ahead.

Those who do not subscribe to any religious tradition may find their own way to the source within themselves, which can be accessed by meditation and by centering prayer. *Meditation,* then, is a place of spiritual preparation for *mediation,* and indeed for entering on any difficult challenge, whatever our role.

Meditative preparation enables us to be centered when we enter into *mediation*. It involves emptying the mind and focusing on what is, observing present experience without interfering with it. The shift of consciousness that happens in preparatory meditation makes it possible to see things not ordinarily seen, because without this practice our focus is more likely to be on the outside of the self, says mediator Lois Gold.[7] Working from the center allows the creative side of the brain to emerge, bringing about new perceptions and perspectives. Centering carries us from a conscious awareness of the possible factors at play, to a calm place or emptiness, and finally, to a creative openness to the personalities, their attitudes and needs, and to the dynamics that will shortly unfold within the meeting. As we take our place, in the center of the storm of conflict, we may bring our own centering to the chaos.

What is this chaos like? It depends both on the parties, what they bring from their own personalities, and on the dynamic between them.

DISCOVERING THE CONTENDERS WHERE THEY ARE

Being there for somebody.
William E. Diehl

Who will we meet across the table? People come to mediation with a wide variety of attitudes, emotions, assumptions, and expectations, depending on their personalities and previous experiences with each other. They carry "master narratives" and themes derived from their worldviews, their values and beliefs, which grow from the socio-cultural world in which they are embedded.[8]

Let's review some of the attitudes that parties may bring to the table. Many of these are already familiar from the earlier pages of this book.

The Dominating Client

First, there are people who dominate, who clothe themselves in a mantle of power over others. This attitude is seldom conducive to a collaborative process designed to obtain outcomes that meet the needs of everyone involved. Strangely, as noted earlier, where two individuals with a habitual competitive, dominating style come together, there can be a paradoxical quality about the encounter: a negative interdependence.

Where both sides of the confrontation use coercive power against each other, each may explain their tactics as necessary because they see themselves as victims of the other person's actions. Alternatively, they may have always acted in a coercive way, because they believe that otherwise people will take advantage of them. And their prophecy, of course, will likely come true, because their approach influences the other's response. As we saw when we examined the patterns of escalated conflict (Speed Leas, see page 99), the two sides come to be mirror images of each other. Vamik Volkan has pointed out that "The more we want to be completely different from the enemy, the greater the resemblance, however unconscious. And the more we long to distance ourselves from the enemy, the more our excessive preoccupation with him, the more tightly we are tied to him, consciously and unconsciously."[9] Each sees him- or herself as especially vulnerable to attack by the other.

A sense of personal vulnerability is often found between adversaries who use a competitive approach, whether they come as individuals, as members of groups, or as national representatives. This feeling of insecurity may be one reason why mediators who seek to balance power meet frequent resistance. Sometimes one has to start the "balancing" act by empowering the apparently powerful, who feel exposed when challenged in their assumptions. The mediator needs to acknowledge their legitimate claims and reduce any sense of defenselessness.

The Privileged Client

Then there are those who are used to enjoying a place of privilege. They may believe that the world is basically just,[10] because it has fulfilled their worldview. As a result, they may believe that a change in relationships and social structures will not be for the better. They may assume that people get what they deserve and deserve what they get. Change and conflict is seen, therefore, as a diversion from the norm, created by modifiable external forces. Their aim will be to return to the previous state. They will think it's their duty to "fix" things for the proper ordering of society by measuring and harnessing the wayward activities of others. Such clients may expect the mediator to act on the same premise. The client will likely be slow to engage with the mediator in exploring the opponent's feelings or underlying needs, which may reflect quite a different perspective.

The need to maintain honor where someone of status feels he or she has been shamed in some way can be another closely related cause of resistance. As we saw in the section on "face-saving," this is a potent factor in many conflicts. To be aware of the influence of honor and the need to maintain or regain face is the first step in dealing with it effectively.

For clients who are used to privilege, the process of mediation, if they buy into it, can be a valuable learning opportunity indeed (note the case of the board-staff mediation on page 112), granting them a new perspective on how the collaborative process can improve relationships, reduce risk, and reestablish the harmony and morale they desire. The mediator may help the parties to redefine the meaning of prestige, fair apportionment of assets, and respectful relationships.

The Legally Minded Client

Other clients are determined to exercise their *rights*. These people may expect and want an adversarial, legal-type process. The mediation process, in its aim to get the two sides to work together, may therefore appear at variance with their mindset, which seeks to prove the fault of the other.

Clients with this intention may be afraid of full disclosure, as any admission of responsibility might put them at a disadvantage. To avoid this problem and to facilitate discussion of all relevant factors and events, it is prudent, when preparing for the mediation, to obtain agreement that the discussion will be held in confidence, and that it cannot be used as evidence in court, should the mediation fail to come to a satisfactory agreement. Mediating in the shadow of the legal system tends to be a confining experience. Yet the very fact that the parties are sitting down in mediation, indicates the possibility that the clients are prepared to yield what they feel is their right, if doing so can bring a better outcome for all concerned.

The Overcompliant Client

Some clients are overcompliant, believing that cooperation means gracefully giving up their claim to a fair share of resources, or foregoing recognition of their legitimate point of view before it is fully articulated. Strangely enough, good-hearted people may assume this posture when they ready themselves to learn about and practice collaborative conflict management. Their desire to be cooperative, to be "nice," is so prominent that they are prepared to concede at every turn, even on matters essential to them. They become so flexible that the other side never learns what was so important, or why the issue was raised in the first place.

During an introductory workshop on conflict management for a group of colleagues, I asked the participants to role-play a negotiation. When the role-play was finished, I asked individual members how things had turned out. Most teams had discussed the topic from each person's perspective and had come to a satisfactory agreement. But one member of a pair said, "It didn't work. I conceded everything of importance, but the more I offered, the more he took." I then asked the other person how the negotiation had gone for him. "We got what we needed," he said, "but the other guy didn't seem very happy!"

Bending over backwards seldom leads to a clarification of positions, values, or needs, let alone mutual respect. Outcomes based on such automatic concessions are seldom satisfactory for long. The losing side risks becoming resentful, while the winner remains puzzled that victory turned out to be so easy, yet was apparently unacceptable.

People who habitually demonstrate a fluid response to challenge get blown around by conflicting external pressures, and sometimes by their own unexamined values. Any efforts they make are likely to be half-hearted and will limit their growth and the effectiveness of their interactions.

Sometimes, the mediator may discover too late that one side has made a concession which they now regret, but can no longer easily retract. Individuals are responsible for their own actions, crazy or misguided though they may seem to others. A plan to re-evaluate any concessions at a later date may open the opportunity for their review.

Another reason clients may be too compliant in mediation is because they fear the other party. If they have been abused, for example, they may fear, and in fact actually risk, further violence if they ask for their fair share of an asset, or for respectful treatment. Mediation will seldom be appropriate in these cases.

It is especially important to screen carefully for this possibility when mediating with couples who have split up or who are contemplating it, or who are even just trying to get along. If, despite such screening, the attitudes or behaviors of either party during the session suggest that safety is an issue, then immediate steps must be taken to prevent any incident that could leave either side more vulnerable than before. Remember, too, that physical assault is not the only form of violence; verbal abuse can be even more spirit quenching. Be prepared to terminate the session quickly, if necessary. The mediator will also need to ensure that the vulnerable one is afforded protection for as long as needed. Some tough actions may be necessary.

Sometimes, the people who come to mediation are still suffering the consequences of having been victimized, either by the individual they are to meet at mediation, or by a group or ruling class of which the individual is seen as a representative. This association in the mind of the vulnerable may relate to the time leading up to the session, or to further in the past, to memories of past generations. In such cases, the mediator must decide whether the meeting can serve a useful purpose, and if so, how.

In other situations, the victim may have recovered his or her resilience, and be well able to meet the other. But the possibility remains that some outburst may occur, triggered, perhaps, by some unintended remark by the other party or by the mediator.

Obviously, any of these categories of people may be meeting with any other. So one dominant person may meet with another dominant person, or a dominant person may meet with a compliant person. The mediator's role then turns more to balancing power and getting each party's story validated by the other. Sensitivity to the historical and cultural background of the clients is essential for understanding their attitudes and worldview, which will inevitably bear on even the simplest-appearing disputes. This pertains especially when the parties are from different cultures or ethnic groups, or when either is from a different background from that of the mediator. Differences of religion, class, educational level, gender, and employment status will all have a bearing on the approaches and apprehensions of the parties.

The mediator may, of course, be faced with lesser problems! None of the above factors may exist to any discernable degree. The mediator may have the agreeable task of working with people who wish to enter genuine dialogue, but who have found, when working on their own, that mutual misunderstandings have not been clarified. Sometimes the mediator may encounter clients who just want to get the job done, the transaction completed. Some will wish to keep their dialogue to material issues and fair exchange. If this is truly the case, then the mediator will respond accordingly. But even the issue of a hundred dollar fence repair can have undertones of honor and grace and spirit (see the case of neighbors Fred and John, page 88). Sometimes it is easier to divide a million dollars than a hundred. Then there are the clients who want and are ready to build a new relationship (see couple scenario, page 137) and with whom it is a pleasure to work. In such meetings, being present and needed is an awesome experience.

Summary

The mediator assists the parties to tell and hear their stories. Where each side really listens to history, context, and significance, each may realize they are portraying very different perspectives on the same event, because each story has been created out of their own search for meaning and order. Thus the narratives of each become freshly heard and reinterpreted.

These new insights will guide subsequent understandings, appreciation, and decision-making. This process provides grace, as it respects the honor of and gives a voice to each. Dialogue creates openness to change, to the discovery of new possibilities, and a willingness to integrate them, through efforts to create new, sustainable realities.

PART FOUR

HEALING IN
THE AFTERMATH

XV

FORGIVENESS & APOLOGY

History, despite its wrenching pain,
Cannot be unlived, but if faced with courage
Need not be lived again.
Maya Angelou

We have now come to the time in our conflict story when forgiveness, healing, and reconciliation may bring about a renewal of spirit, traumatized and challenged through difficult times. It is the beginning of a future with the possibility of hope and promise. Yet even in this phase, when we expect the storm of conflict to be dying down, difficulties and turbulences continue to present themselves. To suppose that this time of bringing it all together is an easy one, would be to display the naïveté of which O'Murchu spoke in Chapter 10.

FORGIVENESS

To forgive is to change the world.
Peggy Noonan

To begin with, let's understand that forgiveness is a widely misunderstood term, with several different meanings attached to it. To forgive seems at first glance to be such a simple act. "If only we would all forgive each other, then our problems would all go away!" we might say. These are the outcomes we artlessly pray for, and may even expect of the aggrieved party. "If only everyone else would extend the necessary goodwill, then the world would be a more peaceful place!" If only! But much more than goodwill is necessary, if genuine forgiveness is to be offered and accepted, or authentic reconciliation accomplished. The path to forgiveness and reconciliation is a complex one, yet if we walk it, we can transform the darkest times in our relationships with others.

Theologians preach forgiveness as a good thing in itself. Conflict managers, including John Burton and Roger Fisher, whom we have already met in these pages, advocate it for different reasons. Forgiveness is a key to peacemaking, they say, more powerful than any coercive strength or economic adjustment. Anglican Archbishop Desmond Tutu, Chairman of the Truth and Reconciliation of South Africa, goes so far as to say that in the particular circumstances of his country's dilemma, there could have been "no future without forgiveness." These writers, who have such formidable experience in the wider world, assert that even hard-nosed practitioners of Realpolitic are beginning to acknowledge that forgiveness is an integrating force for peace, because it makes possible both short-term and long-term benefits for all parties.

A readiness to give and receive forgiveness and to seek reconciliation is a measure of our primordial wish for reconnection with a moral personal life, for reconnection with each other, and with the Creator Spirit. This potential readiness speaks to our capacity – and our need – to build sustainable I-Thou community, and soul-satisfying conditions of interdependence.

Until now, our principal concern in these pages has been to discuss situations where the actions of people toward or against each other have not been criminal. When speaking of forgiveness, apology, and healing, however, any distinction between civil and criminal behavior becomes less clear-cut. For someone to need forgiveness or to offer it, someone else has been hurt, and someone has done the hurting. Whether the hurt lies within or outside the dictates of the law may be less important than the deeply personal aspects of the interaction.

The other side to forgiveness is apology. Does the one necessarily require the other?

The relationship between these two concepts is complex and draws on many of the taken-for-granted expectations that one person may have of another.

Where Apology and Forgiveness Might Arise

Apology and forgiveness challenge us with the most profound questions about who we are and how we wish others to see us. They direct our attention to issues of truth and justice, shame and honor. We cannot change the past, but we can come to terms with it, understand it, and search for the courage to move on. Through forgiveness and apology, we liberate our souls from the need for personal vengeance, or from any perception of ourselves as victim. But they by no means represent an easy road.

When we speak of apology and forgiveness, we encounter several degrees of meaning, depending on the circumstances.

Apologies are often offered and accepted in the normal course of communication, following clarification of some misunderstanding. In this context, apology and its acceptance operate within a framework of social norms and practices. This graceful give and take abounds in the unnoticed patterns that shape our everyday expectations and discourse. Here there will have been no breach of honor, betrayal, or other sense of injury, so the quick apology will cause no ongoing concern to either party. "That's okay," we say, and move on.

At other times, the offense may really be more severe, enough to cause the person who has been hurt some considerable anxiety. Yet the injured person's response may still be still to deny the offensive act or its resulting harm. Such denial, inappropriate in the circumstances, would be to pretend tolerance and closeness. To the extent that it does not reflect true feeling, it produces instead a distancing and superficiality in the relationship. As David Augsburger points out, this action is at variance with our espoused values of authentic forgiveness.[1] Rather, it speaks to our preference for avoidance. Thus we cover up feelings, avoid confrontation, pretend superiority, and suppress conflict – not to mention foster resentment and alienation. Are not our spirits entombed by such practices?

When people who have been harmed come to us and ask what they should do, very often we are quick to recommend forgiveness. This social attitude is enhanced, perhaps, by the many writings and stories we read about extraordinary acts of forgiveness. These accounts, and the expectations derived from them, tend to create a perception that every hurt person should follow suit and offer forgiveness unconditionally. Yet if this course were followed, the victim could not come to terms with the affront, and the slow process of healing a traumatized soul could not begin.

What does forgiveness mean? Forgiveness does not mean bringing us back to where we were, as if nothing had happened. Something has happened, something hurtful. The fabric of interwoven lives has been torn to a greater or lesser extent. The past harm will not lie down and disappear. Rather, as Desmond Tutu points out, it has an embarrassing and persistent way of returning to haunt both the present and the future.[2] Unless it has been dealt with adequately, it returns and holds us hostage. Entrapped in the past, our future is tainted with unresolved pain. Unresolved injury affects our attitudes toward many other aspects of our life, and may even distort our personality in ways we might rather avoid, if we knew how. Yet to forgive in any sort of reflexive way will not ease the pain.

Gina O'Connell Higgins, who has come to terms with the deep hurts she suffered in her growing up years, outlines the defects of reflexive forgiving. To forgive automatically, she says, is tantamount to condoning and becoming complicit in the evil done. It is a betrayal of one's self, giving the lie to one's own ethical convictions. It is to deny the intense personal anguish, self-doubt, and soul searching, which are necessary on the road to recovery. It means brushing aside the depth of the hurt that has been experienced, and avoiding the need to recognize the pain. Reflexive forgiving means denying one's sacred identity.[3]

It may also mean submitting to the expectation of an abuser who feels entitled to an easy pardon. Reflexive forgiveness suggests that the perpetrator need not show remorse, genuine regret, sorrow, or empathy for the individual harmed, nor any intention to provide reparation for the harm done, where this is possible.

Forgiving and Forgetting

Victims are sometimes expected by their friends, their self-appointed judges, and by the wider society, to move beyond the pain, to not only forgive, but also to *forget* the injury, to put the past to rest. This expectation is likely to traumatize them further.

What do people mean by forgetting? Forgetting is ordinarily understood as an erasure from consciousness. Not an easy thing to do intentionally – the more one tries to focus away from a topic, the more it is recalled! The expectation that victims should self-inflict amnesia on themselves, should forget unacknowledged grievous harm, requires not only difficult mental gymnastics, but aggravates the original injustice.

Perhaps those who suggest "forgiving and forgetting" mean otherwise. Maybe they hope that the victim will deal with the problem in private, so that it doesn't have to be a constant topic of conversation. The word "forgetting" has been misapplied here: "suppression of anguish" may be closer.

Some erosion of memory may well occur naturally at a later stage, where the forgiving has followed adequate recognition of the hurt by the offending one, and the issue has been addressed honestly and openly. The pain is thereby lessened and a phase of healing can begin. If this happens, the victim may indeed find that the incident is no longer so constantly in his or her thoughts. It will have become less relevant in the midst of other priorities, taking its place in the recollections of the past.

The journey toward forgiveness and healing may begin when the offender expresses responsibility, regret, and repentance. It may begin as each listens to the story of the other – perhaps the offender will hear the sense of violation and loss of security experienced by the victim; perhaps the victim will hear a degree of understanding on the part of the offender. Genuine reconciliation will come from an intense experience of truth that emerges from the in-between of the meeting. It will explore the ramifications of justice denied and its consequences.

Out of this searching process, forgiveness may not derive so much from an expectation, but rather from a discovery, from an experience that a transformation in interpretation, understanding, and attitude has taken place. The opportunity to tell and hear these stories may have begun the healing.

Desmond Tutu tells the following story. A White officer of the South African apartheid defense forces was seeking amnesty for his role in the notorious Bisho massacre of Blacks. At the Truth and Reconciliation Commission hearing, which Tutu chaired, amnesty, but not pardon, could be granted if the one seeking it was prepared to make a full disclosure, and the deeds appeared to be more derived from the politics of the time than from any criminal intent.

On that day, the hearing room was packed with angry Blacks who had either been personally injured, or who had relatives who had been apprehended by South African apartheid officers and never heard of again.

The officer giving evidence on his own behalf acknowledged that his men had indeed given orders to open fire on the unarmed Blacks. The tension became so thick you could, as they say, cut it with a knife. The audience could not have been more hostile.

Then he turned to the audience and made an extraordinary appeal: "I say we are sorry. I say the burden of the Bisho massacre will be on our shoulders for the rest of our lives. We cannot wish it away. It happened. But, please, I ask specifically the victims not to forget, I cannot ask this, but to forgive us, to let the soldiers back into the community, to accept them fully, to try to understand also the pressure they were under then. This is all I can do. I'm sorry, this I can say, I'm sorry."

That crowd, which had been close to lynching them, did something quite unexpected. It broke out into thunderous applause! Unbelievable! The mood change was startling. The colonel's colleagues joined with him in apologizing and when the applause died down, I said:

"Can we just keep a moment's silence, please, because we are dealing with things that are very, very deep. It isn't easy, as we all know, to ask for forgiveness and it's also not easy to forgive, but we are people who know that when someone cannot be forgiven, there is no future."[4]

The officer's transformation may well have occurred long before the courtroom scene. Even more astounding, however, was the transformation within the courtroom. The audience accepted the apology as an authentic act of contrition. How great was the spirit within that assembly!

In genuine exchanges such as this, each person may be seen by the other, no longer as a monster impervious to change, but as a fellow human being who can be viewed apart from the atrocious act. This discovery of the other's humanity may happen through grace, out of "nowhere," and represents a resurgence of hope. With that resurgence may come the faith that the future can indeed be different.

Why would a person forgive in any intentional way? Because, says Desmond Tutu, it's in the person's own best self-interest. Forgiveness gives people resilience, enabling them to survive and emerge as whole beings, despite all apparent or real efforts to demean or dehumanize them. For the victim, it gives release from anguish, liberating their future; for the perpetrator it means freedom from guilt, allowing them to live the future openly and with authenticity. When we extend forgiveness, we make possible our own developing maturity and self-respect; we become able to give up our dependence on anger or the desire for revenge. Forgiveness removes any constraint upon the promise of the future because of the past. Yet the decision to forgive must always come from the one harmed, without pressure from others, however well-intentioned.

Forgiving means extending grace and demonstrating that it is more demanding than the law. How could this be? Surely the knowledge that one has grievously erred, but has been forgiven by the victim, is a far stronger motive to reform and live in search of atonement than any punitive ordinance imposed by a court of law.

Forgiving and receiving forgiveness is seldom a one-time thing. It is more often a process that continues throughout life, as thoughts about hurtful episodes rise again, causing us to reflect on them and move on once more, with a little more work done, a little more ease of heart.

When is it best to forgo forgiveness? There will be times when it is inappropriate for the wronged individual to extend forgiveness. This may be the case when issues of justice and accountability are still unresolved.

Sometimes, one party is out of phase with the other. One person may believe that he or she has told enough, but the other person believes he or she has not *heard* enough. The offending party may still believe that the incident is insignificant, or that his or her motives were wrongly interpreted, but that is not how the receiving party experiences it.

Then there is the situation where people who have been victims cannot bring themselves to shed the victim role, because they see no other possibility. They may wish to retain the false comfort of the aggrieved, perhaps afraid to take on the painful task of emotional and spiritual recovery and growth.

Others find the world such a threatening place that they dare not speak their pain. Sometimes meeting the other party face-to-face would prove to be too traumatic. In these situations, pastoral care and counseling will be necessary in order to help the victim reach a point where they feel empowered and healed enough to face their assailant – if they ever find the courage to do so. One must always respect the wishes of the weaker, dishonored party. He or she must always be allowed to choose what is right for him or her, in any particular time and place. If the friend or counselor honors the choice of the victim *not* to engage, yet offers it as one option, the victim may, paradoxically, find the courage to enter the fray. He or she may then, hopefully, discover that liberation of soul which authentic meeting and, most of all forgiveness, can bring.

Religious Injunctions to Forgive

The holy texts of most religions speak of mercy and compassion as key to the restoration of right interpersonal relations. Buddhism directs our attention to this goal through its focus on harmony, nonviolence, interpersonal responsibility, and compassion. Though the current repressive social policies of many Islamic countries don't reveal it, the Qur'an presents an authentic vision of a humane, compassionate, and all-embracing social order.[5] This teaching comes from the same source as the Judaic scriptures. In both the Qur'an and the Hebrew scriptures, believers must atone for any wrongdoing they have committed, in order to earn Allah's or Jehovah's forgiveness. In Hinduism, according to David Augsburger, an attitude of forgiveness is evidence of an enlightened acceptance of the situation in which one finds oneself.[6]

Further to the East, while Confucianism has been codified into a rigid, hierarchical system, the principles taught by the original fifth-century BCE sage placed emphasis instead on an injunction to repay hatred with uprightness, virtue with virtue.[7]

Perhaps the most pointed religious teaching on forgiveness is found in the Christian gospels, where Jesus instructs his disciples to forgive 70 times seven – i.e., on all possible occasions. Yet surely Jesus, the personification of *agape* love, could not have meant that a victim is required to forgive oppressors unconditionally or automatically. (Jesus had suggested other ways to deal with evil, such as walking the extra mile, thereby overcoming oppression with generosity – a practical example of the Confucian principle.) An alternative interpretation of Jesus' instruction to forgive 70 times seven recognizes that Jesus was Jewish, and that in Judaism, atonement, shalom (which means peace), and right relationships with the Creator, are emphasized strongly. Acknowledgment of wrongful action by the perpetrator, and forgiveness by the person hurt, is an essential part of living in community. In *agape*, forgiveness would come, not as an imperative, but from a freely offered graciousness. Here the one extending the forgiveness might even anticipate the guilty one's atonement.

All of this is illustrated in the great parable of forgiveness Jesus tells about a father and his prodigal son (Luke 15:11–24). In the story, the son first admits his fault to himself, then confesses it to his father, potentially subjecting himself to his father's just wrath. But even before the son confessed, the father had been searching the horizon for him and when he saw his son coming down the road towards home, ran to him and welcomed his return. Because, as the father said, "he was lost, and now is found." In this interpretation, the son was met with love and forgiveness, because his journey home meant that he was prepared to face his father's justice.

The gift of forgiveness surely represents the deepest and most spiritual level of human interconnection. The person who offers forgiveness comes to a place where he or she is prepared to see beyond the deed to the individual, to set aside the balance sheet and to move toward reconciliation. As Miroslav Volf has said, "only those who have been forgiven and who are willing to forgive will be capable of relentlessly pursuing justice without falling into the temptations to pervert it into injustice."[8]

APOLOGY

It is never easy to say "I am sorry":
they are the hardest words to articulate in any language.
Desmond Tutu

For the offending one to ask for forgiveness or to apologize for significant harms done is no less demanding than for the harmed one to extend forgiveness or to accept the apology. Where a guilty person's dignity is quite fragile, for instance if it has been balanced on a pedestal to which he or she has pinned honor and identity, an acknowledgment of imperfection might well destroy that delicate ego. An apology in its full meaning implies that the offender has to revisit and acknowledge the wrongful act and the subsequent harm done. Asking forgiveness humbles the transgressor. Denying the error is always a temptation, for there is always the chance that the offender can "get away with it." After all, as long as the action is passed off as justified, no pardon is necessary. To ask or accept forgiveness is to confess guilt – not only to another person, but also to oneself. Asking for forgiveness implies an acceptance of responsibility. Also, for the request to be meaningful, the guilty party must speak the truth in expressing sorrow and regret, while promising not to repeat the mistake – and then they must keep the promise.

Asking for forgiveness from the one hurt has other risks; the victim may spurn the gesture. Moreover, an admission of fault may lay the individual open to legal action. While this risk is real, it may also be overstated. Expressing responsibility may be interpreted as a friendly gesture, as a wish to share in the dilemma posed by the harmful act and to reconnect as an imperfect human being with the one who has been harmed. Legal suit has often been avoided by such action.[9] The wronged one has found a friend, or at least one who acknowledges the predicament – and one seldom sues a friend!

Summary

This chapter has been dosing out some strong medicine. But then, the need is great. When our human relationships break down, we suffer. To face the other person and to attempt to make things right often requires great moral courage. Yet the act can change the world. It can give us hope that we can learn from the past and shake it free. We put ourselves at risk when we extend forgiveness to those who have offended us, or when we, believing we have been at fault, offer apologies. Our gestures, whispering of vulnerability, may turn out to be our greatest strength, evidence of a generosity of spirit, of justice, and of mutual honor. They can pave the way for an authentic reconciliation and mending of our kinship ties.

At last we have come to the moment when we can extend our hand to the other and begin the task of reconciliation and healing. For that, we turn to the next chapter. It is the final one, but really, a beginning.

XVI

HEALING & RECONCILIATION

If you are for peace,
and I am for peace,
give me your hand.
Ruth Patterson

When we've experienced a transformative moment at the heart of conflict and have begun to see the other person with new and more understanding eyes, when apology and forgiveness have perhaps been offered and accepted, we discover the possibility of healing and reconciliation. But what do they look like? What is it to find ourselves and our relationships healed after a difficult altercation? How do we honor the hard work of reconciliation?

HEALING

Give me your hand,
so small a thing to ask,
and yet – so big.
Ruth Patterson

Healing has happened when we come to that place where we have survived the ordeal and then find ourselves perhaps even thriving in the appreciation and transcendence of the challenges life throws at us.

Recall the story of the breast-cancer survivors, who became more dynamic and helpful in their relationships with others as they came to terms with their predicament. Or the account of the childhood survivors of abuse, who rose above their malign past and turned their experience into a commitment to be healers for others. In these instances, the people brought about their own internal healing.

In another instance reported in these pages, from my own practice, a husband and wife worked through enormous heart-work and overcame their previous inequitable relationship to forge a new one based on mutual respect and their deep, underlying love for each other. Here, healing was sealed in the relationship *between* two individuals, as well as within each.

Healing is not always assured, of course, as we saw in the case where a board member withdrew from the fray. The individual in question could not work through her changed perception of herself, nor could she use that moment of truth to enhance the quality of any future service to the organization.

From our newspapers and TV screens, we learn how widely gross violations of human dignity and rights still persist on the international scene. In comparison, our attempts to redress these wrongs and clear the path for physical as well as spiritual recovery seem so puny. Yet we can gain hope from the work of the post-apartheid South African government, which has avoided an anticipated reversal of violence between the new regime and the former oppressors. Out of the traumatic experience of listening to the stories of the victims and acknowledging their truth, we saw that healing could emerge, often unexpectedly.

Speaking about healing and reconciliation from the sidelines, as we do here, is a risky affair. We cannot expect others to find the means to heal themselves, or to heal their relationships out of some fountain of goodwill, especially when their wounds may be grievous indeed. Yet we can, through our own everyday acts and professional practices, work to mend ourselves and to provide the sacred spaces where healing and reconciliation may be fostered.

I believe that healing is the natural order of things, an essential part of our life force. Given the right environment, we may discover that healing comes about as a spontaneous event. Let's look for a moment at physical healing as an analogy of the more soul-oriented restoration a spiritual approach to conflict attempts to bring about.

When a doctor sets out to mend a broken bone or torn bit of skin, he or she does not bring about healing directly. Rather, the doctor's task is to remove obstructions such as bacteria or other foreign elements that have no place there, to lay bare and clean the wounds, then to bring the gaping edges together and allow the body to heal itself through the gift of its own life force. In prosaic terms, the body has a self-righting capacity, a drive toward an equilibrium of health, which in physiological terms is called "homeostasis." With the alien objects removed, the natural healing powers of the body can do the rest. The doctor provides the conditions that permit the body to return to optimal functioning.

If the medical condition is chronic or long-standing, complete healing of the physical tissues may not be possible, yet much can be done to improve the overall situation. Here, health professionals act most effectively when they appreciate and foster the gifts and strengths of the person they are treating. And for the clients, healing happens most optimally when they recognize and accept the reality of their dilemma, appreciate their powers of adaptation and resiliency, and actively share in their own recovery. The breast cancer survivors and the victims of childhood abuse rose above their situations and became healers. In the latter case, there never was "homeostasis" in their situation, but these resilient people transcended their traumatic childhood experiences.

Working through conflict toward emotional and spiritual healing is a participatory affair for everyone involved, helpers and helped alike. It is about creating the sacred place between individuals and within communities where the present dilemma can be acknowledged and where the parties can to commit to removing the obstacles, to re-entering relationship and building together a future of hope.

Obstacles to Healing

Obstacles, yes! It necessary, at the start of the journey to reconnection, to identify those matters that keep parties separate from each other. If left unrecognized, or if seen as insuperable blocks, they stand in the way of healing the spiritual and emotional trauma.

First, the problem may be internal to the sufferer; some victims tend to accept their role and obstruct the process by hanging on to their victim-hood. They may do this unconsciously, because some hidden benefit is served, such as gaining sympathy for their plight. It takes courage to leave behind outmoded beliefs, debilitating support systems, and self-handicapping behaviors. Spiritual healing involves removing the blinders of habitual, limiting ways of operating. With blinders off, the individual may be encouraged to see that a different future is possible, and may find the resilience to pursue a healing path.

The second, more severe obstacle for the sufferer relates to the constant intrusion of old memories of the wounds and the people who caused them. This can be an interpersonal obstacle, forming a wall between individuals who come together to resolve the issues between them. Sometimes the perpetrator is already dead, and the victim must come to terms with his or her own predicament, so that the past does not continue to destroy the future.

Where the memory of past traumas is deeply felt by a whole community, it will have entered their psychological and spiritual life. It will have become embedded in their traditions and stories, giving them a sense of identity which may be difficult to change or move beyond. History records too many instances of one community committing atrocities against another, leaving a legacy of bitter memories that threaten to define the future. The Balkans are a recent case in point; Rwanda is another. In his book *People Behind the Peace: Community and Reconciliation in Northern Ireland*,[1] Ronald Wells cites Ireland's tragic history at the hands of British colonial power. In North America, the history of our own relationship with aboriginal peoples is one of pain.

As in the case of individuals, the collective memories these communities harbor serve as obstacles to healing as long as they go unaddressed.

There is hardly a part of the world that does not have its own searing memories of woundedness, and a need for reconciliation. Yet even when the beleaguered side regains its power, there may be new problems. As the healing process develops for one side, the other side may experience an increase in anxiety. Its members may become defensive in attitude and perhaps continue to justify their previous behavior because they are unsure of their role in the new climate. After all, the status quo before the attempt at reconciliation may well have served their perspective better that the present situation. They may feel, in consequence, like victims. But healing is not a zero-sum proposition. Genuine healing will happen only when each party takes responsibility for healing the other; each will gain a new sense of transcendence in the process of reaching out to the other and of being accepted by them. If each side allows this to happen, the whole community shares in a sense of accomplishment and the realization of a future together, previously present only in the dreams of imaginative and brave hearts.

Agents of Healing

Community healing may be started by leaders who accept responsibility in the name of their predecessors. Equally if not more important, because they are more closely involved, are the grassroots communities who decide that the violence must end, and who meet with members of the other factions to build a momentum for peace. By coming together and swapping stories that acknowledge their pain, they create a mutual spiritual empathy. An example of this can be found in Northern Ireland, where dozens of community-based organizations are working together on shared work projects, integrated schools, recreational facilities, and ongoing seminars and pastoral healing.

Mediation and facilitation are often thought of as problem-solving processes, but they can be agents of healing, too, addressing both the objective and the subjective or spiritual aspects of the protagonist's needs. Practitioners in the field have important roles to play in the promotion of spiritual healing among individuals and communities in conflict. The mediator can assist the whole process by creating a sacred space for a full and sensitive dialogue between the hurt people. The goal is to help the parties unlock their isolating identification with their pain and to shift the frames that have entrapped them. Lois Gold, who brings a healing perspective into her mediation work, insists that mediators can "Emphasize the hope and a belief in the potential for success."[2] Hope energizes a person's resources. By describing the possibilities for future success or change, mediators can create an expectancy that may increase the likelihood of behavior — conscious or unconscious — that will lead to that success. We cannot underestimate the power of tapping into the universal desire for wellness that exists in even the bitterest of conflicts.

Even as the process develops, the injured one and the perpetrator may begin to regain honor in their own eyes and in the eyes of the other. They may each begin to recognize where hope and resilience can be found, to grow in maturity as a result of the experience, and to embrace the life-giving force on which they can build the future. In the case of deep spiritual wounds, however, this process of restorative healing can take months, even years.

Healing comes about as we decide to forgo the role of victim and to move through the wounds, not to disregard them or the experiences they bring. Healing requires faith, dedication, and a commitment that some other future is possible. Its empathic quality enables the parties to be gentle with their own and others' imperfections, to be trustworthy and trusting, to tap into their resources of wisdom and moral development, to make choices consistent with personal values. It enables the parties to rediscover their capacity to be curious, compassionate, and joyful.

Healing is a consequence of a rediscovered spirituality. It comes about when both sides discover that their enemies are human beings like themselves, equally vulnerable to guilt and shame, capable of enjoying honor and extending grace. It can occur in the most seemingly intractable conflicts when each discovers that they need their adversaries for their own completion.[3] That is an amazing proposition! It is a truth that grabs the imagination!

RECONCILIATION

*More than a cessation of violence,
reconciliation involves a fundamental restoration of the human spirit.
As a spiritual rather than a technical process, it cannot be foreshortened;
it keeps its own timetables.*

R. Scott Appleby

As we move from the phase of healing to that of reconciliation, we stress the intentional side of the equation. Reconciliation entails the restoration of trust in a relationship between two or more people through mutually trustworthy behavior.[4] Before reconciliation can happen, the urge to blame or incriminate the other must be let go of, and a soul-searching decision made to embrace the other, figuratively if not physically. Promises will be exchanged and honored.

Rituals

How do we bring ourselves as conflict managers, and those with whom we work, to this transformative event? Any process designed to reach this goal will necessarily involve ritual, to bring the work to that deep soul-level of our being, and to give the process authenticity, authority, and finality. For it is in ritualized processes that we discover and enhance the meaning of our relationships with one another. Ritual re-mythologizes our narratives and enhances our experiences of transition and change.[5] Through ritual, we attempt to address the full truth of the experience, a truth that remains beyond complete comprehension, even beyond language, because it is metaphysical. Rituals communicate in a special way, using symbols and metaphors, rather than mere words, to convey images of truth. They bring all our senses into play to reach meanings too deep for mere rational, objective problem-solving.

Rituals and similar acts of a symbolic nature have been almost totally neglected in Western-based secular conflict studies and practice – although they continue to play a significant role within the legal system. However, in our attempt to develop rituals for spiritually based conflict management, we may draw on several other, more primordial sources. Modern-day anthropological research has identified the verbal and nonverbal rites and liturgies that religious institutions and indigenous societies have developed from time immemorial and still use today. These may be usefully adapted for our use and provide a birthing ground for transformation and reconnection.

For instance, the highly sophisticated South African Truth and Reconciliation Commission was based on the long-standing belief of the indigenous people of that country in *Ubuntu*. This teaching says that the dignity of one person is linked to the dignity of all. Thus, indigenous South Africans already possessed a mindset that allowed them to demonstrate an unusual willingness to confront the past, trusting that to do so would bring about healing and reconciliation. Other truth commissions have operated in Central and South America, and each has succeeded to the extent that the process enabled participants to hear each other's story, to recognize each other's humanity, and to start, however imperfectly, the task of rebuilding their nations.

A classic indigenous ritual is the Hawaiian process of *Ho'oponopono* for family reconciliation. It is worth recounting here, because it illustrates themes that can be found throughout the world. David Augsburger outlines the process in some detail in his book *Conflict Mediation across Cultures*.

The several ritualized stages include the family's initial agreement to come together.

- The meeting begins with a prayer for divine assistance.
- All participants make a commitment to search themselves for their own motivations. Problem identification includes identifying layers of secondary hurts and conflicts. Cooling-off periods may be called as tempers flare.
- Sincere confessing, willing forgiveness, and promise of appropriate restitution follow.
- A "cutting off" ceremony, in which the problem is declared closed, never to be brought up again, allows the release of or abandonment of hurts.
- A mutual, reciprocal agreement follows.
- The closing phase may include a summary of the proceedings and a reaffirmation of the family's enduring bonds.

- Finally there is a closing prayer.
- A traditional meal to which all have contributed is shared.
- The family resumes its normal life and activities.[6]

George Irani and Nathan Funk describe the rituals of the Arab-Islamic peoples of Lebanon.[7] Private justice may be administered through informal networks in which local political and/or religious leaders determine the outcome of feuds between clans and individuals. Communal religious and ethnic identity remain strong forces in social life, as do patron-client relationships and patterns of patriarchal authority. Group solidarity, traditional religious precepts, and norms concerning honor and shame retain their place. The Middle East practice of *sulh* has its origins in tribal and village contexts. Its rituals address both the process of restorative justice and the outcome sealed by that process. In common with the Hawaiian process, each side pledges, after the stories have been told and acknowledged, to put behind them everything that happened in the incident and to initiate new and friendly relations.

Such processes are essential to existence in the harsh living conditions of the desert. Robert Axelrod's suggestion that survival and evolution occur through cooperation among groups[8] finds confirmation in the practices of indigenous peoples.

In Western culture, our religious traditions may provide the base from which we can design new rituals of reconciliation. For example, when contending parties come together, the meeting may start with prayer, directed *meditation*, or centering silence. A reading from scripture may bring the members to a common understanding of their relationship with their Creator and each other. Confession and contrition are characteristic requirements of religious reconciliation processes. Then may come the moment of renouncing previous wrongdoing and poisonous communication patterns. The meeting will usually conclude with a prayer or blessing, and perhaps a meal to celebrate the rebuilding of community.

Another element missing from our secular world, but present in the rituals of the indigenous peoples of Canada, is our sacred connection to the environment and our place in nature. Many indigenous rituals include the use of sacred visual symbols such as candles; plants and shells; sacred scents, such as incense or sweet grass; the sounds of chants and music, and sacred movement in the form of dance. All of these are incorporated at the appropriate parts of the meeting.

In designing new rituals for our secular times, the facilitator will be breaking new ground. He or she will be engaged in a Daoist-like process that attempts to "build the container to hold the fire of all the souls present," as my colleague Richard McGuigan has put it.

The design will, of course, include an appreciation of the different traditions, attitudes, and power relationships that are held by and exist between the parties who will attend the meeting. Where cross-cultural mediation is to take place, we need to be especially aware of the sensitivities of each side to their customary practices. We may need to assure the individuals that the process is designed to bring them all to their desired and collective goals, in a manner that lends security, honor, and authenticity to their endeavors. For church members in conflict, or for workshops in connection with church groups, I have found that a spiritual approach is willingly accepted. People find new meaning when the old texts are applied to everyday problems.

In the wider society, where conscious attention to ritual has been so often neglected, we must take special care to describe the process and its meaning to potential participants, and insist on a genuine commitment from those who plan to be there.

My colleagues Richard McGuigan and Sylvia McMechan have elevated the development of rituals that enhance the sacred within mediation to a fine art. They have found such rituals particularly effective when dealing with intractable conflicts. In particular, they have developed a ritual that has been used successfully in meetings between indigenous tribal groups and government staff members. Because of its success, they have adapted it for use with mainstream organizations dealing with particularly difficult internal problems.

McGuigan and McMechan start by meeting with each of the parties to learn for themselves about the situation, its history, and context. They also take the opportunity to describe to the parties what they can expect at the planned gathering. The novelty of the approach takes a little getting used to! They then gain a commitment from all potential participants that they will attend the whole event – and leave their cell phones and other distractions behind! McGuigan and McMechan ask the participants to help make the event meaningful and fruitful for all present.

The "container to hold the fire together" includes even the selection of the meeting place. It is chosen for its aesthetic appeal and ability to make everyone can feel welcome and nurtured. The layout of the meeting room is prepared with care. Chairs and tables are arranged in a semi-circle and natural emblems of our West Coast – stones and boughs of pine and salal – decorate the tables. Some of these objects, symbolic of our connection to the earth and all of nature, surround a lighted candle, which provides a sacred focus at the front of the group.

The opportunity to make reconnections is fostered by assigning seats, at both mealtimes and meetings, to mix up the constituencies and to provide for informal interconnection throughout the days of the meeting.

A period of silence or prayer or guided meditation opens the formal part of the gathering and centers the thoughts and hearts of those present.

The business part of the meeting consists of familiar routines, such as the setting up of guidelines that build safety and mutual trust. Everyone commits themselves to confidentiality, to the use of non-adversarial approaches, and to equal participation, with mutual understanding and healing as the goal.

McGuigan and McMechan provide the framework for the discussion by presenting themes from needs theory, which we examined earlier in this book. The participants then have an opportunity to identify how this framework fits with their own circumstance, in a variety of group discussions.

The meeting is not directed solely to find solutions, but to begin a transformed relationship. Throughout the meeting, participants engage in a significant and powerful effort to walk through the fire, to begin to understand each other, to heal and then to transform their relationship. Networks for further initiatives may be fostered. Long-term shared goals for the whole community may be started. "Individuals find themselves called upon to remain personally centered in the heat of difficulties, and to practice integrity, sometimes in the form of apology and forgiveness," says McGuigan.

The meeting may end with a prayer or a ritual of cleansing, with members standing in a circle to receive the symbolic water dish or sacred smoking herb.

At the end of the gathering comes the time for celebration. The crowning event is a celebratory meal together, where people can bring their charged-up energies and exchange in a communal atmosphere stories about what the meeting has meant. It is an experience few of them will forget.

Other closing rituals may be appropriate for other groups and practitioners. For example, the group might decide to record the hurtful incidents on pieces of paper and then burn the paper in the sight of all. Or they may celebrate though musical performance and singing or dancing. They may decide on a game that allows them to sublimate previous hostilities into peaceful competition. Such possibilities may emerge spontaneously from the energy and goodwill of the group.

Alternatively, the ritual may be just a simple handshake, which can indeed be powerfully symbolic. As poet and pastor Ruth Patterson of Northern Ireland states, a handshake between former enemies is "so small a thing to ask, and yet – so big."

In the context of a spiritual approach to conflict management, rituals will be used to bring closure to a painful incident, honor the past and celebrate the potential of the future. They will confirm the transition that has taken place, celebrate the new reality, and honor the achievement of reconciliation. People may thereby create anew the scaffolds that will reconnect them to their moral frameworks and to the elemental questions of human existence, and support them as they work together in the future.

Summary

Genuine forgiveness cannot be an imperative in the face of injustice, but a freely offered gift which acknowledges the humanity of both the forgiver and forgiven. Without it, there is no hope that our future can be brighter than our past.

Healing and reconciliation may come through an acknowledgment of past suffering, an intention to discover each other's humanity. And reconciliation can be cemented by the use of sensitively designed ritual, so that, as Ruth Patterson suggests, we can recognize that we are "being called toward a future bright with hope and promise." Perhaps a handshake is all it takes.

CONCLUSIONS

What are we to conclude about spirituality and conflict? Spirituality is that divine force that inspires and animates us. Challenges bring forth the spirit, as we become newly aware of who we are; as we become aware of resilience and our ability to care, forgive, rebuild relationships, and create fresh beginnings. Tapping into our spiritual resources at times of hardship enables us to discover what it is to truly live in the world and connect with that Universal Spirit, which is both immanent and transcendent, within us and around us.

Matthew Fox, our mystical creation-minded theologian, insists that spirituality is a dirtying of the hands, a stretching of the heart, an openness to the inner mystery. True spirituality is about power, though it is not about the power of domination or threat, nor is it about the relinquishing of power to others. Instead, spirituality speaks to the power of creativity, justice, and compassion, which can be manifested in all persons. It is about grounding persons and communities in the powers that will enable them to survive and even flourish in the midst of adversity. It is about re-creating relationships. It is resilient and healing. It brings us through the dark night of the soul to transformation.

As the prophet said so long ago, we have a choice "Therefore, choose life!"

> *Now we are changed*
> *making a noise*
> *greater than ourselves*
> *to be worthy of the lesson*
> *all duly noted*
> *all forgiven.*
> Kathleen Norris

APPENDIX

MEDITATION ON A QUARREL

I am sitting quietly, having set time aside to ponder a disagreement with a relative, friend, or business associate.

Let me think now, to myself, about that person and about where things are not quite right between us,
or about where there is an obvious disagreement which remains unresolved.

Let me get in touch with my anger, my sense that all is not well.
There may be more than meets the eye behind my chagrin.
Why does it bother me so much?
What does this conflict mean for me, and
what does it tell me about myself?

Let me show the situation and my feelings about it to the Fount of All Being,
so that I can put it in perspective,
so that I can bring my values, my heart, and
my soul to the matter at hand.

Oh Divine Presence, what is it I really *need* – not what I would *like* – in my engagement with this person?
What is my real need in relation to how I view myself,
to how I view the other the person, and
- to what we are quarreling about.

What is the core issue here?
Is it just a failure to deliver a resource as expected,
or something that cuts to the very core of who I am?
Why am I so upset about it?

**Oh Divine Presence, you know my anxieties about
the encounter, because of what might happen.**
Let me number off all those fears and bring them into the open, to you,
to see if they are real.

**Oh Divine Presence, give me clarity of vision
so that I can deal with them wisely.**

Let me look at the whole situation,
the consequences of actions over which I have control,
and those where I may not have control.

**If things work out badly, what will I stand to lose:
just a few dollars, or something more precious?**
Over what would I grieve?
What is so vital to me that no compromise seems possible?
Why?
What does this issue represent that it is truly non-negotiable?

Oh Divine Presence, let me pause and reflect.

**Oh Divine Presence, you know my association with
this person.**
Remind me of where we see eye to eye;
remind me of the quality of our relationships in the past,
and of where we may rebuild;
remind me of my appreciation of him/her as an individual,
of his/her quirks and strengths in our relationship.

**Oh Divine Presence, let me consider the needs of
my adversary.**
How important is this discussion for him/her?
What is it that he/she really needs?
Where might hurt lie for him/her as a result of our disagreement?

**Let me speculate on the fears or anxieties
my adversary may have.**
What things block him/her from talking to me?
What risks does he/she perceive,
and how might I avoid taking advantage of them,
but help him/her instead?

Am I prepared to truly listen to what he or she might say,
however uncomfortable it might be for me to hear?

**Oh Divine Presence, let me now set aside my assumptions
about my opponent,**
and be prepared to hear the truth he/she expresses about himself/herself.
Let me be prepared for surprises!
Let me find a way to talk, equally, in terms he/she might be prepared
to acknowledge, about what is important to me.

**How, Divine Presence, can I make it easier for
both of us to talk about this problem?**

**Oh Divine Presence, let me search my mind to see if there are
other people affected by this quarrel.**
Do they have needs I should be sensitive to?
Oh Divine Presence, bring them to my mind and my heart.

Oh Divine Presence, let me be sure of my facts and reasons,
before I call another to account.

**Oh Divine Presence, give me the strength
to carry through with the discussion**
in a way that reflects your love and endurance.
Oh Divine Presence, clear my mind of vengeance, bitterness, and pride,
and open my heart to the possibility of forgiveness and reconciliation.

ENDNOTES

Introduction: The Place of Spirituality in Conflict
1 Ursula King, "Spirituality," in *A New Handbook of Living Religions*, J. J. Hinnells, ed. (London: Penguin Books, 1998), 679.

Chapter I – Defining Our Terms
1 John W. Burton and Frank Dukes, *Conflict: Practices in Management, Settlement, and Resolution* (New York: St. Martin's Press, 1990), 8.
2 Speed Leas, *Moving Your Church Through Conflict* (Washington: The Alban Institute, 1985).
3 Ken Wilber, *The Eye of Spirit: An Integral Vision for a World Gone Slightly Mad* (Boston, MA: Shambhala, 1998), 2, 8.
4 Werner Heisenberg, *Physics and Beyond* (New York: Harper and Row, 1971).
5 King, "Spirituality," 667.
6 Leonard Boff, *Ecology and Liberation: A New Paradigm* (Maryknoll, NY: Orbis Books, 1995), 36, 105.
7 Daniel G. Scott, "Spirituality, Education, and Narraturgy" (Ph.D. Thesis, University of Victoria, 1998), 213.

Chapter II – Modernism & The Self-Fulfilling Prophecy
1 Richard Tarnas, *The Passion of the Western Mind: Understanding the Ideas that Have Shaped Our Worldview* (New York: Ballantine Books, 1991), 220.
2 Alvin W. Gouldner, "Anti-Minotaur: The Myth of the Value-free Sociology," in M. Stein and A. Vidich, eds. *Sociology on Trial* (Eaglewood Cliffs, NJ: Prentice Hall, 1965). See also Matthew Fox, "A Mystical Cosmology: Toward a Postmodern Spirituality," in *Sacred Interconnections: Postmodern Spirituality, Political Economy and Art,* D. R. Griffin, ed. (New York: State University Press, 1990), 15.
3 David R. Griffin, ed. *Spirituality and Society: Postmodern Visions* (New York: State University Press, 1988), 2–3.
4 Ken Wilber, ed. *Quantum Questions: Mystical Writings of the World's Great Physicists* (Boston, MA: Shambhala, 1985), 9–10, 150.
5 Kenneth R. Melchin, *Living with Other People* (Ottawa: St. Paul University, 1998), 27–29.

6 Robert Axelrod, *The Evolution of Cooperation* (New York: Basic Books Inc., 1984), 125.
7 Lynn Margulis and Dorion Sagan, "Exploring Our Interconnectedness," *Context,* 34 (1993): 18.
8 Lee Jussim and Jacqueline Eccles, "Teacher Expectations II: Construction and Reflection of Student Achievement," *Journal of Personality and Social Psychology,* 63 (1992): 947.
9 John W. Burton, "Conflict Resolution as a Political Philosophy," in *Conflict Resolution Theory and Practice: Integration and Application,* D. J. D. Sandole and H. van der Merwe, eds. (New York: Manchester University Press, 1993), 57.

Chapter III – Postmodernism

1 David R. Griffin, ed. *Sacred Interconnections: Postmodern Spirituality, Political Economy and Art* (New York: State University Press, 1990), xi, 172.
2 Martin Heidegger, *The Question Concerning Technology: Heidegger's Critique of the Modern Age,* W. Lovett, trans. (New York: Harper and Row, 1977).
3 Griffin, *Spirituality and Society,* x.
4 Lee Butler, "From Eagle to Dove" *Turning Point* (Spring 1999): 4.
5 Louis de Broglie, "The Aspiration Toward Spirit," in *Quantum Questions,* K. Wilber, ed. (Boston: Shambhala, 1985), 121.
6 Tim O'Riordan and James Cameron, *Interpreting the Precautionary Principle* (London: Earthscan Publications Island Press, 1994).
7 Rollo May, *Man's Search for Himself* (New York: W. W. Norton, 1973), 14.
8 Julian B. Rotter, "Generalized Expectancies for Internal Versus External Control of Reinforcement," *Psychological Monographs* 80 #1 (1966): 1–27.
9 Mary Clark, *Ariadne's Thread: The Search for New Modes of Thinking* (New York: Macmillan, 1989), 317.
10 Fritjof Capra, *The Turning Point: Science, Society and the Rising Culture* (New York: Bantam Books, 1982), 48, 108.
11 Wilber, *Quantum Questions,* 8–9.
12 Ken Wilbur, *The Eye of Spirit,* 2, 8.
13 Thomas Franck, *The Power of Legitimacy Among Nations* (Oxford: Oxford University Press, 1990), 242._
14 Burton, "Conflict Resolution as a Political Philosophy," 57.
15 Jay Rothman, *Resolving Identity-Based Conflict in Nations, Organizations and Communities* (San Francisco: Jossey-Bass Publishers, 1997), 12–18.

16 K. J. Holsti, *International Politics: A Framework for Analysis* (Englewood Cliffs, NJ: Prentice Hall, 1992), 83.
17 Michael J. Bopp, "The Nuclear Crisis: Insights from Metatheory and Clinical Change Theories," in *Transformation in Clinical and Developmental Psychology*, D. A. Kramer and M. J. Bopp, eds. (New York: Springer Verlag, 1989), 235.
18 Gina O'Connell Higgins, *Resilient Adults: Overcoming a Cruel Past* (San Francisco: Jossey-Bass Publishers, 1994).
19 Shelley E. and Jonathan D. Brown, "Illusion and Well-being: A Social Psychological Perspective on Mental Health," *Psychological Bulletin* 103 (1998): 193–210.
20 Cynthia Bourgeault, *Mystical Hope* (Boston: Cowley Publications, 2001).

Chapter IV – Religion

1 Richard Holloway, *Doubts and Loves: What Is Left of Christianity* (Edinburgh: Canongate, 2002), 47, 69.
2 Preston Jones, "Quebec After Catholicism," *First Things First* (June/July, 1999): 12–14.
3 Anthony Giddens, *The Consequences of Modernity* (Stanford: Stanford University Press, 1990), 105.
4 Ursula King, "Spirituality," 679.
5 D. L. Carmody and J. T. Carmody, *Peace and Justice in the Scriptures of the World Religions* (New York: Paulist Press, 1988), 44.
6 Johan Galtung, "Conflict Resolution as Conflict Transformation: the First Law of Thermodynamics Revisited," in *Conflict Transformation*, K. Rupesinghe, ed. (New York: St. Martin's Press, 1995), 54.
7 Richard H. Tawney, *Religion and the Rise of Capitalism* (New York: Penguin Books, 1922), 117.
8 Ibid, 229.
9 Michael Lerner, *Spirit Matters* (Charlottesville, VA: Hampton Roads, 2000), 47.
10 Gustavo Gutierrez, *A Theology of Liberation: History, Politics, Salvation* (Maryknoll, NY: Orbis Books, 1971), 129.
11 Robert K. Greenleaf, *Servant Leadership: A Journey into the Nature of Legitimate Power and Greatness* (New York: Paulist Press, 1977).
12 Bennett J. Sims, *Servanthood: Leadership for the Third Millennium* (Cambridge, MA: Cowley Publications, 1997).
13 R. Scott Appleby, *The Ambivalence of the Sacred* (New York: Roman and Littlefield, 2000), 91.

14 George Irani, "Rituals of Reconciliation: Arab-Israeli Perspectives," *Mind and Human Interaction* #11.4 (2000): 226–245.
15 Brian Victora, *Zen at War* (New York: Weatherhill Inc., 1997).
16 Matthew Fox, "A Mystical Cosmology: Toward a Postmodern Spirituality," 15.

Chapter V – Culture

1 David W. Augsburger, *Conflict Mediation Across Cultures: Pathways and Patterns* (Louisville, KY: Westminster/ John Knox Press, 1992), 7, 275.
2 Edward T. Hall, *Beyond Culture* (New York: Anchor Books, 1989), 107.
3 Irani, "Rituals of Reconciliation," 226–245.
4 Victor H. Li, *Law without Lawyers: A Comparative View of Law in China and the US* (Boulder, CO: Westview Press, 1978), 42.
5 Galtung, "Conflict Resolution as Conflict Transformation," 54–55.
6 John P. S. McLaren, "The Origins of Tortous Liability: Insights from Contemporary Tribal Societies," *University of Toronto Law Journal* Vol. 25 (1975): 42–93.
7 Stephen Diamond, "Redeeming Our Devils and Demons," in *Meeting the Shadow*, C. Zweig & J. Abrams, eds. (New York: G.P. Putnam and Sons, 1991), 180.
8 Evan Imber-Black and Janine Roberts, *Rituals for Our Times* (New York: Harper-Collins, 1992), 32–33, 37–38.
9 Clifford Geertz, *The Interpretation of Cultures* (New York: Basic Books, 1973), 112.

Chapter VI – Honor, Grace, & Face

1 Paul Adams and Paul Koring, "Rebuilding Jenin Camp a Delicate Task," *The Globe and Mail*, 4 May 2002.
2 Julian Pitt-Rivers, "Postscript: The Place of Grace in Anthropology," in *Honor and Grace in Anthropology*, J. G. Peristiany and Julian Pitt-Rivers, eds. (Cambridge, UK: Cambridge University Press, 1992), 217.
3 Caryl E. Rusbult and Paul Van Lange, "Interdependent Processes," in *Social Psychology Handbook of Basic Principles*, E. T. Higgins and A. W. Krugslanski, eds. (London: Guilford Press, 1996), 564–596.
4 Dale T. Miller and Rebecca K. Ratner, "The Disparity Between Actual and Assumed Power of Self-interest," in *Journal of Personality and Social Psychology* 74 (1998): 53–62.
5 Pitt-Rivers, "Postscript: The Place of Grace," 220.
6 J. G. Peristiany and Julian Pitt-Rivers, *Honor and Grace in Anthropology*, 12–13.

7 Arthur Koestler, *The Ghost in the Machine* (New York: MacMillan, 1967), 234, 281.
8 Jim Wallis, "Light in the Darkness," *Sojourners* (November-December, 2001): 7–9.
9 Marcus J. Borg, *The God We Never Knew* (San Francisco: HarperSanFrancisco, 1997), 111.
10 Borg, *The God We Never Knew*, 168.
11 Michael Ignatiev, *The Needs of Strangers* (New York: Viking, 1985), 64.
12 Pitt-Rivers, "Postscript: The Place of Grace," 220.

Chapter VII – Human Emotions & Needs

1 James D. Whitehead and Evelyn E. Whitehead, *Shadows of the Heart: A Spirituality of the Negative Emotions* (New York: Cross Road, 1995), 50.
2 Ibid., 8.
3 Ron Potter-Efron, *Angry All the Time* (Oakland, CA: New Harbinger Publications Inc., 1994), 44.
4 Leas, *Moving Your Church Through Conflict*.
5 Bernie Wiebe, a report on "Sharing Common Ground: Culture and Conflict in Canada," *The Network: Interaction for Conflict Resolution*, Vol. 4. No. 3 (1992): 20.
6 Loraleigh Keashley, "Identity and Conflict," *The Network: Interaction for Conflict Resolution* Vol. 4 No. 1 (1992): 13.
7 Terrill A. Northrup, "The Dynamics of Identity in Personal and Social Conflict," in *Intractable Conflicts and Their Transformation*, L. Kriesberg, ed. (Syracuse: Syracuse University Press, 1989), 68.
8 Herbert C. Kelman, "The Interdependence of Israeli and Palestinian National Identities: The Role of the Other in Existential Conflicts," *Journal of Social Issues* 55 (1999): 581–600.
9 Abraham H. Maslow, *Toward a Psychology of Being*, 2nd ed. (New York: Van Nostrand Reinhold Company, 1968).
10 Paul Sites, "Needs as Analogues of Emotions," in *Conflict: Human Needs Theory*, R. Burton, ed. (New York: MacMillan, 1990), 10.
11 See among others, M. E. Clark, "Meaningful Social Bonding as a Universal Human Need," in *Conflict: Human Needs Theory*, 34.

Chapter VIII – Coercive Power

1 Desmond Tutu, *No Future without Forgiveness* (New York: Doubleday, 1999).
2 Arnold Mindell, *Sitting in the Fire* (Portland, OR: Lao Tse Press, 1995), 21.
3 Phyllis B. Kritek, *Negotiating at an Uneven Table* (San Francisco: Jossey-Bass, 1994), 30.
4 Carol Gilligan, *In a Different Voice: Psychological Theory and Women's Development* (Cambridge, MA: Harvard Press, 1982), 43.
5 Leslie Shanks and Michael Schull, "Rape in War: The Humanitarian Response," *Canadian Medical Association Journal* 163 (2000): 1152–6.
6 Vamik Volkan, J.V. Montville, D. A. Julius *The Psychodynamics of International Relationships Vol. II: Unofficial Diplomacy at Work* (Lexington, MA: Lexington Books, 1990), 5, 161.
7 L.Y. Abramson, G. I. Metalsky, and L. B. Alloy, "Hopelessness Depression: A Theory-Based Subtype," *Psychological Review* 96 (1998): 358–372.
8 Kenneth Boulding, *Three Faces of Power* (San Francisco: Sage Publications, 1989), 25, 109.
9 Mechthild Hart, "Liberation through Consciousness Raising," in *Fostering Critical Reflection in Adulthood,* J. Mezirow and Associates, eds. (San Francisco: Jossey-Bass, 1990), 48.
10 Gina O'Connell Higgins, *Resilient Adults,* 19.
11 Kenneth Cloke, *Mediating Dangerously: The Frontiers of Conflict Resolution* (New York: Wiley and Son, 2001), 140.
12 W. E.Vine, *The Expanded Vine's: Expository Dictionary of New Testament Words* (Minneapolis: Bethany House Publishers, 1984), 1196.
13 Mindell, *Sitting in the Fire,* 91.
14 Walter Wink, "The Third Way: Reclaiming Jesus' Non-violent Alternative," *Sojourners* (December 1986), 28–30.

Chapter IX – Integrative & Spiritual Powers

1 Boulding, *Three Faces of Power,* 109.
2 Fox, "A Mystical Cosmology," 16.
3 William C. Eichman, "Meeting the Dark Side in Spiritual Practice," in *Meeting the Shadow,* p. 134.
4 Gerald Gold, *Gandhi: A Pictorial Biography* (New York: Newmarket Press, 1983).
5 Rollo May, *Power and Innocence* (New York: W. W. Norton, 1972), 111.

Chapter X – The Development of Faith & the Experience of Spirit

1 Diarmuid O'Murchu, *Reclaiming Spirituality* (New York: The Crossroads Publishing Company, 1999), 11.
2 Matthew Fox, "A Mystical Cosmology: Toward a Postmodern Spirituality," 26.
3 Matthew Fox, *The Coming of the Cosmic Christ* (San Francisco: Harper and Row Publishers, 1988), 49.
4 Robert Sternberg, *Wisdom, Its Nature, Origins, and Development* (New York: Cambridge University Press, 1990), 13.
5 Mihaly Csikszentmihalyi and Kevin Rathunde, "The Psychology of Wisdom: An Evolutionary Interpretation," in *Wisdom, Its Nature, Origins, and Development*, 31.
6 Daniel Robinson, "Wisdom Through the Ages," in *Wisdom, Its Nature, Origins and Development*, 13.
7 Daniel G. Scott, "Spirituality, Education, and Narraturgy" (Ph.D. Thesis, University of Victoria, 1998), 213.
8 John Barton, *Ethics and the Old Testament* (London: SCM Press Ltd., 1998), 16.
9 Rupert Ross, *Return to the Teachings* (Toronto: Penguin, 1996), 258.
10 Jimmy Carter, *Talking Peace: A Vision for the Next Generation* (New York: Dutton Children's Books, 1993), 17.

Chapter XI – Conflict Management through Systems of Law

1 Harold J. Berman, *The Interaction of Law and Religion* (New York: Abingdon Press, 1974).
2 Ibid., 26.
3 Kenneth Cloke, *Mediating Dangerously: The Frontiers of Conflict Resolution* (San Francisco: Jossey-Bass, 2001), 144.
4 Tutu, *No Future without Forgiveness*, 106ff.
5 Bennett J. Sims, *Servanthood*, 62.
6 Morton Deutsch, *Distributive Justice* (New Haven: Yale University Press, 1973), 38.
7 Tom R. Tyler and Maura A. Belliveau, "Tradeoffs in Justice Principles: Definitions of Fairness," in *Conflict, Cooperation and Justice*, B. B. Bunker, J. Z. Rubin and Associates, eds. (San Francisco: Jossey-Bass, 1995), 291.
8 Robert Folger, Blair H. Sheppard, and Robert T. Buttram, "Equity, Equality, and Need: Three Faces of Justice," in *Conflict, Cooperation and Justice*, 261.

9 David Lerman, "Underlying Principles: Restorative Justice and Jewish Law," *Full Circle: Newsletter of the Restorative Justice Institute*, Volume 2 Issue 2 (April 1998): 2.

10 Nawal H. Ammar, "Restorative Justice in Islam: Theory and Practice," in *The Spiritual Roots of Restorative Justice*, M. L. Hadley, ed. (New York: State University of New York, 2000), 161.

11 David R. Loy, "Healing Justice: A Buddhist Perspective," in *Spiritual Roots of Restorative Justice*, 81.

12 Howard Zehr, *Changing Lenses* (Waterloo, ON: Herald Press, 1990), 139.

13 John Paul Lederach, *Preparing for Peace: Conflict Transformation across Cultures* (Syracuse: Syracuse University Press, 1995), 22.

Chapter XII – Managing Conflict by Negotiation & Mediation

1 Roger Fisher and William Ury, *Getting to Yes: Negotiating Agreement without Giving In* (Boston: Houghton Mifflin, 1981), 6.

2 Ibid.

3 Robert A. Bush and Joseph P. Folger, *The Promise of Mediation: Responding to Conflict through Empowerment and Recognition* (San Francisco: Jossey-Bass, 1994).

4 Ibid., 20.

Chapter XIII – Identity-Based Conflict Management

1 Jay Rothman, *Resolving Identity-Based Conflict*.

2 Arnold Mindell, *Sitting in the Fire* (Portland, OR: Lao Tse Press, 1995).

3 Kelman, "The Interdependence of Israeli and Palestinian National Identities," 581–600.

4 Rothman, *Resolving Identity-Based Conflict*, 29.

5 Martin Buber, *I and Thou* (New York: Touchstone/Simon and Schuster, 1970/1996).

6 Mindell, *Sitting in the Fire*, 47.

7 Bertram Spector, "Deciding to Negotiate with Villains," *Negotiation Journal* (1998): 43–59.

8 Nelson Mandela, *Long Walk to Freedom: The Autobiography of Nelson Mandela* (Boston: Little Brown and Co., 1994), 272.

9 Mindell, *Sitting in the Fire*, 162.

10 Theodore Roethke, *In a Dark Time* (New York: Doubleday & Co. Inc., 1966), 236.

11 R. Scott Appleby, *The Ambivalence of the Sacred*, 91.

Chapter XIV – The Mediator in Action

1 Thomas Moore, *Care of the Soul* (New York: HarperPerennial, 1992), 135.
2 Peter M. Senge, *The Fifth Discipline: The Art and Practice of the Learning Organization* (New York: Doubleday, 1994), 237.
3 Melchin, *Living with Other People*, 27.
4 Kabir Helminski, *Living Presence: A Sufi Way to Mindfulness and the Essential Self* (New York: Penguin Putnam, 1992), 57.
5 Galtung, "Conflict Resolution as Conflict Transformation, 54
6 Martin Buber, *Between Man and Man* (London: Kegan Paul, 1947), 126.
7 Lois Gold, "Influencing Unconscious Influences: The Healing Dimension of Mediation," *Mediation Quarterly* Vol. 11, No. 1 (1993): 55–66.
8 Gerald Monk, *Narrative Mediation: A New Approach to Conflict Resolution* (San Francisco: Jossey-Bass, 2000), 41.
9 Vamik D. Volkan, *The Need to Have Enemies: From Clinical Practice to International Relationships* (New Jersey: Jason Aronson, 1988), 5.
10 Melvin Lerner, *The Belief in a Just World: A Fundamental Delusion* (New York: Plenum, 1980), 11.

Chapter XV – Forgiveness & Apology

1 Augsburger, *Conflict Mediation across Cultures*, 271.
2 Tutu, *No Future without Forgiveness*, 303.
3 Higgins, *Resilient Adults*, 28.
4 Tutu, *No Future without Forgiveness*, 150.
5 Nawal Ammar, "Restorative Justice in Islam," 161.
6 Augsburger, *Conflict Mediation across Cultures*, 269.
7 Edwin Hui E. and Kaijun Geng, "*The Spirit and Practice of Restorative Justice in Chinese Culture*," in *Spiritual Roots of Restorative Justice*, 99.
8 Miroslav Volf, *Exclusion and Embrace: A Theological Exploration of Identity, Otherness and Reconciliation* (Nashville: Abingdon Press, 1996)
9 Stephen B. Goldberg, E. D. Green, and F. E. Sander, "Saying You're Sorry," *Negotiation Journal* Vol. 3 (July 1987): 221–224.

Chapter XVI – Healing & Reconciliation

1 Ronald A. Wells, *People Behind the Peace: Community and Reconciliation in Northern Ireland* (Cambridge, UK: William B. Eerdmans, 1999), 46.

2 Gold, "Influencing Unconscious Influences," 55–66.

3 R. Kegan, *In Over Our Heads: The Mental Demands of Modern Life* (Cambridge, MA: Harvard University Press, 1994), 319.

4 Michael McCullough, *Forgiveness: Theory Research and Practice*, Michael McCullough, Kenneth I. Pargament, and Carl E. Thoreson, eds. (New York: Guildford Press, 2000), 229.

5 Imber-Black and Roberts, *Rituals for Our Times*, 268.

6 Augsburger, *Conflict Mediation across Cultures*, 213.

7 Irani, "Rituals of Reconciliation: Arab-Israeli Perspectives," 226–245.

8 Axelrod, *The Evolution of Cooperation*, 88.

INDEX

A

aboriginal **69, 116, 144, 214**
abuse **46, 121**
   children **119**
   women/children **118**
action **171, 175**
Adams, Paul **80**
adversarial model **166**
advocates **150**
African National Council **179**
agape **59**
   love **60–61, 208**
agreed-upon rules **44**
alienation **41–42, 48, 58, 68, 136, 159, 184**
Allah **61–62, 158, 207**
altruism **83, 130**
Ammar, Nawal **158**
Angelou, Maya **200**
anger **96, 99, 107, 227**
   power **97**
   stress **98**
   pacifist communities **101**
antagonism **171, 173**
apartheid **110, 205**
apathy **11**
apology **200–202, 209, 221**
Appleby, R. Scott **62, 184, 217**
ARIA **173, 183**
Aristotle **95, 150**
Arnold, Matthew **27**
asceticism **53, 191**
assimilation **76**
atom **39, 40**
attitudes **11, 111, 168, 179, 191–192, 220**
   need for change in **34**
   social **203**

Augsburger, David **67, 202, 207, 218**
authenticity **98, 220**
authority **125**
autonomy **44, 106**
awakening
   collective **51**
   spiritual **134**
Axelrod, Robert **31, 219**

B

Bach, Richard **134**
balance
   dynamic **156**
Balkans, the **214**
bargaining position **163**
Barton, Archbishop Arthur **52**
Baruch Bush, Robert A. **166**
behavior **33, 111, 123, 215**
   altruistic **82**
   conscious **216**
   self-perpetuating **33**
   unconscious **216**
belief **11, 20, 23, 33, 37, 45, 48–49, 65, 77, 140, 182, 192, 218**
   evolutionary theory **30**
   fulfilled **34**
   individualism **73**
   just world **193**
   system **102**
benefits **130**
   mutual **125**
Berman, Harold **151**
betrayals **118**
   imagined **19**

Bhagavad Gita **40**
Bin Laden, Osama **184**
Borg, Marcus **89–90**
  grace **90**
Boulding, Kenneth **117**, **125**
Bourgeault, Cynthia **47**
Boyle, Robert **28**
Bradley, General Omar **39**
Brody, R. A. **99**
Brown, Jonathan **47**
brutality **124**
Buber, Martin **174**, **190**
Buddha, the **49**, **54**
Buddhism **50**, **53**, **158**, **190**
  community **55**
  compassion **55**
  Eight-fold Path **54**, **190**
  forgiveness **207**
  harmony **54**
  non-violence **55**
bullying **118**
Burton, John **19**, **34**, **44**, **201**
Bush, Robert **166**
Butler, General Lee **39**
Buttram, Robert **158**

C

capitalism
  rise of **58**
Capra, Fritjof **42**
caring
  mutual **61**
Carter, Jimmy **147**
centering **188**
change **75**, **96**, **174**, **216**
  (see also attitudes)
  environment **106**
  power **123**
  rituals **217**
  social **120**, **179**
changing the game **122**

children
  abuse of **46**
Christianity **56**
  domination **58**
  exploitation **58**
  forgiveness **208**
  chosen people **57**
  compassion **60**
  harmony **54**
  love defined **58–59**
civil disobedience **128**
Clark, Mary **42**
Cloke, Kenneth **120**, **153**, **166**
codes of law **20**, **73**, **157**
Cold War **39**
collaboration **31**, **44**, **130**
  and evolutionary theory **31**
collusion **102**
commitment **125**, **141**, **167**, **176**, **180**
communication **23**, **162**, **172**, **202**
  in escalating conflict **102**
  non-verbal **156**
communities **46**, **51**, **98**, **103**, **153**, **156**, **213**, **225**
  global **15**
  intentional **106**
  pacifist **101**
  good of **127**
  rebuilding **219**
compassion **83**, **86**, **126**, **145**, **159**, **225**
competition **34**, **117**
  evolutionary theory **31**
compromise **147**, **163**
conflict **18**, **131**, **136**, **153**, **161**
  challenge of **13**
  circular process
    Buhddist idea **20**
  definition of **19**
  destructive patterns **101**

dynamics 37
emotions 103
escalation 99, 108, 173
evolutionary theory 31
externalization 174
family 137
internalization 174
international 102
interpersonal 48
professional groups 101
religious groups 101
resolution 157
legal system 150
spirituality 47, 225
conflict management 15, 35,
   61, 62, 93, 125, 143, 151,
   166
   ARIA 173, 182
   bargaining 163
   honor, grace, and face 80–81
   identity-based 163, 171
   interest-based 163
   mediation 161–162
   negotiation 162
   spiritual approach 163, 188, 222
   transformational 168
   Western approaches 165
Confucianism 49
   forgiveness 207
connectedness 12, 25, 51
   dependancy 82
   essential 48
   human 106
conscience 127–128
consciousness 49, 87, 126, 134,
   193, 204
Cooper, William 56
cooperation 32, 117, 128, 164
counter-threat 117
court system 150
creation 32, 135, 141, 158
   stewardship of 59

creativity 14, 47, 126, 130,
   141, 182, 225
   and anger 96
Crusades 50
Csikszentmihalyi, Mihaly 142
culture 21, 66–67, 107, 151, 168,
   192, 219
   as a network 68
   clash of 76
   community-focused 69
   customary practices 74
   defining 68
   identity 76, 173
   individualism 68, 102
   North American 68
   of silence 118
   power of 77
   ritual 74
   violence 115

D

Darwin, Charles 30
Dass, Ram 188
de Broglie, Louis 40
defiance 118–119
democracy 185
Descartes, Rene 28
despair 11, 48, 104, 111,
   136, 139, 140
Deutsch, Morton 157, 164
development
   of children 118
   spiritual 126, 133, 181
   spiritual and ARIA 180
dialogue 20, 45, 162, 197
Diehl, William E. 191
dignity 106, 218
disempowered 120
dispute vs. conflict
   defined 19

Divine Creator Spirit **12, 16, 21, 24, 26, 38, 43, 47–48, 50, 53, 58, 61, 64, 81, 89–91, 98, 127, 133, 190, 219, 227**
domination **124, 130**
dualism
  body-mind **48**
Dukes, Frank **19**
dynamic
  group **163, 191**
  mediation **188**

E

Eccles, Jacqueline **34**
Eckhart, Meister **135**
ecosystem *(see also creation, nature)*
  threats to **110**
Einstein, Albert **10–11, 22**
emotion **95, 104, 107, 151, 192**
empowerment **130, 135, 168, 193**
emptiness
  inner **41**
encouragement **118, 125, 143, 153, 167, 214**
energy
  life's **126**
  potential **144**
equality **185**
essence
  spiritual **133**
essential
  self **190**
ethics **127, 144, 152, 203**
  and scientific discoveries **40**
ethnic cleansing **110, 116**
evolution **30**
  cooperation/collaboration **32**
experience
  immediate **47**
  life **51, 145**
  mystical **141**
  spiritual **133**
  transformative **135**
expertise **73**
exploitation **29**

F

face **80, 87**
  honor **87**
  loss of **71, 73, 87**
  saving **87**
facilitator **147, 162, 176, 180**
faith **126, 133, 140**
  healing **216**
  vs. belief **46**
families **119, 172**
feminism **48**
Fisher, Roger **163–164, 201**
flight **117, 121**
Folger, Joseph P. **87, 158, 166**
Follett, Mary **164**
force **34**
forgetting **204**
forgiveness **25, 159, 200–204, 206, 209, 221**
  and forgetting **204**
  genuine **222**
  reflexive **203**
Fox, Matthew **134–136, 141–142, 182–183, 225**
  and spiritual development process **138, 181**
Franck, Thomas **43**
freedom **25, 120, 125, 143, 179**
  of others **61**
freedom fighters **120, 177, 179, 184**
Freud, Sigmund **11**
fundamentalist **61, 86**
Funk, Nathan **219**

G

Gablik, Suzi 33
Galilei, Galileo 28
Galtung, Johan 54, 190
Gandhi, Mahatma 117, 125, 127, 156
Geertz, Clifford 75
genocide 45
Gibbon, Edward 63
Giddens, Anthony 51
God *(see also Divine Creator Spirit)*
  as love 59
  as dominator 56
  existence of 38
  law of 54
  logic 38
  people as image of 59
Gold, Gerald 127
Gold, Lois 191, 216
Golden Rule 49
Good Friday Accord 176
government 118, 178
  colonial 129
grace 80–81, 93–94, 197, 216
  between people 91–92
  concept as free gift 90
  Divine 81, 89
Greenleaf, Robert 60
Griffin, David Ray 37–38, 42
guerilla warfare 184
Gutierrez, Gustavo 60

H

Hall, Edward 69
Harvard Negotiating Team 164
Hawaii 219
healing 126, 130, 136, 199, 200, 203–204, 210–215, 221, 223, 225
hegemony 128

Heidegger, Martin 38
Heisenberg, Werner 22, 42
  Uncertainty Principle 48
Helminski, Kabir 190
high-context societies 71–72, 84
Higgins, Gina O'Connell 46, 119, 133, 203
  reflexive forgiveness 203
Hinduism 40, 129
  forgiveness 207
Hobbes, Thomas 30, 159
holistic 35, 143, 169
holocaust 110
Holsti, K. J. 43–44
Holsti, Ole 99
homeless 80
honor 81, 84–85, 94, 175, 210, 216, 220, 222
  collective 175
  face 87
  sacred 51
hope 13, 45–47, 65, 90, 98, 136, 140, 143, 171, 174–175, 213, 216, 223
hopelessness 11, 48
human(ity) 11, 23, 38, 133, 162, 179
  community 45
  connectedness 106, 174
  dignity 34, 212
  needs 31, 44, 95
  rights 185
  spirit 10, 15, 79, 151
humiliation 26, 44
humility 25

I

idealism 34
identity 19, 20, 25, 41, 47,
    81, 85, 98, 101,
    107, 120, 140, 142,
    161, 171–172, 175
    celebration 61
    cultural 67, 76
    nature of 172
    spiritual 133
Ignatiev, Michael 91, 103, 176
Imber-Black, Evan 74
individualism 29, 58, 68
    low-context societies 72
    tough love 60
injustice 104, 119, 123,
    128–129, 135, 204
integrity 47, 190, 221
intention 83
interconnectedness 44, 130
International Commission on
    Intervention and State 116,
    122
International Commission on
    International Law 45
invention 171, 175
I-Thou relationships 174
Irani, George 219
Irish Republican Army 121
Islam 62, 90, 184
    Allah 62
    forgiveness 207

J

Jefferson, Thomas 109
Jesus 49, 59, 122, 155, 208
jihad 62
Jones, Preston 51
journey
    spiritual 135

Judaism
    forgiveness 208
Jussim, Lee 34
justice 11, 25, 34, 44,
    62–63, 101, 120–121,
    125–127, 129, 151, 157–159
    179–180, 185, 208,
    210, 225
    denial of 81
    restorative 33, 158, 219
    social 129, 130, 185
    just world 193

K

karma 54, 190
Keashley, Loraleigh 101
Kepler, Johannes 28
King David 145
King Jr., Martin Luther 127
King, Ursula 49
knowledge 142
Koestler, Arthur 85
Koring, Paul 80
Kritek, Phyllis 114

L

Landmines Treaty of 1997 45
language 15, 68, 173
law 206
    spirit of 157
    unjust 128
leadership 121
    healing 130
    paradoxical 61
    servant 61
Leas, Speed 99, 192
legal systems 76, 100, 140,
    150–152, 157–159, 161,
    166–167, 206, 217
    spiritual approach 151
    truth 153

Lerman, David **158**
Lerner, Michael **59**
life
    enhancing **48**
    meaning **47**
logic **73**, **82**, **106**, **143**, **156**
    modernism **28**
loneliness **139**
love **128**, **158**, **176**
    defined **60**
low-context societies **72**, **84**
    autonomy **72**
    individualism **72**
Loy, David **158**

M

Mandela, Nelson **121**, **127**, **179**
Mangan, James Clarence **49**
Manhattan Project **40**
Margulis, Lynn **32**
martyrdom **123**
Maslow, Abraham **106**
maturity **142**
May, Rollo **127**
McGuigan, Richard **220–221**
McMechan, Sylvia **220–221**
meaning **38**, **47**, **156**, **171–172**, **217**, **221**
    life **107**
    patterns of **48**
Médecins Sans Frontières **115**
media **118**
mediation **103–104**, **137**, **140–141**, **159–162**, **165–169**, **173**, **183**, **195**, **197**
    cross-cultural **220**
    dominating client **192**
    legally minded client **193**
    overcompliant client **194**
    privileged client **193**
    problem-solving **168**
    responsibility of **163**
    rituals **220**
meditation **26**, **191**
    centering **191**
    directed/guided **219**, **221**
    on a quarrel **227**
Melchin, Kenneth **29**, **190**
mentors
    spiritual **176**
Merton, Thomas **135**
metaphysical **43**
Middle East, the **171**, **219**
militarism **39**, **48**, **185**
Miller, Dale **83**
mind **23**
    conscience **97**
Mindell, Arnold **111**, **120**, **171**, **176–177**, **179**, **180**, **183**
mobility
    of people **75**
modernism **26**, **35**
    ethics **28**
    monastic model **52**
    rationality **95**
    self-fulfilling prophecy **27**
    re-evaluated **35**
morality **26**, **128**, **158**, **167–168**
Moses **49**, **63**
motivation **23**
motivator **87**
Muhammad **49**, **62**
Muslim **50**, **129**, **158**
mystery **93**, **134**, **140**
    inner **225**
mystical **43**, **48**, **146**
    experience **141**
    truths **144**
mysticism **145**

N

narcissism 42
nature 220 *(see also creation)*
 modernism 28
Nazi Germany 110
needs 19, 103, 153, 157, 172,
 182–183, 191
 and emotions 104
 basic 98
 hierarchy
  Maslow, Abraham 106
 human 106 *(see also humanity)*
neglect 46
negotiation 161–162
 problem-solving 166
networks 25, 32, 68, 144, 158
 personal 70
new birth 136, 139
Newton, Isaac 28
Nietzsche, Friedrich 38
nihilism 12, 38, 40–41
 global consequences 39
 negative thinking 41
non-cooperation 128
non-government 45
nonviolence 127–128
Noonan, Peggy 200
Norris, Kathleen 225
North, R.C. 99
Northern Ireland 176, 178, 214
Northrup, Terrill 102
nuclear weapons 40, 162
 threat of 45
nuclear winter 39
nurture 221

O

O'Murchu, Diarmuid 134,
 136, 180, 200
 Spiritual Development Schema 138

Oppenheimer, Robert 40
oppression 29, 35, 46,
 97–98, 111, 130
 international 120
oppressor 114, 120, 123
optimism 47
 naïve 136, 139

P

pain 119, 126, 130, 135,
 137, 139, 153, 175,
 203–204, 207, 214, 216
parenting 172
 close bonds 69
 community-focused 69
 conflict 70
 rites and rituals 70
partners 175
Patterson, Ruth 211, 223
peace 11, 25, 34, 63,
 126, 131, 135–136, 159,
 161–162
 building 67
 inner 126
 making 61, 103, 177, 201
Peristiany, J. 80, 84–85
perpetrator 124
pilgrimage 51
Pitt-Rivers, Julian 80, 84–85
Pittacus 109
Plato 49
politics
 international 43
 realism 34–35
 religion 50
 positional-bargaining process
  163
 women 118
post-traumatic stress disorder 116

postmodern **12**, **37**, **42–43**, **88**
  constructive **42–43**
  deconstructive **38**, **46**
  defined **37**
Potter-Efron, Ron **98**
poverty **110**, **111**, **129**
power **26**, **40**, **44**, **125**, **136**
  absolute **162**
  coercive **11**, **34**, **109–118**, **125**, **159**, **161**
    defined **109**
    society-supported **111**
  colonial **129**, **214**
  compassion **225**
  constructive **136**
  creativity **225**
  destructive **110–111**, **130**, **136**, **225**
  integrative **125–127**, **129**, **130**
  secular **184**
  spiritual **125**, **127–130**
  to change **34**
  transformative **129**
powerlessness **40**
prayer **126**, **218–219**, **221**
prejudice **128**
problem-solving **164**, **217**
process
  healing **215**

Q

Qur'an **62**, **90**, **185**
  forgiveness **207**

R

rage **120**
Rathunde, Kevin **142**
rationality **95**
Ratner, Rebecca **82**
Rawls, John **157**
realists **34**

reality **21**, **26**, **28**, **37**, **42–44**, **46**, **91**, **140**, **156**, **222**
  construction of **75**
  grace **93**
  shared **93**
  transcendent **43**
reconciliation **200–201**, **204**, **210–212**, **215**, **217**, **222**
  family **218**
redevelopment
  spiritual **126**
Reformation **57**
refugees **80**, **86**, **110**, **121**
  Palestinian **81**
relationships **23**, **26**, **34**, **66**, **68**, **82**, **99**, **113**, **125**, **139**, **142**, **159**, **165**, **169**, **225**
  agape love **60**
  anger **98**
  conflict **10**
  spirituality **10**
  break down **210**
  family **69**
  mature **140**
  respect **140**
  social **92**
  transformed **221**
  trust **217**
religion **21**, **29**, **48–49**, **86**
  backlash **51**
  dark side **50**, **57–58**, **104**
  forgiveness **207**
  non-theistic **53**
  theistic **53**
religious institutions
  and the State **63**
  need of **65**
resilience **25**, **46**
resistance **172**
resonance **171**, **174**, **182**
responsibility **22**, **26**, **41**, **148**, **169**, **174**

revenge 111, 119–120
rewards and punishments 41
rigidification 102
risk 45, 102, 118, 124, 130, 209
rituals 44, 48–52, 221–222
    closing 222
    non-religious 52
    symbolism 75
    transforming 52
    customary practices 74
    indigenous peoples 219
    reconciliation 217
Roberts, Janine 74
Robinson, Daniel 143
Roethke, Theodore 182
Rolheiser, Ronald 25
Rothman, Jay 15, 44, 171, 180–183
    ARIA process 181
Rotter, Julian 41
Rukeyser, Muriel 144
rules 151
Rusbult, Caryl 82
Rwanda 45, 214

S

sacred 51, 98, 128, 213, 220
    scripture 52
safety 175
Sagan, Dorion 32
Schull, Michael 115
secular
    rituals 220
security 11, 34, 44–45, 48, 106, 121, 150, 161, 185, 220
self-centered 42
self-concept 47
self-determination 153, 167
self-empowerment 139, 167
self-esteem 47, 87, 168
self-fulfillment 23, 106
self-fulfilling prophecy 33, 90, 117
self-interest 58, 82–83
self-knowledge 126, 143, 189
self-worth 161
Senge, Peter 189
September 11, 2001 12, 86, 127, 177–179, 183
shame 120, 177
Shanks, Leslie 115
Sheppard, Blair 158
Siddharta, Gautama 54
silence 156, 221
    centering 219
Sims, Bennett 154
Sites, Paul 15, 106
social action 120
social structure 32
society
    community-based 172
    contemporary 75
    diversity 77
    pluralism 159
Socrates 152
solidarity 130
    group 116, 219
    spirit of 119
soul 23, 26, 64, 96, 130, 151
    dark night 47, 136, 139, 182, 225
    destruction of 13, 116
    essence 15
    liberation of 207
Source 141
    (see also Divine Creator Spirit)
South Africa 110, 154, 212
South African Truth and Reconciliation Commission 218
space
    sacred 215
Spector, Bertram 178
Spencer, Herbert 30

Spirit *(see Divine Creator Spirit or God)*
spirit **45–46**, 76, **97–98**,
    107, 111, 130, 143,
    156–157, 169, **174**, 210
  and anger 96
  crisis of 176
  crushed 117
  enhancing 130
  honor and grace 94
  honoring 176
  of cooperation 32
  renewal 200
  resiliency of 124
spirituality **25,** 65, 98, 133, 142,
    216, 225
  and conflict 10
  awakened 134
  commitment 25
  defined 25
  depth 136
  development 133, 136
  embracing 48
  forgiveness 208
  honor and grace 81
  journey **134–136**
  new forms of 13
  power 125
  ties 83
St. John of the Cross **135–136,**
    190
status 73, 106, 152
  need of 44
status quo 118, 130, 215
Sternberg, Robert 142
storytelling 23, 144, 147, 204
Stutman, Randal K. 87
submission **117–118**
suffering 128
suicide 119
survival 31, 107, 172, 225
  and anger 98

survival of the fittest 30
symbolic
  act 82
symbolism **105–106**, 217
  culture 75
  visual 220

T

Tarnas, Richard 27, 37
Tawney, Richard 58
Taylor, Shelley 47
technology 23, **35,** 58
  birth of 28
terrorists 120, 127,
    177–179, 185
Thatcher, Margaret 178
Thoreau, Henry David 153
threat 102, 116, 122
tough love 60
transcendence 24, 52, 157, 225
  grace 81
  mystery 29
transformation 22, 48, 81, 103,
    126, 134, 140, 146, 160,
    166–168, 174, 211, 218, 221,
    225
  dark side 126
  forgiveness 204
  grace 90
  individuals 167
  society 167
  use of images/metaphors 14
  wisdom 48
transitions 74
treaties 44
  treaty-keeping 44
trust 44, 144, 151, 177
  mutual 221

truth 24–25, 50, 65, 91,
    125–129, 141–144, 148, 151,
    155–156, 160, 185, 209,
    212, 216
  empirical 154
  evolutionary 155
  mythical 155
  paradoxical 156
  relational 154
Tse-tung, Mao 71
Tutu, Archbishop Desmond 127,
    154, 201, 203–206
Tzu, Lao 49, 161

U

United Nations 45
United Nations High Commission
    for Refugees 121
United Nations Security Council
    116
Ury, William 163–164

V

values 38, 126, 146, 151, 182,
    184, 192
  core 144
Van Lange, Paul 82
vengeance 19, 100, 120, 180, 202
Via Creativa 140, 182
Via Negativa 136, 137, 139,
    182–183
Via Positiva 136, 137
Via Transformativa 136, 139, 182
victimhood 118–120, 123–124, 214
victimization 116, 118, 196
violence 115, 118–119, 212
  domestic 118
Volf, Miroslav 208
Volkan, Vamik 116, 192
von Clausewitz, Karl 110

W

Wallis, Jim 86, 184
war mythology 58
weapons
  nuclear 110
welfare
  of people 44
Wells, Ronald 214
Whitehead, James 96
Whitehead, Evelyn 96
Wiebe, Bernie 101
Wilber, Ken 21, 43
Wink, Walter 122
wisdom 48, 131, 142–143
women's movement 118
world
  as a machine 11, 27, 43
  concern for 53
  dilemmas 143
  negotiation 120
  right relationship 49
  secular 219
World Court 45
World War II
  nuclear weapons 39
worldview 21, 38, 77, 192
  future 48
  international 102
  modernism 27, 28, 95
  nihilistic 48
worldwide
  cooperation 127
worthlessness 119

Z

Zehr, Howard 158